Rural Studies

Rural Studies

An Annotated Bibliography from Global to Regional

Prepared by:

Global Center for Rural Studies,
CoE, RUSA, Utkal University

Navaneeta Rath, Rashmita Sahoo,
Archita Bala Patra, Bishnuprasad Mohapatra,
Chinmayee Mishra, Subhrajit Rath

GYAN

UTKAL UNIVERSITY
Satyam Param Dheemahi
NAAC A+ University

ISBN: 978-81-212-6143-2

Published, 2021

Published by

Gyan Publishing House
5, Ansari Road
Daryaganj, New Delhi-110002
Phone: 011-47034999, 9811692060
www.gyanbooks.com
E-mail: books@gyanbooks.com

Printed at: Gyan Press, Delhi.

Contents

Professor Sabita Acharya
VICE CHANCELLOR

UTKAL UNIVERSITY
(NAAC 'A' Accredited)

UTKAL UNIVERSITY
VANI VIHAR, BHUBANESWAR - 751004
ODISHA, INDIA
Tel. Off : (0674) 2567700
Mob : 9437015893(O)
9438423366(P)
E-mail : vcuu@rediffmail.com
vc@utkaluniversity.ac.in

No. VC/ 58 /2021, Date: 05.08.2021

Foreword

This gives me immense pleasure to write the forward for the book "Rural Studies: An Annotated Bibliography from Global to Local" compiled by the Global Center for Rural Studies of Utkal University. This Center of Excellence under RUSA is dedicated to undertake research on rural studies, document the languishing rural traditions and to innovate strategies for rural construction and development.

This present annotated bibliography compilation has been undertaken by the faculty members and researchers of the university working under the aegis of Center of Excellence on Global Center of Rural Studies. The book has been classified into three sections where studies on rural societies from global to regional have been placed. The studies have been taken up from various social science disciplines which projecting specific methodology adopted by various disciplines for rural studies. The theoretical foundation upon which rural studies have been built up has also adorned the pages of the book. Both from temporal and spatial point of view the book seems to be exhaustive to cater to the needs of the students, researchers, academicians, policy planners and development activists.

I wish all success for this endeavour.

5/8/2021
(Sabita Acharya)

Res: VC Bunglow, University Campus, Bhubaneswar - 751004, Phone: 0674 - 2567240

CENTRAL OFFICE
POST-GRADUATE COUNCIL
UTKAL UNIVERSITY

Prof. Basanta Kumar Mallik
Chairman
P.G. Council

Gram : UTKALVIHAR
Uni.Fax-(0674) 2581850
Phone: (0674) 2567036
Mobile : 09437484999

Foreword

India is a Nation of the villages. Rural Social Structure is organised on the basis of Caste system and untouchability. Its economic life has sustained with the agriculture, village crafts and itinerary trades. Rural communities are classified into landlords, landholding peasants and landless agricultural labourers. The multifaceted evils of caste, class and gender have still persisted in Indian villages till today in twenty-first century. In the post Independent India, of course, infrastructural developments have taken place in villages, the rich and small peasants have made thatched houses, the poor people have been benefitted by the Indira Awas Yojana and Pucca village roads have been connected with the urban centres; the people's socio-cultural life and their mindset stagnant with their medieval feudal thinking.

Gandhiji felt that the soul of India exists in Indian villages and therefore he considered the villages have been republics since very early time and it could be better organised under the Panchayatraj system in modern times. But B.R. Ambedkar with his critical perception saw the "village republics are ruination of India". Thus he said on the character of village societies in the Constituent Assembly:

"No doubt the village communities did not care to consider what little part they have played in the affairs and the destiny of the country and why? Their part in the destiny of the country has been well described by Metcalfe himself who says: 'Dynasty after dynasty tumbles down. Revolution succeeds to revolution.

Hindus, Pathan, Moghul, Maratha, Sikh, English are all masters in turn but the village communities remain the same. In times of trouble they arm and fortify themselves. A hostile army passed through the country. The village communities collect their little cattle within their walls and let the enemy pass unprovoked".

He further remarked, "Such is the part the village communities have played in the History of their country. That they have survived through all vicissitudes may be a fact. But mere survival has no value. I hold these village republics have been the ruination of India. What is the village but a sink of localism, a den of ignorance narrow-mindedness and communalism? I am glad that the Drafts Constitution has discarded the village and adopted the individual as its unit." (CAD, VII, p. 38). This criticism is largely justified in the light of performance of village panchayat as wherever they have been established in the country.

It gives me an immense pleasure to learn that the Global Centre for Rural Studies, functions under RUSA programme, Utkal University is going to publish a book i.e. "Annotated Bibliography of Rural Studies from Global to Rural." There are very few studies on villages or on problems of Rural India. This Bibliography will throw light on different new areas of studies on villages in Europe, American societies and India as well. We hope, with the spectrum of such studies the long awaited problems of rural society would be resolved and the stagnant culture would be dynamic upon the urge of time. This compilation will be of enormous help and inspiration for the researchers, policy makers and academic in their chosen ways of journey.

I congratulate the noble endeavour of Prof. Navaneeta Rath, Coordinator and Dr. Rashmita Sahoo, Coordinator for their innovative initiative and wish a grand success.

17.8.2021
(Basanta Kumar Mallik)
Chairman, P.G. Council

Foreword

30-07-2021

Prof. Prabodh Kumar Hota
Coordinator, RUSA.
Utkal University, Odisha

This gives me immense pleasure to see the manuscript or the Book **"Rural Studies: An Annotated Bibliography from Global to Regional"** prepared by the Global Center for Rural Studies, a Center for Excellence under RUSA. It befits the very name and vision of the center for excellence. The book carries the intellectual efforts of the fellows who are the young researcher of the university under the leadership of the Coordinator and the co- coordinator. It is one of the first efforts of our Center for Excellence under RUSA.

The book has tried to compile the historic and the updated works on rural society from a global, national and regional perspective. It has tried to look at the studies on the rural societies from a multidisciplinary angle. This volume thus contains significant writings from the large body of literature on various aspects of rural society, multiple viewpoints of the diverse methods and techniques adopted to study the different domains of rural society. It portrays the multi-sided and complex nature of rural society across nations. This book thus provides the crucial theoretical projection about the rural societies of both developed and developing countries. The bibliographies with annotations chosen in this volume will help students to understand the diverse aspects of rural life and stimulate their interest to undertake further studies on this subject. It will also act as a handbook for policy planners, development theorists and activists to take a multidimensional perspective in their designing and implementation of rural development projects, policies and programmes. I congratulate the members of the Global Center for Rural Studies for this academic production and wish the book to stimulate more studies and research on rural societies.

Prof. Prabodh Kumar Hota

Coordinator, RUSA

The Prologue

The present annotated bibliography compilation is the maiden compilation and academic production of the Global Center for Rural Studies, Utkal University. This is a Center for Excellence created under the aegis of Rastriya Uchhatar Sikshya Abhijan, Government of India. The idea for architecting such an academic project originated in the minds of the lead authors and was soon attested by the co-authors who were no less than the enthusiastic research students of the Department of Sociology and the Department of Analytical and Applied Economics. The very titling of the book is done to relate the book to the name of the Center for Excellence. After a long pondering and careful thought and exchange of ideas, we could arrive at a unanimous decision to make the annotations on rural studies to ensure the interdisciplinary of the book and to bring many facets within its fold.

It took us for about six months to complete the project. The very purpose of editing such a volume was to provide a list of "must reads" to the teachers, researchers, policy planners, rural activists, N.G.Os and C.S.Os who can develop a broad vision on the issues plaguing rural society, the nature of policy venture required by them, their resources and curses. We ourselves have faced the dearth of a good annotated bibliography when we have entered into writing on rural society. This was the experience of the author during the days of her persuasion of research, of the co-authors when they have tried to take up some rural issues for their research writing.

The volume comprises of a review of various studies on rural society across countries and provinces. An attempt has been made to compile the literature that has been generated through books, articles, blogs, statistical reports, proceedings, working papers, and monographs on rural society in different countries, India and our home state Odisha since the beginning of rural studies. This annotated bibliography is an interdisciplinary one which has tried to accommodate studies relating to rural society, its tradition, transition, continuities and changes from various dimensions i.e. political, social, economic, management and policy perspectives. The volume is divided into three sections. The sections are based on spatial studies i.e. international studies, national studies and regional studies conducted in our state Odisha.

The **first section** comprises of the international studies on Rural Society which is drafted by Prof. Navaneeta Rath and Shri Subhrajit Rath. Subhrajit Rath is an economist by training and a researcher scholar of the Department of Analytical and Applied Economics. This section includes a wide variety of studies conducted since the post Second World War period till date. The section basically focuses on studies conducted on rural society from a Global perspective. There are studies from U.S.A. which is said to be the origin of rural studies. Studies are also from the Latin American countries and Asiatic countries which have a predominant rural population and rural space and where rural development experiments are always on. In their attempts to bring into the best available research studies on rural society, the authors have tried to bring forth the World Bank Working papers, seminar and workshop compilations too. Many of the studies make a situational analysis, study of the impact of various development models, some make an analysis of the impacts of modernisation on rural societies, some make policy analysis, some of them make an analysis of good practices and success stories and some make an analysis of failure stories.

Section two carries a short review of the studies from an Indian context. This section has been fashioned by the pens of Shri Bishnuprasad Mohapatra and Miss Chinmayee Mishra, research scholars from the Department of Sociology. The authors have tried to compile as many studies as they have been able to from different perspectives. They have taken a pan Indian perspective in this section. They have brought into the fold of their compilation the theoretical models of rural development practised in India, the rural development plans and programmes implemented by different states and their efficacy evaluation, the rural issues and challenges in India and the state specific studies.

The **third section** places the studies on Rural Society from Odisha. This section has been developed by Dr. Rashmita Sahoo, Co-Coordinator, GCRS and Ms. Archita Bala Patra, a research scholar from the Department of Sociology. Both the authors have taken the pain to bring out the available studies on rural societies in Odisha. Studies on rural society in Odisha do not have a strong compilation till date. So, this section will contribute significantly to the researchers, policy planners and academia to take the existing insights from this annotated bibliography.

The very purpose of the preparation of this volume has been to bring a compilation of rich materials on rural studies under a common canvas. There has been a dearth of such a compilation in the academic achieves to guide scholars, students, policy planners and teachers. The review essays, articles and books are expected to benefit the readers, researchers and students to navigate through the many annotations (which are listed in various sections). The bibliographic material was drawn from social scientific journals, government reports, book chapters and conference proceedings, books, edited books, blogs. But the compilation has its own limitations. We have tried to bring as many books as we could into the ambit of various sections. But we do not back out to admit that due to the paucity of time, due to the critical period in which we were engaged in writing the book our access to libraries, achieves were curtailed to a great extent. So, we have not been able to bring many more books, articles and papers which are out of our sight and availability. Hope this book will serve as an academic resource base for scholars working on rural societies.

The authors

Acknowledgement

We deeply acknowledge the contributions of many individuals and institutions in bringing this book into its present form. Among them, the first and foremost to whom we acknowledge and extend our profound thanks and gratitude is our esteemed Vice Chancellor, Prof. Sabita Acharya for providing us all support and encouragement to go ahead with such a publication from the Global Center for Rural Studies, a centre for Excellence of RUSA. It was who made the lead author a part of the CoE which gave an impetus and idea to go for such an authorship. Her continuous encouragement, dynamism, drive, motivation and extension of all needed support has created an enabling environment for us to have an academic production of this sort.

We gratefully recognise the intellectual support of our Chairperson P.G. Council, Prof. Basant Kumar Mallik for his scholarly guidance and input from time to time to bring about this publication in this present form.

We also gratefully express our thanks to Prof. Prabodh Kumar Hota, Director RUSA for providing us all support and setting deadlines to go about with good academic productions. This acted as wonder and we were on the job.

We acknowledge the great help rendered by our publisher, Gyan Publishing House, New Delhi. The Managing Director and the members of the publishing house were very prompt and could keep their promise of the deadline and brought about the book in its concrete form.

We are indebted to countless researchers and academicians whose seminal works we have browsed through. Their works have become the rich resources of the book.

Finally, we express our humble gratitude and endless indebtedness to the ***Almighty*** without whose benevolent support we could not have come together for this academic production. He is the authority who has made the preparation of this book possible.

Section-I
Rural Studies: A Global Perspective

1. Adamides, G. & A. Stylianou, 2013. "ICT and Mobile Phone Use for Agricultural Knowledge Sharing by Cypriot Farmers." AGRIS on-line Papers in Economics and Informatics, **Czech University of Life Sciences Prague, Faculty of Economics and Management, vol. 5(2): 1-8.**

The researcher has taken a stratified random sample of 250 farmers from the Republic of Cyprus by collecting data through face-to-face interview method. The main objective of the paper is to identify the farm and farmer preferences of sources of agricultural information in general, with focus on mobile phones and ICTs. The results show that nearly 98% of the farmers in Cyprus use the mobile phone as a source of agriculture information. Furthermore, it is found that there are no differences between educational groups and between crop farmers and their livestock counterparts concerning mobile phone usage. This research is silent about the factors affecting the usage of mobile phones.

2. Agarwal, S., S. Rahman, & A. Errington, 2009. "Measuring the determinants of relative economic performance of rural areas." ***Journal of Rural Studies*, 25(3), 309-321.**

Based on the empirical data collected from 149 rural administrative units in United Kingdom this study identifies and critically analyses economic performance of rural programs and policies through factors like; productivity, employment and labour market participation. The 3SLS method is used to estimate the relative significance of factors such as; human, cultural, social and environmental capital in the performance of rural policies. In this paper authors advocate on the applicability of both the method of estimation and study findings to other set of rural units in UK and other economies globally.

3. Agrawal, A., & N. Perrin, 2009. "Climate adaptation, local institutions and rural livelihoods." Adapting to climate change: thresholds, values, governance, 350-367.

This study explores into the role of local and rural institutions in making adaptation practices viable in relation to climate induced risk particularly by rural poor. It is evidenced from past that the very success of adaption practices among rural masses is critically dependent on the prevailing formal and informal local institutions. Moreover, this paper also tries to integrate the role of external interventions in strengthening rural framework on climate risk resilience.

For the empirical analysis this study has drawn more than 100 adaption practice related cases both from the UNFCCC and National Adaptation Programmes of Action (NAPA) database. The comparative study of these selected adaptation practices reveals inadequate role of different national governments in promoting local climate induced risk resilience by poor masses, even though the role of governance and institutions have been identified as the key driving forces of such adaptation efforts. If the adaptation practices are to be localised, so the designing and implementation of programme and policies need to integrate local institutions along with external interventions in order to enhance the effectiveness.

4. **Agu, M.N. 2013. "Application of ICT in Agricultural Sector: Women's Perspective."** ***International Journal of Soft Computing and Engineering (IJSCE)*** **ISSN: 2231-2307, Volume-2, Issue-6, January 2013: 58-60.**

In this study the researcher has taken women of Nigeria as respondents who constitute 60 – 80 percent of labour force engaged in agriculture starting from production, processing and marketing of food. The researcher tries to find out the problems faced by women labourers. Rural women labourers face multiple problems. The scholar notes that women labourers having the availability, accessibility and affordability to ICT facilities are better empowered than their counterparts deprived of ICT facilities.

5. Albrecht, Don E. and Steve H. Murdock. 1990. *The Sociology of U.S. Agriculture: An Ecological Perspective.* Ames: Iowa State University Press.

The twin authors try to indicate that technology drives U.S. agrarian structure. Change in agrarian structure boosts changes in the agrarian communities. The authors basically look into the technological progress bringing prototype changes in the agricultural practices which has pervasive influence on rural communities. The book makes an analysis of the agricultural environment and describes the strong interlinkage between technology and agriculture. It reviews some important technological developments and their consequences for agriculture and rural society. Some of their important pronunciations relating to agrarian structure in the book include the rising farm size, reductions in farm numbers, and lowering demand for farm labour. They make a startling revelation that between 1930 to 1985 whilst the population of the USA doubled; the farm population has come down by over 82 percent.The authors conclude that rural USA is likely to continue in a state of flux in the coming decades. Sophisticated forms of technology such as biotechnology and information management technology, coupled with organisational changes and increased international competition are going to cast numerous changes in farm practices. There will be a diversification of agricultural niches, and new positions like part-time farming will be rising in the rural society. This is likely to bring economic modernisation and social transformation in rural U.S.

6. Albrecht, Don E. 1998. "The industrial transformation of farm communities: implications for family structure and socioeconomic conditions." *Rural Sociology* Vol. 63, No. 1 (Spring 1998): 51-65.

This article on the basis of its analysis of 281 Great Plains counties that were agriculturally dependent in 1940s, examines the consequences of industrial transformation of farm communities. Industrial transformation has become a powerful force to change the socioeconomic conditions and family structure in the rural space. Non-farm employment is noted to be the major cause of rural decline. The author on the basis of his analysis of 281 Great Plains counties those were agriculturally dependent in 1940. The researcher concludes from his observation that the communities remaining agriculturally dependent had extensive population declines, they also had higher rates of employment, lower poverty rates, higher proportions of married couple households, and income levels equal to counties now economically dependent on nonfarm industries. Counties dependent on service industries are found to do the worst overall on the socioeconomic and family structure indicators. They exhibit the features like higher proportions of residents living in poverty, lower rates of employment and fewer married couple households. However, the article is empty of policy prescriptions.

7. Albrecht, D. E. 2007. "Small town in global society." *Southern Rural Sociology*, 22(1), 1-14.

The author in this article tries to posit the major transformation rural America is experiencing with the process of globalisation. Rural societies are forced to transform from "Small Town in Mass Society" to "Small Town in Global Society." Mass societies are getting transformed into global societies due to the loss of the relevance of location or space. The space dichotomy is getting eroded with the forces of globalisation. Globalisation with its key features like opening of borders, market expansions, information revolution and rapid dissemination of ideas have led to economic transformation and amenity availability. In this context, the rural societies are struggling hard to survive by transforming themselves and many of them also have undergone a process of extinction. Finally, the author tries to urge upon for a dialogue among community leaders and development specialists and summon them to prepare effective plans and programmes to enable to communities to deal with these critical issues.

8. Allen, J. C. and D. A. Dillman 1994. *Against All Odds: Rural Community in the Information Age.* Boulder: Westview Press.

This book contains the outcomes of an ethnographic case study of a small town, Bremer in rural Washington. The major highlight of the book lies in illustrating through a portrait of the town that community can exist in rural towns in the Information Age. This book clearly asserts that community is not dead. The book opens with a strong theoretical framework. The authors present their own model of community organisation and change. The authors look at community organisation and change through three eras of social and economic changes i.e. community control, mass society, and the information era. The case study town of Bremer is in fact very consciously dedicated to preserving its own sense of community and uniqueness by rejecting government grants in favour of community solutions, by creating a community club that takes on government-type responsibilities, by organising a town fair, and the presence of community calendars in local households that list residents' birthdays and anniversaries. The book begins with background on the town and a chapter that introduces the theoretical framework. The authors have made interesting analysis of the values, norms and behaviours that make up a small community. The general theme of the book is clearly pointed toward proving not only that community continues to be viable in the information age, but that rural success will be achieved more easily through local community involvement in governance and development. This book does not focus on poverty in rural areas, claiming instead that it is Bremer's lack of poverty that has allowed the community to remain strong. Thus, the book gives an insight into what it takes to be a rural success, rather than focusing on what causes failures.

9. Almstedt, Å., P. Brouder, S. Karlsson, & L. Lundmark, 2014. "Beyond post-productivism: from rural policy discourse to rural diversity." ***European countryside*, 6(4), 297-306.**

This article outlines the scope of multifaceted economic activities in rural development particularly in the case of post-productivism. By making a clear distinction between the post-productivism to post-production and productive activities this study recommends for a rural transformation of nature from mere primary production to diverse economic activities for a wider regional development.

10. Anderson, J. R., & G. Feder, 2003. "Rural extension services, World Bank Policy Research Working Paper" 2976, World Bank, Washington, DC.

The key focus of this study is to examine the policy need for public investments on rural extension services particularly in agriculture and its intra-agency variability. Authors in this policy paper have devised a conceptual framework in explaining the nature of farmer's demand for extension services, characteristics of organisational and political set up in facilitating such services at rural units, different extension modalities, and their perceived as well as actual effectiveness under intra-agency structure. Through review of empirical literature on the impact of rural extension services this paper suggests for a decentralised local delivery system which needs to be public funded for poorer countries and to introduce incentive mode of delivery by private facilitators in order to improve the scope and performance of rural extension services.

11. Angelsen, A., P. Jagger, R. Babigumira, B. Belcher, N. J. Hogarth, S. Bauch, & S. Wunder, 2014. "Environmental income and rural livelihoods: a global-comparative analysis." ***World Development*, 64, S12-S28.**

Based on the primary data collected from 8000 sample household of 24 developing countries, this study examines the role of forest based natural resource dependency in the regional economy and its inequality. The study reveals that 28 percent of total household income is sourced from the natural environment, of which 77 percent are from natural forest. The low-income households are dependent more on such income sources like; fuel woods and other forest products. Therefore, the share of environmental income is more for low-income households compared to those of high-income households.

12. Annes, A., & M. Redlin, 2012. "Coming out and coming back: Rural gay migration and the city." ***Journal of Rural Studies*****, 28(1), 56-68.**

Unlike any commonly practiced rural-urban migration this study highlights some of no-economic dimension of rural-urban migration particularly of gay population from rural America and France. With the help of semi-structured case study of 30 sample respondents this study finds that the urban space is never be considered as a final destination for rural gay population as it is simultaneously favourable and repulsive for them. Such rural-urban migration significantly contributes in formation of identity of migrants on one hand and on other it helps in the development of an understanding, particularly in the part of non-migrant gay population due to reverse migration from urban to rural.

13. Ansoms, An, 2009. "Re-Engineering Rural Society: The Visions and Ambitions of the Rwandan Elite, ***African Affairs*****", Volume 108, Issue 431, April, Pages 289–309.**

This article analyses the Rwandan elite's visions and ambitions for a wide-ranging re-engineering of rural society. The post-1994 political elite has limited touch with the rural society and the peasant way of life. They are not quite optimistic about the role of Rwanda's small-scale peasant agriculture for its economic future. The article shows how current Rwandan policy makers aim to realize three social engineering targets. They are: first to transform the agricultural sector into a professionalised motor for economic growth, centred on competitive and commercial farm units; second, to artificially upgrade rural life by inserting 'modern' techniques and strategies into local realities, while hiding true poverty and inequality; and, finally, to transform Rwanda into a target-driven society from the highest to the lowest level. The article also indicates the potential dangers, flaws, and shortcomings of this rural re-engineering mission, and illustrates how the state as the engineer superimposes the local without consulting those affected. The article ends up with a pessimistic note that contemporary policies are unlikely to be conducive to poverty reduction.

14. Ardington, E. M. 1988. "Nkandla Revisited: A Longitudinal Study of the Strategies Adopted to Alleviate Poverty in a Rural Community." Durban: Centre for Social and Development Studies, University of Natal.

This working paper is a longitudinal survey undertaken by the researcher and presents the comparison of the findings from a 1985 survey of rural households in the Nkandla district of KwaZulu with the findings of a 1982 survey of the same households. The households were resurveyed to take note of the strategies adopted by them to respond to the changing social and economic circumstances in which they found themselves. The survey periods witnessed, the area suffering from prolonged drought as well as economic recession. The working paper opens with a demographic description of the population of the area and reflects on household structures, and particularly on changes and migration that were restructuring the social life of the region. The subsequent chapter focuses on economic activities, looking mostly at aspects of agriculture and land tenure. Little change is found in agricultural practice and production during the time period. Underproduction related to poverty is found to be caused by labour deficit and the absence of capital, expertise, markets, and the means to plough. Problems related to livestock raising and employment are also discussed in detail. Next chapter looks into the quality-of-life issues that include education, health, water, transportation and communication, fuel, and savings. It also mentions about income distribution and sources of income, which are found to be severely limited in this rural area. Chief income sources are found to be remittance and pensions. The following chapter compares income levels over the three-year period for fifteen households and the causes of their increase and decrease as well. The result shows that rising income marks half of the households, and falling incomes in the other half. The concluding chapter confirms that changes in the economy at the macro level have micro impacts impacting incomes, living conditions and lifestyles in the region. The research paper concludes that agricultural growth has limitations in arresting urban flight and macro planning hardly addresses the needs of local communities. Rural communities need to have their micro local specific plans to deliver better policy results.

15. Argent, N. 2002. "From pillar to post? In search of the post-productivist countryside in Australia." *Australian Geographer*, 33(1), 97-114.

In this paper, researcher considers the applicability of the notion of "post-productivism to describe changing rural conditions under advanced market economies. The term "post-productivism is the brainchild of the British geographers. The author uses it to map the changes taking place in the Australian countryside. The author has been moved by certain phenomenal developments since the World War II i.e. legislation governing the physical management and use of rural resources in Australia was increasingly being influenced by a range of new social values such as growing public/urban concern for the natural/rural environment and an increasing acknowledgement of Aboriginal title in land in Australia, the increasing urban-rural migration leading to uneven rural development and urban migrants moving to rural areas with high amenity value. To the author, these syndromes find a place in the post productivism discourses. The researcher concludes that there is clear evidence of a post-war productivism rural regime operating in Australia and this transition has become more evident since the mid-1980s.

16. Argent, N., P. Smailes, & T. Griffin, 2007. "The amenity complex: towards a framework for analysing and predicting the emergence of a multifunctional countryside in Australia." ***Geographical Research*****, 45(3), 217-232.**

The authors in this paper try to define amenity in a rural context. They also seek to find out the nature of distribution of amenity across the Australian countryside and its impact on demographic, socio-economic and land use change. To them rural in-migration is determined by consumption interests of the people in the Australian country side. The authors begin by suggesting that amenity is a central element of the post-productivist transition and for the recent conceptualisation of the multifunctional rural transition. Both the types of transitions involve an extractive use of land. Land is progressively used for industry, urban residential, recreational or other uses. It is more consumption oriented rather than production oriented in character. This increases the value of rural space in rural Australia. Added to the amenities for recreation the authors also delve out three prominent drivers of in-migration to rural space, namely: beach distance, employment in recreational and related services, and availability of irrigation water resources.

17. Arnold, M. L., J. H. Newman, B. B. Gaddy, & C. B. Dean, 2005. "A look at the condition of rural education research: Setting a direction for future research." ***Journal of Research in Rural Education*****, *20*(6), 1-25.**

This is a meta-analysis of 580 research articles on rural education of USA published during the year 1991 to summer 2003. The study finds only 21 percent of sample articles are fulfilling the criteria of explaining issues related to rural education. Whereas, none of the study are found to be truly experimental according to the quality of research criteria set by McREL. The quality studies identified are of quasi-experimental in nature. Out of 106 articles, those which have used a comparative research design, 10 articles are rated high and 48 come under the medium and lower quality of research respectively as per the stated standard. This meta-analysis also recommends that community involvement in improving educational outcomes in rural America.

18. Ashley, C., & S. Maxwell, 2001. "Rethinking rural development." ***Development Policy Review*****,** ***19*****(4), 395-425.**

This article derives a new narrative on rural development through re-examining of Washington Consensus to post-Consensus debates on food security, agriculture and the rural development. By considering issues like; persistent rural poverty, demographic changes, wider heterogeneity of masses authors suggest some of fundamental principles along with explicit framework on rural development. To them, proper identification of nature of heterogeneity, to use of both large and small farm in arresting the intensity of rural poverty are very essential. Though, the study is empirically confined to the economies of India, Kenya and Brazil but the outcome can be generalised to any of similar economy globally.

19. Ataei, P., S. Hassan, I. Nasim, 2021. "Major challenges to achieving food security in rural, Iran" ***Rural Society*****, Volume 30, 2021-Issue-1.**

This research investigates the major challenges to food security in rural areas of Iran. It uses the Delphi technique run in three rounds with a panel of experts consisting of 27 academic faculty members in the field of food security, rural development, agriculture, and executive staff. The authors find eight factors as the principal challenges to food security. They are: policy, economic, knowledge and information, infrastructural, cultural, access to food, climate conditions, and social challenges.

20. Bardhan, P. K. 1984. "Land, Labor, and Rural Poverty: Essays in Development Economics." Delhi: Oxford University Press; New York: Columbia University Press.

The book's central issues include land, labour, credit, production relations, and rural poverty. The book is being organised into three parts. The first part contains essays dealing with agricultural labour, mostly using econometric analyses. The major focal issues are: determinants of female labour force participation, farm-level determinants of the use of hired labour, and labour-tying arrangements. The second part comprise of issues like land lease contracts and rural land tenure issues, focusing on tenancy and sharecropping. The last part is an anthology of essays on different aspects of production relations in agriculture. It also includes write ups on the relationships between growth and poverty, and poverty and mortality. In this part, the book seems to have departed with its economic character and has brought more sociological considerations into account and discussion. In this part, it deals with sociological issues like the causes of gender differences in child mortality figures. However, it is still basically an in-depth look at the development economics issues in India, and economic issues are the focus. Thus, on the whole, this book focuses on rural development economics in India. It tries to blend formal theoretical analysis with statistical testing, and is more quantitative than adhering to qualitative analysis.

21. Barjis, J., G. Kolfschoten, & J. Maritz, 2013. "A sustainable and affordable support system for rural healthcare delivery." *Decision Support Systems*, 56, 223-233.

This is a comparative study of different rural healthcare system that exist in developing economies and their associate challenges such as; inadequate infrastructure, inefficient caregivers and obsolete technology. The study tries to highlight the comparative effectiveness of home-based care to locally available institutional care along with new technology of tele-medicine and monitoring. The paper concludes with positive outcome of integration of innovation in healthcare delivery system at least in the nature of documentation and monitoring related to patient care at rural and remote areas.

22. Barlett, Peggy F. 1993. *American Dreams, Rural Realities: Family Farms in Crisis.* Chapel Hill: University of North Carolina Press.

The basic thrust of the author in the book has been the farm crisis rural America was witnessing since 1980s and its impact on the rural society and the subsequent social transformation and transition that was following agrarian crisis. The farm crisis of the 1980s came as a violent thunderstorm and challenged the sustainable livelihood of the farm dependent families of rural America. This induced powerful changes in American rural life. While experts predicted that the crisis years would affect the small- and medium-sized family farms, it was seen that it hurt the largest farms as well. Farm indebtedness increased, the farm dependent rural economy started adopting many industrial features like long-term planning, money management, and commitment to a multigenerational agricultural business in the place of short-term gains, expansion, and risk-taking entrepreneurship. The farm economies started taking the features of capitalism with unrestrained capitalism and individualism. This led to changes in the rural family structure, work distribution and personal goal setting and the institution of marriage. The conflict between agrarian value systems and capitalist features thus dismantled the traditional rural life. The entrenchment of industrialist tenets into the farm based rural society became a major source of tension for modern farmers. The impact was far more felt by the women, who are more in touch with their children's material needs and desires. The book ends up in questioning the future of farming in the late-industrial economy.

23. Bascom, A. 2001. "Energizing rural space: the representation of countryside culture as an economic development strategy." Journal of Cultural Geography, 19(1), 53-64.

The author concentrates on examining the way in which

the American rural communities are trying to rebuild their weakened economies. The author adopts a post structuralist perspective, case study research to prove his thesis that changed space identity is a mover for reactivating the rural economies. This they are doing primarily by reconstructing their rural place identities. For this, they are using the resources like local/rural culture, landscape and natural resources, and are introducing marketing tools to attract new types of capital investment, particularly with the establishment of consumption-based activities such as tourism. The author sees that these mechanisms are quite effective in revitalising the exhausted local/rural economies.

24. Beaulieu, Lionel J. and M. David (eds.) 1995. *Investing in People: The Human Capital Needs of Rural America.* Boulder: West view Press.

This edited volume contains a collection of essays which examine the human capital needs and resources of rural America in the context of the economic and social changes taking place in the late 1980s and 1990s. The book basically thrives on the human capital models and structural theoretical models. The first chapter provides an introduction to these theoretical perspectives. It explores several sides of the human capital issue, as well as structural issues. The remaining chapters of the conceptual section of the book provides an overview of human resource conditions in rural America and points out to gap that exists between available human resources and available jobs. The next section of chapters focuses on key economic, social and technological changes that are likely to shape the future viability of rural areas. The book also highlights on the structural shifts and their economic implications for rural areas, on strengthening community to fight against the host of social problems, the possible negative consequences of modern technology on rural communities, while offering a framework for using technology to create sustainable community systems. The chapters on human capital issues in the book also explore the quality of human capital resources across rural America, focusing on deficits. These chapters relating to human capital issues of rural America analyse poverty from a human capital deficiency perspective and bring forth the human capital resources of rural minorities such as rural Native Americans, blacks, Hispanics and women. The problem of worker displacement also finds place in the book and the last chapter in this section looks at the problem of outmigration from rural areas and analyses the impact of the so-called "brain-drain". The final section of the book focuses on policy issues, primarily the investments necessary to strengthen rural America's human capital resources by creating a linkage between human capital and rural development, healthcare, family structures and labour market incentives. Thus, the editors of the book conclude that human capital investment is a precursor to future economic development in rural areas. But it needs to be coupled with investment into jobs that match the human capital resources of the areas.

25. Bebbington, A. 1996. "Organisations and intensifications: campesino federations, rural livelihoods and agricultural technology in the Andes and Amazonia." ***World Development*** **Vol. 24, No. 7 (July 1996): 1161-1178.**

This paper is based on the experiences gained from field-based interaction with rural organisations in Bolivia and Ecuador. It analyses how campesino and indigenous federations engage in agricultural development and natural resource management activities. It argues that necessary intensification will depend to some degree on rural poor campesinos. This rural poor compensation will ensure more secure and expanded rights over resources and improved access to existing and new markets to the rural poor. For this, it is needed to allow the wealth derived from natural resource and agricultural activities to be reinvested in rural areas, creating new income and employment activities. It is argued that modernised forms of indigenous organisations need to play crucial roles in the negotiation of new market relationships, managing the development of on and off-farm technologies, and negotiating new relationships with other institutions. The paper identifies three different trajectories through which campesino federations have arrived at work with technology, and three different natural-resource related roles played by the federation. The paper also suggests that experience shows that these organisations could play an integral role in inter-institutional approaches to agricultural development and rural intensification.

26. Beel, D. E., C. D. Wallace, G. Webster, H. Nguyen, E. Tait, M. Macleod & C. Mellish, 2017. "Cultural resilience: The production of rural community heritage, digital archives and the role of volunteers." *Journal of Rural Studies*, 54, 459-468.

This study emphasises the community-based labour participation in rural development. By considering cases from United Kingdom authors examine the importance of community resilience and its relationship with cultural ethos at rural places in order to bring a transformation regionally. Hence, this study suggests for a cohesive community-based activity with rural digitalisation for a more resilient community.

27. Bell, C. & J. Lyall, (1995). *Putting Our Town on the Map: Local Claims to Fame in New Zealand*. New Zealand: Harper Collins.

In this book, Bell and Lyall show how many rural communities in New Zealand have manufactured place identities which in turn have contributed towards local/regional differentiation, economic gain and enhanced community well-being. They trace the beginning of constructing distinct place identities in New Zealand, to the early years of 1990s when rural communities were fighting against the forces of the global/ rural economic recession. To both Bell and Lyall the new cultural landscape that emerged in the rural areas welcome the visitor to the areas and gave an opportunity to the rural areas to display an element of local cultural pride and identity. In this connection they cite the examples of Te Puke and its giant-sized kiwi fruit, Pokeno and its claim to be "bacon country", Dannevirke as Viking country (Scandinavian heritage), Westport and mining, Taihapeas the Gumboot City.

28. Bell, D., & M. Jayne, 2010. "The creative countryside: Policy and practice in the UK rural cultural economy." ***Journal of Rural Studies*, *26*(3), 209-218.**

This paper observes the policymaking behaviour and research extension of several of creative industries at rural United Kingdom. In creative industries a proper policy design is required which to blend effectively cultural, social and economic element at specified rural unit. Finally, the authors underline a proper design of rural plan and policies as the key element to good practices and the wider regional development.

29. Bell, D., R. Phillips, D. Shuttleton, & D. Watt, 2000. "Eroticizing the rural." ***De-centering sexualities*, 83-101.**

In this book authors are critical about the issues related to sex and sexuality particularly with rural masses. They address varieties of sexual experiences in a rural setup compiled internationally on disciplines like; history, culture, law, lesbian and gay studies. Such studies help in improving the socio-economic structure at rural space by breaking through its orthodoxy

30. Bell, D., & G. Valentine, 1995. "Queer country: Rural lesbian and gay lives." ***Journal of Rural Studies*, 11(2), 113-122.**

Departing from the usual rural centric fundamental issues, this study attempts to explain the problems associated with sexuality of lesbians and gays residing in the countryside. It identifies the issue of sexuality leading to several of structural difficulties. The authors have reviewed the history of homosexuality in a rural setup from fiction and cinemas. The study finds that majority of homosexual people are adjusted to their place of origin and local conflicts while some try to find an exist route to change the existing unfavourable scenario. Few of them have opted for urban life and in recent their number is continuously increasing.

31. Bell, M. M. 1994. *Childerley: Nature and Morality in a Country Village*. Chicago: University of Chicago Press.

This book provides an ethnographic portrait of the residents of Childerley, an "exurban" English village. Childerley is an exurban village in the outskirts of London. It is a two hours journey from London to reach the village. The village has 475 residents. The most striking feature of the village is the residents of the village have rejected urban living in favour of the benefits of the village. The residents of Childerley are found to have taken pride in their rural habitation, in their natural environment, and they use nature as a source of their identity and moral understanding. The book demonstrates the importance of two kinds of moral thinking in the villagers' lives. The first type of moral thinking is based on ideas the villagers consider to be socially derived. The second is based on truths they consider to be above and free from the polluting interests of social life. The book relies heavily on the villagers to explain for themselves why they choose to live in Childerley, and what makes it a coherent entity. The book explores the meanings of class and community through the eyes of its residents. It finds the feudal character of Childerley, but the resentment to class. Other themes explored in the book include the residents' construction of rural/urban differences, the countryside's strong conception and connectivity to nature, and the distinct identity of the village in the minds of its residents. The book also analyses community behaviour from a gender standpoint. Thus, interconnectedness of people and ideas within the changing rural environment are the main thematic concern of the book.

32. Bell, M. M. 2007. "The two-ness of rural life and the ends of rural scholarship." ***Journal of Rural Studies*, 23(4), 402-415.**

This theoretical work is a revisiting of two fundamental approaches of defining the 'rural'. The 'first rural' and 'second plural'. When the former is confined to the space related material moment, latter one describes the rurality on the ground of moment of ideas. These two dimensions of rurality can be understood under discourses like; modernist and post-modernist views that prominently prevail in USA and European rural scholarship respectively. Finally, the approach of rural-plural tries to integrate both the space and idea based approaches of rurality by lessening their excludability on different grounds of applicable and acceptability.

33. Bell, P. &P. Cloke, 1989. "The changing relationship between the private and public sectors: privatisation and rural Britain." ***Journal of Rural Studies*, 5(1), 1-15.**

In this paper, the authors explore the theoretical and ideological background of privatisation. They draw evidences from Britain after the introduction of the privatisation policy by Margaret Thatcher. Their concern lies in the examination of the impacts of privatisation on rural space of U.K. The authors describe privatisation as a move to shift responsibility for the management of various elements of production and consumption from the public sector to the private sector. The principal impacts of privatisation observed by the authors are: the rising need for rural communities to help-themselves; fulfilling roles and providing services which were previously provided by local governments, emerging risks for the people who were on the margins. The authors also outline an exploratory research agenda for rural researchers who might be interested in examining the future impacts of privatisation on rural places.

34. Bernstein, H., B. Crow, & H. Johnson, (Eds.) 1992. *Rural livelihoods: crises and responses.* Oxford University Press, USA

This book initiates the debate on survival of rural people in developing countries particularly in the course of rural changes after the Second World War. Even if in the rural spaces of these countries there was the growth of agricultural output but there was no growth in livelihood security. Hence, rural livelihoods in the rural spaces were noted with crisis. Scholarly contributions made in this book also discuss issues like poverty and rural inequalities along with various dimensions of rural transformation on the ground of space, society, economic, politics and development.

35. Bessiere, J. 1998. "Local development and heritage: traditional food and cuisine as tourist attractions in rural areas." *SociologiaRuralis*, 48, 21-34.

In the present article the writer examines the social, cultural and economic transformation of rural France. This has taken place as a corollary of the "culinary (cookery) heritage" industry coming into prominence throughout the countryside of France. The researcher argues that place-bound cultural markers like local food products and associated services have been used to widen and revitalise the dying economy of rural France.

36. Betz, C. & R. Perdue, 1993. "The role of amenity resources in rural recreation and tourism development." *Journal of Park and Recreation Administration*, 11(4), 15-29.

The authors in this article bring the resource management perspective into account. They examine the link between amenity resources (such as local scenery, heritage and culture) and rural tourism development. They strongly put forth the view that amenities are the means to handle recreation management and recreation management creates tourist potentials. Rural tourism enterprises and marketing strategies enable the rural space to become efficient tourism destinations. The researchers base their arguments on three major surveys conducted in 1989 in a south-western state of North America.

37. Bhandari, P. B. 2013. "Rural livelihood change? Household capital, community resources and livelihood transition." ***Journal of Rural Studies*, 32, 126-136.**

In this article the author tries to identify a number of factors i.e., from resource endowment to socio-economic and cultural background those are vital in livelihood transformation of an agrarian setting. Apart from these macro variables, this study also examines the role of micro-level household factors and of communities on rural transition. The household data from 1996 to 2001 are collected from a rural agrarian space of Nepal. The empirical analysis reveals that the variables such as; available in house labour force, family-owned cultivable land and the ownership of livestock are impeding the process of livelihood transition of farm households to other alternatives. However, the author records that the presences of non-farm households at community level significantly contribute to the livelihood transformation at rural space of Nepal.

38. Bijker, R. A., T. Haartsen, & D. Strijker, 2012. "Migration to less-popular rural areas in the Netherlands: Exploring the motivations." ***Journal of Rural Studies*, 28(4), 490-498.**

In general, the rural deficiency and urban adequacy of life's necessities are key factors of rural-urban migration but, if it is the case of migration from urban to rural then the scenario is much fitted into the concept called, rural idyll. Nevertheless, this phenomenon is not exploring the cases of such urban to rural migration at less popular rural areas. Based on the survey data collected from 664 respondents of four urban units at North Netherlands, this paper identifies factors beyond rural idyll contributed significantly. The study reveals that factors like;

individual preferences on comfort and low-price houses are the major driver of migration to less popular rural areas Among high income groups, clean environment is a major decisive factor for this type of migration.

39. Bilsborrow, R. E. 1992. "Rural poverty, migration, and the environment in developing countries: three case studies" (Vol. 1017). World Bank Publications.

The author of this article brings into discussion three case studies across developing countries namely; Latin America, Indonesia and Sudan. It explores issues related to rural poverty, internal migration and environmental degradation and ends with suitable policy recommendations on checking population growth, managing land resources to environmental sustainability through specific research curriculum and enforced practices of conservation.

40. Bob, Sam B. 1998. ***Participation of the Poor in Rural Development Programmes: Selected Case Studies.*** **New Delhi: Discovery Publishing House.**

Being authored by a government official in charge of rural development programmes in the state of Andhra Pradesh, this book highlights on the participation of the poor in rural development programmes. The field views of the author find a place in the book. Its major concern lies in exploring the rural development programmes and their conceptual frameworks. The book attempts to highlight the participation of rural poor in developmental strategies to improve livelihoods. The book starts with a conceptual framework of participation, brings into discussion the various theories of participation, presents the government's operational definition of participation as envisioned by the Indian government and outlines the government's approach. This approach is then examined through a case study done in a district of Andhra Pradesh where the author worked. The chapter concludes that the poor respond positively to the participatory nature of the scheme, and reap favourable results from the schemes and programmes. The next chapter analyses the strengths and weaknesses ingrained in the development programmes in India and their shortcomings in reaching out the targeted population. The book then proceeds to look at technological change in agriculture, particularly with reference to the Green Revolution in India and Africa. It then compares decentralisation experiments in India and Kenya, and ends with a chapter on common property resources and the tragedy of the commons. However, the book fails to generate a linkage between the unconnected chapters and to establish a solid conclusion. But it is pregnant with field views and unfolds many ground realities.

41. Bosworth, G. 2006. "Counter urbanisation and Job Creation: Entrepreneurial in Migration and Rural Economic Development." Centre for Rural Economy Discussion Paper Series No. 4. Centre for Rural Economy, University of Newcastle upon Tyne.

The researcher in this article expresses that rural in migration is becoming phenomenal. This pronunciation is based on a survey research conducted in the North East of England which establishes that over half of the owners of rural micro-businesses were in-migrants who had moved at least thirty miles into their new rural locality, their growth-oriented approach vis-á-vis their local counterparts, their business networking outside the community and important links within. As such, the author concludes that in-migrant entrepreneurs provide both supply and demand to the local and regional economy, contribute significantly to the diversification of rural economies, thereby offsetting economic and social decline associated with the agricultural downturn. The author argues that the rural policy-makers need to acknowledge the value and importance of this relatively new sector of the regional rural economy and its contribution to the countryside.

42. Bosworth, G. 2012. "Characterising rural businesses–Tales from the paperman." ***Journal of Rural Studies*, *28*(4), 499-506.**

This article outlines the distinct features of rural entrepreneurship and its intangible characteristics through a case study of a paper on business unit at rural United Kingdom. Beyond financial elements, the author highlights specific features of rural businesses which are operated at rural places, cater to the need of its population and deals with rural products. The study concludes with some specific socio-managerial policy framework rural business can be strengthened and will be more value added without much financial investment.

43. Bourke, L. and A.E. Luloff, 1997. "Women and leadership in rural areas." ***Women and Politics*** **Vol. 17, No. 4 (August 1997): 1-24.**

This article explores female leadership in rural areas. Female leadership in rural societies if often an ignored issue. Conventional discourses hardly gave significance to it. However, in this study, the researcher examines rates of female leadership, the nature of perceptions of female and male leaders, and attitudes of the rural community towards women as local leaders in several rural regions. This is based on an empirical study undertaken in four regions of rural Pennsylvania. These four regions are not uniform and differ in levels of urban presence and pressure. The results arrived at is an outcome of the quantitative analysis of the data, as well as qualitative analysis of the interviews undertaken. Findings reveal that men still pre-dominate rural leadership positions. Rural community accepts men as leaders than women. Growth of women leadership is a recent phenomenon and the types of women leaders who emerge, vary by site. However, the author concludes that rise of women leadership is the need of the hour and attention need to be paid to that.

44. Bowen, S., & K. De Master, 2011. "New rural livelihoods or museums of production? Quality food initiatives in practice." ***Journal of Rural Studies*, *27*(1), 73-82.**

This article explores the motivations behind restoring and preserving the traditions and heritage of local rural products particularly after the stated commitments of European Union under its Common Agricultural Policy. To understand the meaning and basis of heritage, tradition and extra-local commodification of rural products, case studies are evaluated from France and Poland. Among others, this study underlines the quality-of-product factor as an essential in preserving local livelihood at rural space against extra-local food system particularly when the traditional agricultural practice is economically marginalised. Further, the authors have suggested reducing product diversities, creation of static culture, shifting of local to extra-local market for rural products, and envisaging the means through which these practices will help rural masses to look beyond the mere museum of production and to adopt new rural livelihood practices.

45. Bowler, I. & J. Everitt, 1999. "Production and consumption in rural service provision: the case of the English village" pub. In N. Walford, J. C. Everitt & D. Napton. (Eds.), ***Reshaping the Countryside: Perceptions and Processes of Rural Change (Chapter Twelve)*****. United Kingdom: CABI Publishing.**

In this article, Bowler and Everitt attempt deal with restructuring that has undertaken in rural Britain with their focus on village pub. The authors try to point out that changing policies of the government, the landing of more role players as producer's production process with its diversification of products and styles of serving and consumption behaviour and clientele with urban tourist becoming the dominant consumers village pubs have undergone a process of restructuring. For centuries, the village pub served as an important cultural/social institution in the British countryside. The authors report that in recent times many rural pubs have either closed down or have changed significantly in their physical form, in terms of the services they offer with the focus on recreational/ entertainment service for non-rural people. The English village pub has changed from being the focal point of rural social life, into a centre for recreation and entertainment for urban outsiders. Such changes, they argue, are the result of four large scale and interconnected processes, namely:

- The investment policies of national and international brewing companies.
- The United Kingdom policies and regulations for the brewing industry.
- Changing social behaviour of the new rural service class, and
- Changes in the leisure behaviour of the non-rural population.

46. Boyle, P. J. & K. Halfacree, 1998. ***Migration into Rural Areas: Theories and Issues.*** **Chichester: John Wiley.**

Counter urbanisation and rural in-migration are the thrust of this book. The authors of this book compiled a wide range of studies with the purpose of explaining the processes underlying the phenomenon. The book mainly focuses on rural migration patterns in the UK and Europe, with just two contributions from further afield, one from Australia, the other from the United States.

47. Bradshaw, T.K. 1993. "Multicommunity networks: a rural transition." ***Annals of the American Academy of Political and Social Science,*** **Vol. 529 (September 1993): 164-175.**

This article speaks about the external influence on rural communities due to their dependence on the outside societies. These external forces drive changes in the rural communities in

America. Due to these influences, American rural communities are gaining new positions within the global economy. It identifies and discusses three changes in the character of communities that make the transition to the new rural reality often difficult. These are: decreasing rural dependence on central places, the regional linkage of specialised places, and the external origin of local problems and resources. Examples of the linking of towns in regional networks include the locations of large discount stores between rural communities to service multiple places at once. Most difficult for rural communities to comprehend is that local problems and resources are becoming external to the tight-knit communities. These changes create new development challenges that the article suggests should be met with a two-pillar paradigm. Firstly, development must be focused at the local level, with the local community taking the lead in mobilising outside resources for community benefit. Secondly, the approach must be multifaceted in purpose and scope. The article then proposes a new community leadership model for development, including multijurisdictional leadership, strategic planning, resource mobilisation, sharing, economies of scale, specialisation, and leveraging. It concludes that policies for rural development need to provide more mechanisms for this type of multifunctional and multijurisdictional response.

48. Bramwell, B. 1994. "Rural tourism and sustainable rural tourism." ***Journal of Sustainable Tourism*, *2*(1-2), 1-6.**

In this article, the author demonstrates the need of sustainable tourism practices under the distinctiveness of rural tourism in the developed nations with special reference to Western Europe. Considering the economic interest of growth of tourism, host communities and the environmental impact, this paper suggests for an integrated and inclusive model of sustainability which includes external managerial skills along with active participation of local communities, training and promotion for indigenous entrepreneurship.

49. Brandth, B. 1995. "Rural masculinity in transition: gender images in tractor advertisements." ***Journal of Rural Studies, 11*(2), 123-133.**

This article explores the scope of understanding masculinity particularly in farming sector where still there exist labour divisions on the basis of machine and technology. The central idea of this study is to understand the definition of masculinity in rural agriculture. As agriculture is fundamentally linked with maleness, so its related components can be connected with male identities. Since, tractor is an important and basic technological intervention in farming sector, this article studies the gender images in the advertisements of tractors and associate taglines. This study finds a strong link between technology and masculinity, as tractor possesses many male characteristics. But, with the advancement of technologies, tractors are no more associated with driving precision or horsepower and can be operated through a computer which can reduce the gender orientation of the gadget and can be easily female operated. Thus, the study concludes that technological advancement needs to blend the goals of gender difference reduction and occupational success.

50. Brems, C., M. E. Johnson, T. D. Warner, & L. W. Roberts, 2006. "Barriers to healthcare as reported by rural and urban interprofessional providers." ***Journal of Interprofessional Care, 20*(2), 105-118.**

This article attempts to identify factors that hinder the healthcare delivery system at rural setting of Alaska and New Mexico. The authors have resorted to interview and focus group discussion tools and have taken 1555 healthcare professionals as their sample. They examine the factors such as; resource constraints, complex nature of patients, accessibility, lack of training as a cause for an inefficient healthcare delivery even at urban areas. The study discovers that crunch of resources, shortfall of infrastructure, limited accessibility, lack of training and the overlapping role of service provider in rural areas paralyse their delivering capacities.

51. Brown, David L.; D. R. Field and J. J. Zuiches, (eds.) 1993. *The Demography of Rural Life*. University Park, PA: Northeast Regional Center for Rural Development.

This edited volume contains papers from a 1991 Madison, Wisconsin symposium organised to honour the rural demographer Glenn Fouetté. The volume contains an overview of the rural demography and rural sociology disciplines as well as the major substantive areas of rural study. Essays included in the book discuss on population redistribution; migration and spatial inequality; urbanisation; demography of agriculture; applied demography and rural sociology; and reflections on rural demography. The uniqueness of the essays lies in the fact that each essay is followed by several short reactions and critiques of it. The major insights that emerge from the book include population decline in rural areas due to migration and economic redistribution, as well as the decline of farm populations. The book gives a good overview of the state of rural demography, but fails to offer a large amount of in-depth analysis of the rural situation or policy suggestion.

52. Brown, David L. and Louis E. Swanson (eds) 2003. *Challenges for Rural America in the Twenty-First Century*. University Park: Pennsylvania State University Press

The book is an edited volume prepared in the context of the profound changes the rural society was witnessing since the twentieth century. Demographic and economic changes were bringing profound changes not only in the lives of the rural people, but in the overall rural scenario of the country. The book defines these changes and interprets their implications for the future of rural America. All the authors have not only tried to elaborate the drastic and dramatic changes, but have discussed thoroughly on the role of present public policy and talk about the public policy needs to handle and manage the situations in future. The volume is produced as the "decennial volumes" co-edited by presidents of the Rural Sociological Society and is published in the Society's Rural Studies Series.

53. Bryant, C. 1989. "Entrepreneurs in the rural environment." *Journal of Rural Studies*, 5(4), 337-348.

The author in this article claims that the role of local agency in the study of contemporary rural change should not be downplayed. He picks up the example from Atikokan, a small town in north-west Ontario. This place was witnessing an economic decline in the wake of two iron ore mines being closed. To overcome the situation, a not-for-profit association was formed to try to identify new opportunities for development in the town. The idea emerged to produce and sell classic replica automobile. Gradually, the community owned company started production. He shows how the formation of the new community company raised the confidence of local people in their ability to bring about development and to secure their own social and economic well-being in a globalising setting. Bryant believes that entrepreneurs have an important role to play in encouraging new economic activity in rural areas by identifying and developing new enterprises. In doing so, the local people contribute to helping their own population realise their potential and make them shoulder responsibility and take initiative to influence their own destiny. This inspires local people to develop their own enterprises in what Bryant (p. 346) calls a new "entrepreneurial community". Thus, the paper brings to forefront certain facets of this entrepreneurial growth which includes the decisions made by entrepreneurs, be they farmers, non-farmers, or even local governments, in a local rural context and advances the view that these decisions are invariably influenced by the broader political, social, and economic environment.

54. Bryant, L., & B. Pini, 2009. "Gender, class and rurality: Australian case studies." *Journal of Rural Studies*, 25(1), 48-57.

This research paper contextualises the interlinkages between gender and class on the background of rurality. For empirical analysis, data are collected through semi-structured interviews of farming households in Australia. The case study method is also used to derive the qualitative aspect of rural morality on gender, class and their interconnections. The study shows how the class is a representation of social ranking of occupational scale, ownership and the level of consumption, whereas the gendering is a social construct and mainly determined in abstract way on the basis of rural moralities.

55. Burkey, S. 1993. ***People first: A guide to self-reliant participatory rural development.*** **Zed Books Ltd.**

This book emphasises the role of agents who are instrumental in rural development. Rural development is based on principles of regional cooperation, community participation, and self-reliance. Rather than identifying only symptoms of underdevelopment, inequality and rural poverty this book tries to prescribe some specific mechanism of wider rural development on concrete theoretical base. There are three sections in the book consisting of 11 chapters. The content of the discussed chapters flows as; from a theoretical base of rural poverty to historical reviews of earlier developmental practices and finally the book concludes with the discussion of the obstacles and risks associated with grassroot development.

56. Burton, R. J. 2004. "Reconceptualising the 'behavioural approach' in agricultural studies: a socio-psychological perspective." ***Journal of Rural Studies, 20*****(3), 359-371.**

This paper investigates the nature and scope of improved socio-psychological theories in rural studies in relation to the adaptabilities among developmental actors. It explains the methodological limitations of behavioural approach in studying rurality, which is largely based on an agent specific process of decision making. Since, rural studies are increasingly important for designing agricultural policies effectively and to meet the requirement of rural farmers, the paper concludes that a positive relationship exists between the improved behavioural approaches in agriculture. Improved behavioural approach includes factors like self-identity and self-efficacy.

57. Butler, R., C. M. Hall, & J. Jenkins, 1998. *Tourism and Recreation in Rural Areas.* United Kingdom: John Wiley.

The authors in this book throw light on the barriers, challenges and opportunities associated with rural tourism and recreation development in rural places. They have drawn the insights from an international perspective, largely from Europe, New Zealand and North America. The authors give an elaborate description of the growth of rural tourism ventures within the context of rural restructuring. The book also examines the policy perspective related to rural tourism, its socioeconomic impact and the issues of sustainability.

58. Campbell, H., & M. M. Bell, 2000. "The question of rural masculinities." *Rural Sociology*, *65*(4), 532-546.

Based on earlier theory of hegemonic masculinity, this paper makes a clear distinction between the masculine-rural and rural-masculine. It tries to establish that such studies on masculinity are complementary to feminist scholarship rather alternative in nature. Hence, this article provides a ground for research in the field of masculinity across the related disciplines.

59. Carter, M. R., B. L. Barham, 1996. "Level of playing fields and laissez faire: post liberal development strategy in inegalitarian agrarian economies." *World Development* Vol. 24, No. 7 (July 1996): 1133-1149.

This article examines the microeconomic linkages between distribution and growth the possible reproduction of rural poverty over time in the context of the rural sector of Latin America. The study has been taken up in the post liberalisation period when markets supersede the state interventions. It has tried to locate the prospects of public policy and collective people's action that has the propensity to modify the nature of growth and distribution in the post liberalisation agrarian market economy. The authors note that the agrarian sector bears a disproportionate share of Latin American poverty in the post liberalisation period. Even if the agro export of the countries witnessed a rapid surge, the rural sector experienced a rapid increase in income disparity. This export boom benefitted a small segment of farmers while the majority experienced the pain. The authors are sceptic about the neo liberal economy and they predict that the laissez faire agrarian economies are going to face catastrophe. They visualise that the neo structuralist perspective that evolves through the neoliberal political philosophy are dirty and dangerous for the small farmers with low wealth. This emerging economy is going to deepen inequality and worsen poverty. So, they call for better public policy intervention and collective action to redress these issues.

60. Carter, M. R., B. L. Barham, & D. Mesbah, 1996. "Agricultural export booms and the rural poor in Chile, Guatemala, and Paraguay." ***Latin American Research Review*****, Vol. 31, No. 1 (Winter 1996): 33-49.**

This article is a fine blend of conceptual framework and empirical analysis. It makes an exploration of the post liberalisation syndrome in the agricultural set up of three countries i.e. Chile, Guatemala, and Paraguay. The authors examine the scenario of export booms in the agrarian products in the three aforesaid Latin American countries. This export boom has yielded a wide range of sectoral outcomes. This has been feasible due to the distinct socioeconomic contexts and varying crop types adopted by the agrarian economies of these countries. To the authors policies play a significant role in the export boom in agricultural economies and they have got the tenacity to include and exclude the rural poor. Policies need to focus on increasing participation of the rural poor in the agrarian transformation. Participation can be stirred by increasing the access to and control of the rural poor over land resources. They can also have a positive impact on rural employment. The first two sections set the conceptual models adopted by the authors to make the subsequent empirical interpretations. The four follow up sections interpret export booms in Chile, Guatemala and Paraguay. The study seems to be a multi-centric study. The authors use data on farms collected from the surveys of rural households in each country. They have also used case studies from various countries under study to substantiate their pronunciations. The final section ends up with a conclusion that agro export needs to benefit the rural poor. Policy reformations are the need to make agro exports rural people centric.

61. Castle, Emery N. 1993. "Rural diversity: an American asset." Annals of the American Academy of Political and Social Science Vol. 529 (September 1993): 12-21.

The author sees the diversity in the American rural society. To him, American rural spaces vary in terms of their natural resource and human resource components. Not only resources vary significantly in the rural societies of the country, but the social problems are also diverse from one rural space to the other. This article insists upon the immense diversity of rural America in order to assess the direction that rural economic development of the country need to take in the future. With an introduction to the heterogeneity existing within rural America and historising the economy of American rural society, the article discusses rural economic policies for the future. The author shows his concern on the declining farming and extractive industries, which affects not only the distribution of space in rural areas, but the handling of rural affairs. It suggests that rural development programmes need to be progressive and forward looking in character as the future rural societies are going to have a different face with newly emerging issues. They clearly voice that farm issues cannot be taken as the sole and the whole rural social problem and rural development strategy need not be only targeted only to farm development nor the Department of Agriculture be treated as the sole agency for social transformation in rural society. The article proposes that rural development need not try to recreate an outdated ideal of rural America. The final section of the article discusses rural entrepreneurship and different types of economic development that will provide a viable model for rural social change and bring solution to many social problems. The last proposition the author makes is that the rural development plans need to be highly adaptable to be successful in mitigating rural issues and bringing meaningful rural interventions.

62. Castle, Emery N. (ed.) 1995. *The Changing American Countryside: Rural People and Places*. Kansas: University Press of Kansas.

This edited book is a collection of essays that provide an insight into the geography, sociology and economy of rural areas in the United States. The book has been edited by Emery Castle, a member to cater to the interests of the college level students as well as the researchers and population having interest in rural studies. The book is classified into eight main sections. The initial two chapters of the book set the background of American rural society and farming as their mainstay, the reflection of rural areas in American literature and culture. The third section of the book analyses the changes witnessed by rural America due urban sprawl and the rapid decline in the farm-oriented economy. Chapter four of the book contributed by John Fraser Hart is very interesting and it tries to negotiate the much-misused definitions of rural/urban and nonmetropolitan/metropolitan. The book elaborates the changing rural economy due to the increasing importance of money, changing job scenario, space, land management and growing industries. The book also reflects on poverty and its causes, brings regional and ethnic diversities into account. The book devotes a section to decision making, rural organisations and institutions. Thus, the book provides an overall scenario of rural society and introduces the readers with the various institutions, issues and interventions undertaken in the rural society.

63. Castle, E. N. 1998. "A conceptual framework for the study of rural places." ***American Journal of Agricultural Economics*****, 80(3), 621-631.**

This paper distinguishes the study of rural America from all other in the sphere of rurality. It looks into the rural population from the angles of their low density, vast diversity, and strong linkages with urban and global structure. The author elaborates the coexistence of prosperity and poverty in rural America. He tries to impression upon the readers that no single rural socio-economic issue is distinctly away from urban or global influences. Therefore, this study devises a new framework to understand American structure of rurality without which it is hard to design any plan and policies.

64. Cernea, M. M. 1991. ***Putting people first: Sociological variables in rural development*** **(No. 9831, p. 1). The World Bank.**

This book redefines the understanding of rural development on the perspective of multilayered agency participation. A well-structured economic system, technological advancement, and agricultural advancement are not always the key element of rural transformation; rather it is the people's participation and acceptability which makes the process viable and sustainable. Social engineering always influences social action and in this behavioural process people's participation is much needed. Further, this book widens the perspective of rural development beyond the mere financial component and advocates for the positive role of communities along with their socio-cultural ethos.

65. Chambers, R. 1974. "Managing rural development: Ideas and Experience from East Africa." ***Institute of Development Studies Bulletin*****, 6(1), 4-12.**

The author discusses how the rural developmental programmes are always subject to resource constraint taking the cases from Kenya. In order to address these resource trade-off or misallocations, this study recommends a number of managerial frameworks related to programme designing and implementation, field staff management, local participation, programme evaluation, research and development, formulation of plan to carry out the rural developmental programmes. Further, author also remarks the criticality of too much of systematic and managerial approach in the realm of rural development which usually sidetracks the less skilled group of population.

66. Chambers, R. 1987. "Sustainable rural livelihoods: a strategy for people, environment and development." in C. Conroy and M. Litvinoff (eds). *The Greening of Aid, Sustainable Livelihoods in Practice*, London: Earthscan.

Based on five case studies related to rural development and sustainability from countries like; Thailand, India, Nepal, Mali and Honduras this study emphasizes the role of bioeconomic intervention for livelihood sustainability in rural areas even against the resource constraints. In order to meet the basic needs of rural population in a sustainable way, the author recommends five elements such as; understanding of issues, priorities people's interest, securing the rights of poorer mass, promotion of self-help approach, skill and continuity of staffs. All these elements need to be taken into consideration in developing strategies for sustainable livelihood programmes.

67. Chambers, R. 1993. *Challenging the professions: frontiers for rural development.* Intermediate Technology Publications Ltd (ITP).

This volume comprises of research articles earlier published by the author over the years which centrally on the role of professionals in delivering effective rural development programmes. The author considers rural development since 1974. To him, rural development since 1974, has adopted new strategies over the old ones, like preferring optimisation goals rather the maximisation, integration of problem-oriented approaches to opportunity-based solving mechanisms, empirical tools on a theoretical foundation. The author also elaborates the professional challenges at ground level in the implementation of programmes with reference to rural heterogeneity, diversified inequality, resource constraints.

68. Chambers, R. 2014. *Rural development: Putting the last first.* Routledge.

This work of author signifies the need of both the scientific expertise and indigenous knowledge for local development. The author talks about the bottom-up approach to development and also the top-down managerial procedure and resource flow. This book further highlights the role of external agencies in putting the developmental goals on a right track by transferring skill, power, controls, and know-hows to local people for a sustainable rural development in long run.

69. Chambers, R., & G. Conway, 1992. "Sustainable rural livelihoods: practical concepts for the 21st century." *Institute of Development Studies* (UK).

This paper extensively debates on rural livelihood sustainability on the assumption of high growth of livelihood requirements in 21st century. This requirement again is subdivided into tangible and intangible assets. In order to have these assets the author advocates for a decent livelihood particularly for rural masses who are usually deprived and are low in capability, accessibility and equity. Additionally, the author suggests that a livelihood practice may be described as sustainable when it has net benefits in terms of restoring and enhancing local as well as global wellbeing. Therefore, study explains multidimensionality of rural livelihood transition in future to come into existence in terms of production, distribution and deprivation. Finally, the author summons both the developmental practitioners and academic researchers, to come up with better and responsible policy design to enhance the local capability.

70. Cheshire, L., Higgins, 2000. "Contemporary strategies for rural community development in Australia: A Governmentality perspective." ***Journal of Rural Studies*** **Volume 16, Issue 2, April 2000, Pages 203-215.**

This paper explores rural community development in Queensland. The author talks about the current discourses on rural development which emphasise upon self-help and bottom-up, community-based initiatives which are said to 'empower' the individual. But in reality, they cut back on public expenditure. These approaches are not new to Australia. Having the 'governmentality' perspective at the foundation, this paper examines the operation of 'govern through community'. With this in mind, three basic research questions are identified by the author. They are;

- How are the notions of self-governing individuals and communities constructed in political discourse?
- What political rationalities are used to justify current levels of (non) intervention?
- What are the discourses, forms and outcomes of empowerment at the local level?

The paper concludes that self-help empowers people on the one hand, but on the other it brings the added burden with the devolution of power to local people.

71. Cheshire, L., V. Higgins, & G. Lawrence, 2006. Guest editorial. "Rural governance in Australia: Changing forms and emerging actors." ***Rural Society*****, 16(3), 231-234.**

This is the editorial for a special edition of the journal Rural Society. This editorial explores new rural governance in Australia. The authors note that over the last 20 years, new actors have come into the playfield of decision-making and service delivery. They are increasingly taking the place of the state. This has no doubt led to a decline in the importance of state authorities. But Government remains heavily present in contemporary forms of governance, via the ongoing structures of Australia's federated system, and the continued role of state, federal and local government agencies in policy formation and delivery. The authors point out that the increasing role of community in governance is not necessarily problem free, nor it is highly democratic. Local citizen's participation is good, but they need to understand their role and prepared to take up the responsibility. Finally, they conclude that when governance shifts to the hands of rural people rural communities become more diverse and competing interest grow in the rural areas.

72. Christenson, J. A. and E. G. Lorraine 1985. "Fifty Years of Rural Sociology: Status, Trends and Impressions." ***Rural Sociology*** **50(4):503–22.**

Christenson and Garkovich note that European rural sociology has its origin from liberal arts. It tends to be more theoretical and philosophical than U.S. rural sociology. They find that U.S. Rural Sociology is more empirical, more quantitative and a better feeder to practical policy designing for rural societies. The authors also see the great contributions of the professional and academic organisations for the growth of the sub discipline. They make a reference to the role of the International Rural Sociological Association (IRSA), established in 1966, the Latin American Rural Sociological Association formed in 1969, followed later by the Australia and Oceania Network and the Asian Rural Sociological Association which have led to a proliferation of research into the rural societies.

73. Clark, D., R. Southern, & J. Beer, 2007. "Rural governance, community empowerment and the new institutionalism: A case study of the Isle of Wight." ***Journal of Rural Studies, 23*****(2), 254-266.**

This article probes into the efficiency and effectiveness of two institutional model of rural development such as; the state-aided model and the community-based institutional model. By examining the case from Isle of Wight, this study concludes in favour of institutions which are backed by local communities with minimal influence from external agencies. These agencies usually aim at enhancing local entrepreneurship through capacity building. Since, we cannot ignore the role of the government in delivering the effective rural governance and community welfare, this study suggests for a new institutionalism by incorporating the merits of both models of rural development.

74. Cleaver, Kevin M. 1997. "Rural Development Strategies for Poverty Reduction and Environmental Protection in Sub-Saharan Africa." Washington, D.C.: World Bank.

This World Bank policy paper sketches the history of donor assistance to agriculture and rural development in Sub-Saharan Africa for a period of three decades. It provides the World Bank insight into development. The policy paper clearly projects that the then development strategies lacked a critical lens. The paper notes the beginning strategies of the 1970s and 1980s under the banner of integrated rural development aiming to promote agricultural commodity development, facilitation of agricultural credit, making provisions of irrigation and overemphasising agricultural services witnessed its tragic failures. The paper summarises the current thrust of government and donor agricultural strategies and identifies the deficiencies in the government models of rural development supported by donor agencies without the addition of their own vision. Flawed designing of the projects, lack of policy vision, exclusion of private sectors and NGOs as role players, fragmentation between donor agencies without a convergence approach and strong commitments of the governments were some of the reasons of the failure of the integrated rural development projects. Further this policy paper notes that lack of proper and sustainable support of the donor agencies for agriculture in these countries coupled with the deficient agricultural strategies of the developing countries of Sub-Saharan Africa contribute significantly for the failure of rural development. This led to a shift in the strategies in the late 1980s. This shifting strategy started emphasising on economic and agricultural policy reform and soliciting greater donor cooperation to float the national programmes for livestock development, agricultural research, forestry, agricultural extension, small-scale irrigation, and rural roads. The government line departments became the nodal agencies to run these programmes. The policy paper has come with some constructive solutions like deeper and drastic agricultural policy reform, donor agencies to be selective in their partner choice among the African government partners, directly supporting private sectors, promoting agricultural marketing and processing, building better institutions, governmental collaboration with NGOs, and support for a broader concept of rural development. The paper is also strengthened by a section in which the authors address criticisms of the World Bank strategies by African government leaders and NGOs.

75. Cloke, P. 1993. "The countryside as commodity: new spaces for rural leisure." In Sue Glyptis (Ed.), *Leisure and the Environment: Essays in Honour of Professor J. A. Patmore* (pp. 53-67). London and New York: Belhaven Press.

In this paper, geographer Cloke conducts a socio-semiotic analysis of rural tourism brochures to provide insights into the increasing commodification and symbolic value of Britain's rural spaces. For the author commodification is a process which transforms rural places into commodities laden with new meanings. The places of agricultural production are transformed into stages for the consumption. This is done to provide rural experiences for tourists. The analysis of rural tourism brochures provides evidence that the contemporary countryside is commonly sold to visitors as a zone of pristine natural landscapes, easy living and ideal family types. Thus, the study shows increasing commodification is dramatically changing the nature of rural space.

76. Cloke, P. 1997. "Country backwater to virtual village? Rural studies and the cultural turn." ***Journal of Rural Studies, 13*, 367-375.**

In this paper, the author suggests that a revival in rural social science is underway. This is linked to the "cultural turn and rise of the post-structuralism perspective in social science. New exciting literatures associated with rural culture and representations of rurality have emerged. Novel topics like rural others and difference, human perceptions of rural landscapes, rural identities, imaginaries and experiences are in their process of evolution. The author focuses on four of these emerging areas of rural scholarship. They are nomenclature as below:

- Nature-society relations (and human-nature engagements).
- Discourses of rural experience and imagination (including work on the diverse nature of rural lifestyles).
- Symbolic texts of rural cultures (i.e., how the rural is represented in the media and how this reinforces common discourses about rurality), and
- Movements (focusing on rural motilities i.e., rural tourism and recreation and alternative rural living).

Cloke finally concludes that it is important to retain a critical edge in rural inquiry.

77. Cloke, P. 2006. "Conceptualizing rurality." ***Handbook of rural studies, 18.***

The author here illustrates how the rural studies of early period are not manifested its dynamism extended from rural idyll to oppressiveness. The theoretical distinctions on rurality from across the disciplines in social sciences is brought into discussion to reconstruct the meaning and concept of rural studies under the changing social, economic and political environment. Further, the article tries to bring a sharp opposition of rural studies as against urban studies and practices.

78. Cloke, P., & Thrift, N. 1987. "Intra-class conflict in rural areas." ***Journal of Rural Studies, 3*****(4), 321-333.**

This paper discusses how the studies related to class conflict has been neglected for decades in spite of an increasing attention given to rural studies globally. The author notes that existing studies on class conflicts basically look at the differences between local communities and in-migrants particularly on the ground of livelihood practice. But this study makes a clear departure from such differentiation and elaborates the class struggle which is intra-class in nature rather than inter-class and such class struggle addresses the deep-rooted structural differences caused by socio-cultural and economic factors.

79. Cloke, P., M. Goodwin, P. Milbourne, & C. Thomas, 1995. "Deprivation, poverty and marginalisation in rural lifestyles in England and Wales." ***Journal of Rural Studies, 11*****(4), 351-365.**

This article tries to re-contextualise the rural issues based on criticisms drawn on the appropriateness of deprivation and disadvantages that prevails in rural England and Wales. The authors clarify that cultural construction plays a significant role along with material deprivation in bringing marginalisation in rural lifestyles. Hence, this study suggests mapping of the intersectionality in the context of material deprivation is needed to understand rurality and its conceptualisation in a wider sense.

80. Cloke, P., T. Marsden, & P. Mooney, (Eds.). 2006. ***Handbook of Rural Studies*****. Sage.**

This handbook aims to bring a new horizon in contemporary social science discourses which is largely dominated by studies related to urban or city life at least until 1970s. Hence, this work is giving a scope for theoretical innovations to both the urban and rural life. More specifically contributors here discuss rural components, its restructuring and profiling of rural policies related to deprivation, exclusion, production, identity, cultural representation and sustainability.

81. Cloke, P., P. Milbourne, & R. Widdowfield, 2002. *Rural Homelessness: Issues, experiences and policy responses.* Policy Press.

This dedicated volume tries to claim high on the problem of rural homelessness. Homelessness is generally considered as an urban centric issue. As most of the studies or policy practices concentrate on only the issue of homelessness in the urban space, they ignore the wider scope of both the theories and practices in addressing a grave issue of homelessness at rural space, where the problem is acute but still invisible. Therefore, this work is mainly based on rural homelessness and its related methodological approaches to set different framework of policy practice and understanding in dealing with rural homelessness.

82. Cohen, J. M., & N. T. Uphoff, 1980. "Participation's place in rural development: seeking clarity through specificity." ***World Development,*** **8(3), 213-235.**

This paper tries to bring clarifications on doubtful performance of developmental debates and policy practices in apprehending rurality and rural poor on the ground of deprivation and marginality. In this developmental discourse the authors are elaborate on the paradigm shift from 1960s to 1970s. During the early period the developmental thinking, capital-investment growth models were overemphasised. Later on, there was a paradigm shift towards people centric basic need approaches. As the current developmental practices are precisely dominated by people's participation, this study formulates a number of rural participatory frameworks on rural development which includes decision making, its implementation, generating benefits and evaluation.

83. Connelly, S., T. Richardson, & T. Miles, 2006. "Situated legitimacy: deliberative arenas and the new rural governance." ***Journal of Rural Studies,*** **22, 267-277.**

In this article the authors develop the notion of "situated legitimacy. In their view, in contemporary times, the notion of legitimacy is complex, perhaps given meaning by different actors in specific contexts. This changed notion of legitimacy is bringing dramatic changes in rural governance. Changing rural system of governance with local partnership model is becoming successful in addressing local economic, environmental and social issues.

84. Connelly, S., T. Richardson, & T. Miles, 2006. "Situated legitimacy: deliberative arenas and the new rural governance." ***Journal of Rural Studies*, 22(3), 267-277.**

With a reference to rural governance in UK and similar economies, this paper revisits the democratic applicability of legitimacy. It verifies the role of governing actors on the changing state of political and social institutions in the rural settings. At residual, the study shows difficulty in drawing specific inferences on the legitimacy of changing principles of rural governance as they are hybrid in nature, and can only justified through complex and competing rationalities. The study concludes that since, the new governance mechanism is dependent on direct involvement of numerous stakeholders, it needs to gear more effort for wider acceptability and the understanding.

85. Coombs, P. H., & M. Ahmed, 1974. "Attacking Rural Poverty: How Nonformal Education Can Help." A Research Report for the World Bank Prepared by the International Council for Educational Development.

Apart from usual and self-evident link between the formal education and development, this paper highlights the importance of nonformal education in rural development to mitigate the incidence of poverty. From the policy perspective, it is the formal education that shares the major budgetary allocation in most of the developing economies. This formal education lacks in imparting sufficient occupational skill and abilities. As these economies are mainly based on agriculture and related livelihood, this study emphasizes facilitation of essential skill development through reallocation of resources from formal to nonformal education without hampering either's objective or scale.

86. Cramer, K. J. 2016. *The Politics of Resentment: Rural Consciousness in Wisconsin and the Rise of Scott Walker.* University of Chicago Press.

The author, Cramer introduces what she means by the "rural consciousness" in the beginning of the book. To her, it is an identity as a rural person that includes attachment to place, a sense that rural communities are ignored by policymakers and do not get their fair share of resources, and a perception that rural and urban people have fundamentally different lifestyles, values, and work ethic. She argues throughout the book that this consciousness is an important part of political opinions and that it creates a sense of justification for resentment of urban elites and the public sector. No doubt, the author has decently described the impact that a rural consciousness has on political opinions of rural Wisconsinites.

87. Curtis, B. 2004. "Rural sociology: a partial review." *New Zealand Sociology, 19*(2), 180-196. This article opens a special issue of the New Zealand Journal of Sociology devoted (in part) to rural sociology.

The paper makes a review of recent debates and trends in the international rural sociological literature. The author poses rural sociology as a sub-discipline and justifies the nomenclature "rural studies" on the grounds of its interdisciplinary character. During the review the author gets a clear impression on the shift in focus of rural studies from rural community to the study of global food chain, new sociology of agriculture, study to the study of agribusiness, farm studies.

The author navigates the recent research on food chains i.e., the complex relationship between (family) farms, local/global processors/factories, local/global agribusinesses and local/global distributors. Here, the author brings into discussion the work of New Zealand geographers including Richard le Heron. The author also makes a reference from the reviews the actor network theory and environmental histories. The author ends with an evaluation of New Zealand rural sociology and concludes that this academic field is shaped by a very small group of institutions and just a handful of scholars in the country.

88. Davis, S., N. Crothers, J. Grant, S. Young, & K. Smith, 2012. "Being involved in the country: Productive ageing in different types of rural communities." *Journal of Rural Studies, 28*(4), 338-346.

This study explores the role of ageing population in rural sustainability through community participation. Based on data collected from 3925 respondents of the age above 50 years in rural Australia, it shows that older people are efficient in maintaining the community link and help in enhancing social capital. But the authors identify that healthcare related issues and lack of facilitation poses limitations in social and civic engagements of elderly people. Therefore, they suggest to promote productive ageing for a well-connected and functional rural community with sustainable social development.

89. Deavers, K. 1992. "What is rural?" *Policy Studies Journal, 20*(2), 183.

The author in this article defines rural in terms of some lags in development indexes. These are: low density and remote settlements, existence of less competitive business entities, and lack of meaningful occupational diversification. The author also talks about intra rural classification based on adoption of livelihood practices. Finally, suggests for developing a proper understanding of the complexity of rural and rurality in order to devise effective developmental plan and policies.

90. de Janvry, Alain; Sadoulet, Elisabeth; Wilcox, Linda. 1989. "Rural labour in Latin America." *International Labour Review,* Vol. 128, No. 6 (Nov-Dec 1989): 701-729.

The article makes an attempt to provide a picture of the changing labour market of Latin America since 1950s. The data are collected from Latin America, the Caribbean, Brazil, Chile and Mexico. The changing labour market and the subsequent change in labour relations are viewed in terms of agricultural transformations. The article is divided into four parts. These parts focus on changes in rural and agricultural populations and the patterns of rural-urban migration; the structure of employment and the importance of wage employment in agriculture; the evolution of agricultural wages and surplus labour; and household incomes and the incidence of poverty. The article views that agriculture is in a process of continuous decline in the rural Latin American countries and thus the share of agricultural labour declining in the total labour force. Rural poverty has been found to be rampant in rural Latin America and absolute poverty paralyses the ruralites dependent on agriculture. At the same time the researchers discover that with no proportionate employment is generated in the rural spaces of the country. This leads to a continuous surge in rural urban migration. The authors suggest that land reforms with distributive justice, stopping over mechanisation of agriculture and creating special rural centric anti-poverty programmes are the need of the hour to stop labour migration in rural Latin American countries.

91. de Ferranti, David, Perry, Guillermo E., Foster, William, Lederman, Daniel, Valdes, Alberto. 2005. "Beyond the city: the rural contribution to development", The World Bank.

This book is an outcome of the study based on original research funded by the World Bank's Office of the Chief Economist for Latin America and the Caribbean. It evaluates the contribution of rural development and policies to growth, poverty alleviation, and environmental degradation in the rest of the economy, as well as in the rural space. As the title suggests it establishes a link between rural and national development.

New findings and are combined with existing literature to enhance the understanding of the how rural economic activities contribute to various aspects of national development. The empirical findings of the book make substantial contributions to the debate over the appropriate design of public policies aiming to enhance the rural contribution to national development, including economic growth, poverty reduction, environmental sustainability, and macroeconomic stability.

92. de Janvry, Alain; Sadoulet, Elisabeth. 1989. "Investment strategies to combat rural poverty: a proposal for Latin America." ***World Development*** **Vol. 17, No. 8 (August 1989): 1203-1221.**

This article attempts to define a rural development strategy for Latin America. The article makes an earnest attempt to profile poverty in rural Latin America. First of all, the authors look at the macroeconomic conditions of the country which is marked by where balance-of-payments deficits and inflationary crises that require the implementation of drastic stabilisation policies and structural adjustment programmes. Secondly, the authors try to look at the long-run structural determinants of rural poverty and the short run impacts which adjustments to the crisis have on the rural poor. The first two sections of the article are dedicated to provide ample quantitative information on the impacts of structural adjustment and the profile of rural poverty. In the next parts, the authors have tried to spell about a strategy for agricultural and rural development that is more responsive to rural poverty and that they expect can be capable enough to make agriculture play a catalyst role in generating foreign exchange, in reducing inflationary pressures, and in creating effective demand for other economic sectors. The development strategy suggested by the authors is tailored to the different types of rural poor and to their specific sources of income. In the final section, the article presents how selective components of rural development programmes need to aim at enhancing productivity growth in small farms, at assisting households on marginal farms to engage in a portfolio of productive activities, at giving the landless and marginal farmers greater access to productive assets, at generating more employment opportunities in agriculture and rationalising rural labour markets, and at creating off-farm employment in activities linked to agriculture located in the rural areas.

93. Donnermeyer, J. F., & W. DeKeseredy, 2013. *Rural criminology*. Routledge.

This book rationalises the need for studying rural criminology. To the authors major rural and small-town settlements account for about 49 percent of the world population. They identify areas like rurality and crime, incident of crime related to food, land and agriculture, drug peddling, and related laws, justice and policy interventions to be studied in details and depth.

94. Douglas, D. J. 2005. "The restructuring of local government in rural regions: A rural development perspective." *Journal of Rural Studies, 21*(2), 231-246.

This article makes a careful review of some public policy interventions at local government of rural Canada. In this connection, it highlights the key role of local government in the discourse of rural development. The authors note that local government is a complex mix of power, resource. But there is still a need for transparency and accountability in policy implementation and its outcome. This can reinforce the role of local agents in delivering effective developmental interventions.

95. Duncan, Cynthia M. (ed.) 1992. *Rural Poverty in America*. New York and London: Auburn House.

This book is edited by Cynthia Duncan, Programme director of the Ford Foundation's Rural Economic Policy Programme. It contains essays on rural poverty in the United States. The book is divided into three sections. The first section makes an economic overview of rural poverty. All of the essays in this section describe rural poverty as primarily a structural, nonfarm circumstance. They see the concentration of rural poverty in the south of the country, varying across race and gender groups. The authors describe that rural poverty is characterised by low earnings and the working poor, with a persistent, slow or never changing quality from decade to decade. The second section contains the case studies captured and developed by sociologists. The ethnographic method is adopted to describe the situation of the people suffering from poverty and their experience. The case studies are drawn from the geographic and ethnic areas in which rural poverty prevails pervasively. These include Appalachia, migrant farm workers, American Indians, and the Northeast and Midwest. The last section focuses on policy prescriptions for addressing rural poverty. It includes the essays to overcome the stereotypes of the rural poor, as well as an essay on empowerment.

96. Duncan, Cynthia M. and Lamborghini, Nita. 1994. "Poverty and social context in remote rural communities." *Rural Sociology*, Vol. 59, No. 3 (Fall 1994): 437-461.

This article looks at social isolation in rural communities and establishes that isolation in poor inner-city neighbourhoods perpetuates poverty. The article makes a comparative analysis of research done in a chronically-poor coal-dependent community in Appalachia with research from a resource-rich community in Northern New England. Four poor and non-poor counties are first described using county-level socioeconomic indicators. The authors make use of in-depth interviews to see how residents perceive the social context in two case-study communities within those counties. It is found that in the New England community, with its more diverse work opportunities and stable middle class to invest in public goods, the poor are not segregated. In contrast in the Appalachian community, limited job options and opportunities bring sharply divided social classes where distancing becomes a marked phenomenon. Interviews with poor women in both communities are used to illustrate these differences. The differing aspirations of women in the communities are also taken into count. The authors land up at a conclusion that it is the social capital and social context of a community that generate supportive and inclusive social relations and institutions.

97. Duncan, Cynthia M. 1996. "Understanding persistent poverty: social class contexts in rural communities." *Rural Sociology*, Vol. 61, No. 1 (Spring 1996): 103-124.

This article establishes that a strong correlation exists between social context and the perpetuation of poverty. In this context, the author studies the social context of rural areas to explain the persistence of poverty within communities and families. It argues that the scale, familiarity among social actors, and bounded nature of rural communities offer unique advantages for understanding the persistence of poverty. So, a deep understanding into the social context of the rural areas is needed to have a proper understanding of poverty. After an introduction to this argument, the article looks at studies of persistent poverty in urban areas as background to study poverty from the social and cultural dimensions. The author brings into presentation and discussion a number of case studies in different rural areas of the U.S. to indicate how low wages and control over labour markets create rigid stratification systems in rural areas. This stratification system generated from the labour market position and wage distribution determine social relations and opportunities. The article ends by instituting the argument that studies of urban poor "neighbourhood effects" and social embeddedness can be extended and improved upon by looking at persistent rural poverty.

98. Du Toit M, Malau-Aduli B, Vangaveti V, Sabesan S, Ray RA. 2019. "Use of telehealth in the management of non-critical emergencies in rural or remote emergency departments: A systematic review." *Journal of Telemedicine and Telecare*. *25*(1):3-16.

The researchers have reviewed 2532 articles published during the period 1996 to 2017 in England. They have taken articles published in English after 1996. The focus of the studies is the emergency duty (ED) staff providing care or the patients receiving care in the rural or remote ED settings, covered by the researchers. Presentations were non-critical emergencies.

99. Dzanku, F. M. (2015). "Transient rural livelihoods and poverty in Ghana." *Journal of Rural Studies, 40*, 102-110

The objective of this paper is to identify factors responsible for livelihood transitions and its welfare trade-off in rural areas. On the basis of panel data collected from 464 households at three different time periods, the author notes that agriculture is the main economic activity of rural Ghana. Though other livelihood options are available along with the agriculture, they seem to be transient due to the considerable gap between existing occupational practices and required competitive vocational skills. The data shows, about 55 percent of sample households are impacted by instability caused due to livelihood diversities and has a high cost for the welfare of economically marginal households. The factors related to geographical remoteness, demographics, education, commodity price differential are important determinants of rural welfare. So, in order to have a more stable rural economy adequate investment on human capital is a much-needed policy intervention which can help in enhancing the rural entrepreneurial capacity in the rural space.

100. Edwards, B. 1998. "Charting the discourse of community action: perspectives from practice in rural Wales." *Journal of Rural Studies, 14*(1), 63-77.

In this article the author draws research insight from his own experience of, and involvement in, a rural community participation initiative in Wales, namely the Jigsaw (or now Jigso) programme. The author realises community participation has remained under researched, even after it has been established as a key aspect of development programmes since the 1980s, it has been initiated in many rural communities and also has been accepted as a key theme in the new governance discourse. The author describes community development as a complex and multifaceted concept and proposes that discourse relating to community development the following propositions into their centrality. These propositions are:

- Which communities participate in initiatives?
- The reasons for their engagement.

The understanding of these two questions can bring a full-fledged idea of community participation in that programme in a particular rural area.

101. Egan, A. F. & A. E. Luloff, 2000. "The exurbanisation of America's forests: research in rural social science." ***Journal of Forestry*, *98*(3), 26-30.**

This paper relates to the syndrome of Ex urbanisation. Ex urbanisation refers to the process of migration of urban residents to near or accessible rural environments. The author sees that this process has taken an upward trend in America since 1980s. An improved quality of life in the countryside becomes the chief fascinating point for the process. But this leads to clash among the ex-urbanised population and the long-term rural residents over land use practices and due to the discrepancy in their attitudes, needs and values that is very different from each other. This process also significantly affects the local forest-based economies, social structures, forest management practices and, in the end, forest policy (or the way rural land is used more generally). Long-term residents over land use practices.

102. Eikeland, S., & I. Lie, 1999. "Pluriactivity in rural Norway." ***Journal of Rural Studies*, *15*(4), 405-415.**

This paper enquires the nature and scope of rural pluriactivity. It tries to explore the rural-urban integration in the labour market, the role of global product market, existence of rural sectoral mix based on the data collected on rural enterprises, labour market and the governance of rural Norway. The empirical analysis confirms that the pluriactivity is a norm for rural Norway which is predominated by its major agricultural enterprises. But the process of urbanisation and labour market integration has affected it in due course. Apart from urban bias, the pluriactivity also found to be male centric. So, the authors suggest it is likely to widen the gender differences at rural areas if not practiced suitably.

103. El Ghonemy, Mohamad Riad. 1990. *The Political Economy of Rural Poverty: The Case for Land Reform*. New York: Routledge.

This book is a depiction of rural poverty with its determinants, triggers and puts a challenge to many of the land reform measures. It contains the author's self-experience as a poverty expert of Food and Agricultural Organisation and case studies drawn from the less developed countries (LDCs) all over the world. The author subscribes to the view that deep rooted institutional structures generate poverty and poverty eradication is only possible with institutional reforms. The author clearly spells out that it is public intervention which can successfully bring institutional reforms and market mechanisms can hardly bring any change. It advocates for land reforms to do away with the institutional monopoly that concentrates land in the hands of the wealthy and restricts the poor's access to land and opportunities. The book opens with an introduction into the issue and is divided into three parts. The first part i.e., "Puzzles and Dilemmas," discovers and describes the link between agriculture and poverty in LDCs; the institutional determinants of poverty and their significance and the way they have been overlooked by the policymakers; the declining demand for agricultural labour, and thus the sinking job market for the rural poor; reversals in development policies that used to favour the rural poor; and the overuse of a myopic framework for policy formulation. This section also contains a description of rural poverty in LDCs. The major focus remaining on the linkage between landlessness and poverty. The second section provides an insight into the concepts like private property; the nexus between rural institutions and rural poverty; the relationship between farm size and production efficiency; and the consequences of land redistribution. This section is more reflective on the needs of land reforms to ensure better opportunities for the rural poor. The last section focuses on the poverty reduction process and factors that block it. It also analyses the achievements of land reforms in some countries in reducing poverty.

104. Ellis, F. 2000. *Rural livelihoods and diversity in developing countries.* Oxford University Press.

This book defines the diversity in rural livelihood and its importance in developing economies. Here the diversity is described as adoption of varieties of livelihood practices to earn household livings. With the ascendancy of such diversities in the livelihood practices in rural areas it became a major concern for developmental studies and local governance. The author also discusses the impact of diversified rural livelihood practices on occupational transition, rural transformation, poverty, rural inequality, environmental sustainability and other related macroeconomic aspects for bringing appropriate policy measures under the discourse of rural development.

105. Ellis, F., & H. A. Freeman, 2004. "Rural livelihoods and poverty reduction strategies in four African countries." *Journal of Development Studies, 40*(4), 1-30.

On the basis of evidences drawn from four African countries (Kenya, Malawi, Tanzania, Uganda), this study highlights the rural adversities such as; low income, asset holdings, livestock, land, high dependency on the production of food crops. But these adversities are found to be more prominent among low-income households those are not practicing diverse occupations. It is the non-farm activities, adequate income provisions, livelihood diversities that distinguish the low- and high-income households in the sample countries. Hence, this study suggests for skill development of farmers, small rural enterprises and rational tax structure at local administration for the survival of economically marginal people.

106. Escribano, M. J. R. 2007. "Migration to rural Navarre: questioning the experience of counter urbanisation". *Tijdschriftvoor Economischeen Sociale Geografie, 98*(1), 32-41.

In this article the author talks about the changes that are noted in the rural areas of Navarre, northern Spain due to counter urbanisation. He makes an in-depth interview with the new arriving population from the urban areas to this rural space. The author describes counter urbanisation as a major rural restructuring process. The author records that this process has led to rural population growth by bringing diversity in the structure of rural population. The article concludes that not only upper-class people are counter migrating to find a better residential environment, but also younger people with fewer economic resources, life styles and less-skilled is also colonising the rural space looking for a cheaper place to live.

107. Esparcia, J. 2014. "Innovation and networks in rural areas. An analysis from European innovative projects." Journal of *Rural Studies, 34*, 1-14.

This study illustrates the scope of innovation in rural development. Nine related cases are analysed on rural innovations. They relate to irrigation, organic farming, energy sector and information technology at rural Europe to verify the impact of such innovation on rural diversification, market or product competitiveness, and the good governance. These projects are found to be efficient particularly with active participation from a larger rural network of stakeholders along with the governmental support. So, the adoption and implementation of innovation requires the right combination of traditional and expert knowledge where an active participation of a strong rural web cannot be ignored for a sustainable local development.

108. Falk, William W. and Shanyang Zhao. 1989. "Paradigms, Theories, and Methods in Contemporary Rural Sociology: A Partial Replication and Extension." ***Rural Sociology*** **54(4):587-600.**

These authors report that rural sociological research is generally more applied and less theoretical than general sociology. They note that rural sociology takes a more paradigmatic stance that is largely "social facts" (e.g., deductive traditions ranging from functionalism to Marxism). They make a calculation that about 92 percent of the articles on rural sociology produced between 1965-1976 have taken this 'social facts' stance while 76 percent articles produced between 1976 to 1985 have adopted this stance. Articles in the social definition (e.g., Meadian tradition) paradigm constituted 6 percent of those published from 1965 to 1976 and 9 percent from 1976 to 1985, while articles classified as a "mixed" paradigmatic perspective made up 1 percent of those published from 1965 to 1976 and 14 percent from 1976 to 1985.

109. Farmer, Frank L.; Ilvento, Thomas W. and Luloff, A.E. 1989. "Rural community poverty: a LISREL measurement model." ***Rural Sociology*****, Vol. 54, No. 4 (Winter 1989): 491-508.**

This article talks about poverty and its alleviation from the individual to the community level. It looks at poverty as a multidimensional concept with an interrelated framework. The article begins with a theoretical discussion that lays out a structural framework for understanding poverty. The progressive discussions in the article try to outline the relationship between the concept and observable variables which is tested empirically. The data are sourced from the Office of Data Analysis and Management. However, the authors finally note that the findings derived from the data hardly conform to the theoretical model. The authors therefore feel that no standardised theoretical model can bring real eradication of poverty. So, the policies aiming at poverty alleviation need to look at community level planning.

110. Fitchen, J. M. 1981. *Poverty in rural America: A case study*. Boulder, CO: Westview Press.

This book represents the outcomes of the years of interactive research of the author on rural America and its problem of poverty. The book rests upon an interdisciplinary approach for studying contemporary rural America. There are two major highlights of the book. They are: identifying the right question and drawing solutions based on empiricism. The book overemphasises the role of community participation for effectiveness of any policy intervention to alleviate rural poverty.

111. Fitchen, Janet M. 1991. *Endangered Spaces, Enduring Places: Change, Identity and Survival in Rural America*. Boulder: Westview Press.

This book authored by anthropologist Janet Fitchen. This book is based on a prolonged ethnographic fieldwork of the author. The author portrays the changes that were taking place in rural America in the late 1980s. The locale of the study is rural New York. The focus is on the local-level reaction of the rural people to the changes and their adaption of the changes. The major changes indicated by the author includes decline of farming and the loss of farmlands; the decline of manufacturing jobs; underemployment and the working poor; and the tightening of the rental housing market in the rural settings of the country. In addition to these issues, the author also points out the worse form rural poverty was taking affecting the interpersonal and community relationships, the changing needs and roles of community services and governments. Finally, the author brings into consideration the issues of identity and survival of rural communities. On the whole, the book provides an intensely personal account of rural New York communities' struggles with poverty and the changing nature of land use and employment options in the late twentieth century.

112. Fløysand, A., & S. E. Jakobsen, 2007. "Commodification of rural places: A narrative of social fields, rural development, and football." ***Journal of Rural Studies, 23*(2), 206-221.**

This paper provides an understanding of rural transition from a non-market to market-based economy. This transition into a market economy no more makes rural areas only a primary production unit rather it leads to increasing commodification of rural goods and services. The authors cite the example of the Norwegian football club, Sogndal Football. This club over the time has not only commodified the game, but also has commodified the countryside where it originated. This study concludes that the process of commodification is externally driven, but control lies with the local communities.

113. Flora, Cornelia B. and Christenson, James A. (ed.) 1991. ***Rural Policies for the 1990s.*** **Boulder: Westview Press.**

This book contains a collection of essays. The contributors include the foremost experts on rural America engaged in policy-relevant research. Its chapters focus on crucial challenges faced by the rural communities like employment, demographics, environment, technology, and globalisation. The book tries to provide an understanding of major problems and recommend some concrete proposals for revitalising rural America. It is a volume designed to address the choices American people which they can translate into programmes of action at the national, state and local levels in order to improve their situations. The chapters are classified into three substantive areas: jobs and the economy, people and services, and the environment. The first section concentrates on an analysis of the issues of capital and economic organisation that particularly impact rural people. The subthemes dealt in these chapters include banking and financing, small businesses, and agricultural labour and policy.

The next group of essays address to the needs of the rural people and special rural populations, such as the aged, the poor, and minorities. These essays also discuss the rural neglects, particularly, education, healthcare, employment, transportation, and other services and bring into the framework the international and domestic issues. The third set of chapters discusses the environment, focusing on land and water in both national and international contexts. Policies having implications for the availability and quality of natural resources are discussed. A final conclusion chapter sums up the main themes of the book, which include the unique attributes and problems of rural areas, the interrelatedness of rural, urban and world policies, and the need for legislation and policies that adequately address the current situation and needs of rural America.

114. Flora, Cornelia Butler; Flora, Jan L.; Spear, Jacqueline D; Swanson, Louis E. 1992. *Rural Communities: Legacy & Change*. Boulder: Westview Press.

The book is a basic level introduction to American rural society. Even people unfamiliar with rural studies can grasp easily the issues posed in the book. This comprehensive introduction to rural America was written as a companion text to a college level telecourse and television series that detailed the experiences of fifteen rural American communities. It makes a very broad selection of issues and frameworks central to rural sociological research. The focus of the book is the community, which is the lens through which larger sociological and economic issues are examined. The book begins with a section that offers an overview of rural communities, focusing on diversity in economies, culture, and family influences. The chapter on Community and Culture is particularly interesting in its discussion of community solidarity and its positive and negative implications for small-town life. The book's clear language presents and introduces sociological concepts in ways that are understandable easily. The book brings into description the community case-studies to effectively illustrate how these concepts are applied to rural studies. The book's second section is economic oriented. It focuses on rural economies, including access to capital, impacts of globalisation and changing consumption patterns. The third section looks at the political and social organisations created to maintain a community and link it to the broader society. Essays enriching this section delineate the dilemmas faced by state and local governments, economic, social and physical structures necessary to support community development, and social infrastructures created to meet the needs of community members. The book's last section uses the community change framework to explore strategies for solving local problems. It looks at power structures in rural communities, techniques for organising, and models for effective community change.

115. Fortmann, Louise. 1988. "Predicting natural resource micro-protest." ***Rural Sociology*** **Vol. 53, No. 3 (Fall 1998): 357-367.**

This article looks at causes of rural-based natural resource protest among rural dwellers. The focus is basically on the timber-harvesting plans. Affluence is measured by average county per capita income. Urbanisation is measured by the size of the biggest city in each county. Consistent with resource mobilisation theory, the article establishes that urbanisation and affluence are the best predictors of rates of protest. Environmental organisation also triggers the protest at rural sites. Reverse migration is not found to be linearly related to protest. The author concludes that natural resource micro protest can be predicted where there is increased proximity of the rural people to natural resource, where natural resources are accepted as a property right of the people, people have a high degree of aesthetic or environmental concerns and where there are organisational forms and resources. These entire combine together to give strength to people's voice and protest action.

116. Fortmann, Louise; Antinori, Camille and Nabane, Nontokozo. 1997. "Fruits of Their Labors: Gender, Property Rights, and Tree Planting in Two Zimbabwe Villages." ***Rural Sociology*** **Vol. 62, No. 3 (Fall 1997): 295-314.**

This article is based on an analysis of tree planting practices by women and men in two Zimbabwean villages. The authors have given a coverage to 27 percent of the households in each of the villages. The authors identify that there are three types of planting sites in these villages. They are: homestead land, individual woodlots and community woodlots. They discover from their survey that women are less likely than men to plant trees on homestead land, the obvious reason advanced by them being that the security of their tenure duration is uncertain on these lands due to the likelihood of change in their marital status. However, women and men are equally likely to plant trees in community woodlots where the duration of their tenure is secure as long as they remain residents of the village. The authors conclude that women's property rights affect their tree planting practices, and thus, this should be a major consideration for researchers and policymakers alike.

117. Galloway, L., J. Sanders, & D. Deakins, 2011. "Rural small firms' use of the internet: From global to local." ***Journal of Rural Studies*****, 27(3), 254-262.**

In process of digitalisation, it is a common theory that local market can only expose to global when it incorporates updated market elements such as the use of internet. This study examines responses collected from six internet service portals and 96 small firms at rural Scotland. The cases demonstrate how it is beneficial for a business to maintain the interest of local business rather fostering the line of activities under the influence of external market alone. Finally, this paper generalises its findings based on the use of internet to place the importance on locally oriented enterprises along with considerable external support for a sustainable market economy at rural space.

118. H. Friedland, W. 2010. "Who Killed Rural Sociology? A Case Study in the Political Economy of Knowledge Production." ***The International Journal of Sociology of Agriculture and Food. 17*****, 1 (Jan. 2010), 72-88.**

In this article the author examines Rural sociology as a case study and brings out the social forces that shape and direct the production of knowledge. The writer feels that Knowledge production is viewed as the product of the nexus of three sets of forces. They are: the rewards and punishments of any system of social control, the system of social control embedded in an institutional network within which knowledge production occurs and the it's institutional relationship to sociology as a discipline.

119. Fuguitt, Glenn Victor; Brown, David L.; Beale, Calvin L and Pfeffer, Max J. 1989. ***Rural and Small Town America. For the National Committee for Research on the 1980 Census.*** **New York: Russell Sage Foundation.**

This is a comprehensive volume and is a part of the Russell Sage Foundation's census monograph series. It aims to educate non-professionals, public officials, planners and others working in public and private agencies, and professional social scientists about the state of rural America and their distinctness. The monograph tries to offer an overview and indicate areas for further analytical work that can be taken up in the context of rural America. Based on the census report of 1980, the write up contains the outcomes of the in- depth analyses made by rural demographers. The compilation basically covers socio-demographic changes like changing population distribution, the growth and decline of small towns in the context of population dispersal, shifts in age-sex composition of rural and nonmetropolitan populations, changes in household growth and structure, fertility, labour force and employment trends, industrial structure and change, income, poverty and farming. However, along with changes, it also takes note of the continuities that mark the American rural society. The monograph also makes a comparative analysis of the variables in the rural context on a longitudinal basis and with urban areas. The diversity of rural areas across regions, different sized places, industries or socio-demographic categories are also adequately discussed in the book. Overall, it gives a very thorough background and introduction to rural America. The basic propositions of the book illustrate that rural areas continue to be unique in their structure, functions, process of change. They differ significantly from their urban counterparts, and justifies that policy focus need to take these uniqueness and distinctions of rural areas into considerations.

122. Gardiner, M. 2008. "Education in rural areas." ***Issues in education policy*, *4*, 1-33.**

This paper gives an insight into the major challenges faced by institutions operated at the rural provinces of South Africa in delivering quality education. In this connection, the author has undertaken a thorough review of the educational policies. From the review of policies on rural education, he discovers that the current policy aims for equal outcome from all the schools operated in the sample provinces. But this is an untenable expectation according to the author as the situations are different according to the geographic location of the provinces. Therefore, the author suggests to develop a policy framework which will facilitate equal opportunities for all the learners but will not expect the same outcome from unequal learners' background.

123. Gardner, J. 1993. "Alternative rural enterprises: non-traditional ventures offer opportunities for rural communities." ***Rural Management*, 2(Spring), 24-25.**

This short article makes an analysis of the emerging entrepreneurship in New Zealand in terms of the non-traditional rural businesses coming up in New Zealand. It is the written version of a paper presented at the 9th International Farm Management Congress (Budapest, Hungary 1993). The author feels that much work has been done on the traditional rural enterprises in the country i.e., those associated with primary production whereas the emergent non-traditional rural businesses are utterly neglected by the researchers. To address the gap, the author surveyed 15 businesses within 150 kilometres of Palmerston North city and took personal interviews. He found a broad spectrum of non-traditional rural enterprises emerging. These include: simple farm stays to complex operations such as manufacturing or running a tourism venture. The author concludes that non-traditional rural businesses provide a supplementary source of farm income, increased revenue for rural communities, and new job opportunities for rural people. Some businesses which involve little initial capital and use existing rural resources grow fasters without much hurdle.

124. Garrod, B., Wornell, R &Youell, R. 2006. Re-conceptualising rural resources as countryside capital: the case of rural tourism. *Journal of Rural Studies*, *22*, 117-128.

The authors in this article propose that sustainable rural development can be best harnessed when local residents and agencies begin to think of their shared/community rural resource as capital. They call it as "countryside capital". To the authors physical and natural capital base of the countryside is a booster to human survival and well-being. They define "countryside capital" as the rural community's available resource inventory i.e., its: natural landscapes, wildlife, soils, agricultural buildings, industrial remnants, local customs, culture and ways of life. They then present a model of interactions between rural tourism and countryside capital where they strongly argue that countryside physical and natural capital need to be converted into products of exhibit and tour operators need to know their symbolic and realistic value to promote tourism. For this sustainable policy of rural resource management need to be developed to convert the rural countryside capital into rural tourism product and generate sustainable income for the rural dwellers.

125. Gautam, Y., & P. Andersen, 2016. "Rural livelihood diversification and household well-being: Insights from Humla, Nepal." ***Journal of Rural Studies, 44*****, 239-249.**

This study tries to make a careful investigation on dimensions of rural livelihood and its scope for rural welfare. The authors have developed a composite index to measure the wellbeing. It comprises of four components and 15 indicators related to livelihood availability, and their income potentiality that prevail in the rural areas of Nepal. The study discovers that households that are based on business, trade and salaried job are sharing major benefits of livelihood diversification whereas, low-income households still are at the margin as they are deprived of such livelihood practices due to lack of sufficient occupational skills. Therefore, the authors conclude that the link between livelihood diversification and household wellbeing is highly skewed and may lead to a wider rural inequality. So, it is high time for public policies to address these issues in a proper manner.

126. Ghai, Dharam and Radwan, Samir (eds.) 1983. ***Agrarian Policies and Rural Poverty in Africa.*** **Geneva: International Labour Office.**

This volume is an outcome of the study undertaken by the authors in different African nations i.e., Kenya, Malawi, Ivory Coast, Botswana, Zambia, Nigeria, Ghana, Mozambique, and Somalia. It compiles nine case studies on poverty, employment and agrarian systems from different African nations. More specifically, agrarian change, differentiation and rural poverty in Africa are the main thrust of the book. It tries to generate understanding of the process and results of rural development in African countries since independence. The information furnished in the case studies are based on both quantitative and qualitative profiles of rural poverty and income distribution.

The research insights developed relate to the impact of state policies with respect to land tenure, public expenditures and resource extraction from the rural areas. Although some common issues are taken up in the case studies, each case study delves out some uniqueness from each rural context. To give some examples, the case study in Kenya thrusts upon the large farms, social justice and development policy, looks at inequalities and the effects of government policies. The case study on Malawi, which has experienced high growth rates, focuses on growth and distribution. For the Ivory Coast the highlight is on export-led development, which has been the driving force behind the country's growth. The case study on Botswana looks at income distribution and poverty, while the study on Zambia identifies why rural development activities have not impacted the rural poor. In case of Nigeria, the focus is on the development of the oil industry and its failure to benefit rural communities despite high growth led by its exports. In Ghana the case study is reflective on stagnation and continuing inequality. In case of Mozambique, the case study looks at the country's experience with development and its impact on distribution and livelihoods in rural areas. Finally, an overview of incomes and poverty in rural Somalia projects an economy that is healthier than previously believed, even though it insists upon subsistence than growth. Thus, all the cases are typical in their own way and they aim at describing the nine countries' development histories and current situations.

127. Glasgow, N., & Brown, D. L. 2012. Rural ageing in the United States: Trends and contexts. *Journal of Rural Studies*, *28*(4), 422-431.

Under the context of the vastness of rural areas of America and its diversities across factors such as; income, employment and demography, this study outlines the ageing process and its wellbeing profile. On the basis of data compiled from Census Bureau and earlier related studies, this paper concludes the significant role of ageing population in shaping rural social capital through active community participation. Hence, rural policies need to pay considerable attention to ageing population at rural areas in facilitating them for both social and civil participation for a sustainable local development.

128. Global Network on Energy for Sustainable Development (GNESD) 2007. Reaching the Millennium Development Goals and Beyond: Access to Modern Forms of Energy as a pre-requisite. ch.1, pp. 1–5.

This article points out that about 1.6 billion of world populations have no access to electricity. 80 percent of these people live in rural areas of developing countries of South Asia, Central America and South America. It speaks about the significance of energy in rural areas. It establishes that without adequate supplies of affordable energy, it is impossible to improve health, education and reduce poverty. So, it suggests to ensure sustainable energy provisions in rural areas for the real development of people and areas of the rural space.

129. Goodwin, M. 1998. The governance of rural areas: some emerging research issues and agendas. *Journal of Rural Studies, 14*(1), 5-12.

In this paper, Mark Goodwin reviews the wider social scientific literature associated with governance. The author notes a deep silence in rural studies on the topic, provides a research agenda for the study of the governance of rural areas.

130. Gorman-Murray, A., K. Darian-Smith, & C. Gibson, 2008. Scaling the rural: reflections on rural cultural studies. *Australian Humanities Review, 45*, 37-52.

In this article, the authors attempt to simplify the understanding of rural and rurality by taking insights from disciplines like; study of rural geography, culture and history. Based on the commentaries from the Australian cases of rural societies, this study advocates for a new line of intellectual development in understanding rurality which can accommodate its complex economic practices into the cultural ethos.

131. Gray, M. L., Johnson, C. R., & Gilley, B. J. (Eds.) 2016. ***Queering the countryside: New frontiers in rural queer studies*** **(Vol. 11). NYU Press.**

This book is a collection of sixteen essays on rural queering. It primarily discusses the wider social characteristics and the historical changes in queer studies rather limited to a narrow description of LGBTQ in rural America. As rural queering was mostly ignored and seems to be invisible in contrast to its urban experiences these essays demonstrate the importance of queer experiences in rural areas. Although, the rural queering is found to be dependent on urban setting for its identity but, this volume successfully elaborates special characteristics of rural queering on the living of LGBTQ people at countryside, on their sexuality, space, and moments.

132. Grimes, S. 2000. "Rural areas in the information society: diminishing distance or increasing learning capacity?" ***Journal of Rural Studies, 16*****(1), 13-21.**

This article emphasises on the adoption of new technology in rural areas within an information society particularly within the boundaries of the European Union. By drawing cases from EU, the author here recognizes the illusion that predominates that teleworking continues to be an urban and semi-urban phenomenon. The study recommends for a careful installation of new technologies i.e., digital support as a supplement for rural enterprises rather substituting the latter. This will enable the rural local interest and entrepreneurs to access the information-based technologies.

133. Gringeri, Christina E. 1994. ***Getting By: Women Homeworkers and Rural Economic Development.*** **Lawrence: University Press of Kansas.**

This book is the by product of an ethnographic study on

women industrial home workers in two rural Midwestern towns. Its basic aim is to assess the impacts of women's involvement in industrial homework on them and their families. The author has given coverage to 80 home workers in her study and has undertaken in depth interview with them. These women home workers are engaged in producing small auto parts at home and are supplementers to their family incomes. The author realises that industrial homework has become a powerful driver of economic development and adopts a tripartite approach to describe the phenomenon. The first approach talks about the local development process which includes the local and state officials and governments as well as private community development corporations. The second approach concentrates on workers' experiences with industrial homework which includes its consequences for their individual lives, Family lives and home and their perceptions of how homework fits into the greater local economy. The third approach has tried to describe the extent to which industrial homework has succeeded in attaining the community's development goals. It has been done through an analysis of the policy process and the data on worker's perspectives. The book also aims at discovering the way women blend their traditional gender roles and confirmation to the gender norms with their economic roles and how their supplementation to the family incomes brings transitions in their status. Thus, the beginning chapter of the book brings the theoretical discourses like modernisation and uneven development theories, gives a conceptual clarity to the concepts like informal labour, histories homework, and describes the state development policy and labour laws relating to homework. The second chapter talks about the role of communities in bringing companies into their space to overcome the economic challenges emerging from farm crisis, increasing debt burdens, to create alternative livelihood options within their boundaries to respond to the income deficit issues and the way low cost have attracted companies to institute their production centers within the rural areas. The ethnographic outcomes and the voices of the interviewees are contained in chapter three and four.

The interviews show that homework has its advantages and disadvantages. The advantages are women remain closer to the family whereas the disadvantages are low wages, long hours of work, and disruption of home chores, unstable contracts, and lack of benefits. The fifth chapter explores the ways in which the local communities subsidize the company's entry into the town in exchange for the hoped-for development and jobs. But it gives birth to the vices of burgeoning of informal work and lack of social security benefits for the workers. A comparative experience of homework at international and national level is placed in the final chapter of the book. Final implications include the need to redefine the development and modernisation theory and to include the real development indicators like education, psychological, sexual and community relational factors.

134. Gwynn, Douglas B.; Kawamura, Yoshio; Dolber-Smith, Edward and Rochin, Refugio I. 1989. *California's Rural Poor: Trends, Correlates, and Policies*. Davis: California Institute for Rural Studies.

This paper outlines the trends of rural poverty in the U.S. and California. It has taken up data from the Population Survey Report. The book establishes that poverty has taken a rising trend during the 1980s. It has been detected to be the highest among the Hispanics during the time cohort of 1981 and 1987. The authors also point out that female-headed families had higher poverty rates than two-parent families. Findings from California reflected in the U.S. Census suggest that 90 percent of California's poor live in urban areas. Poverty rates are slightly higher in rural areas. The native Americans and Hispanics bear the disproportionate burdens of rural poverty in California. Similarly, the elderly and female-headed families have a higher incidence of poverty in both rural than urban areas. However, poverty reduction strategies such as social services and transfer payments such as Food Stamps and Aid to Families with Dependent Children are more in use in urban than in rural areas. On the basis of these information, the paper makes some vital policy recommendations. It suggests to promote research on poverty in rural areas; to assess the impact of state-administered programmes to help maximisation of resources; to increase the number and types of services and client characteristics served by community-based organisations; and to delve out the causes of the increase in poverty and inequality in California.

135. Halfacree, K. 1997. Contrasting roles for the post-productivist countryside: a postmodern perspective on counterurbanisation. In P. Cloke & J. Little (Eds.), *Contested Countryside Cultures: Otherness, Marginalisation and Rurality* (pp. 70- 93). London: Routledge.

Basing his study on the ideas of David Harvey, the author tries to identify and discuss the reasons for, and the impact of, urban-rural migration/counter urbanisation in the post productivist rural era. In this attempt, the author tries to examine the forces leading to the demise of the productivist agricultural regime in Britain and the subsequent rise of the postproductivist countryside. He makes a broad review of the literature on counter urbanisation which signalises that a post-productivism regime has taken hold in rural space. Upon his review of the literature associated with counter urbanisation, Halfacree identifies two major themes which he critically examines, viz: job-led accounts of migration and people-led accounts. The author brings an end to this contributed paper by aligning the productivist/post-productivist debate with broader notions of the societal shift from modernism to postmodernism.

136. Hamin, E. M., & D. J. Marcucci, 2008. "Ad hoc rural regionalism." *Journal of Rural Studies, 24*(4), 467-477.

This paper tries to explore the new dimension of rural

regionalism. It is beyond the 'new regionalism' and is termed as the 'ad-hoc rural regionalism'. This form of regionalism usually has a growth in developed economies like, the United States under the immediate influence of global phenomena. This study draws inferences from the cases collected from rural areas of North America. The authors propose that the ad hoc rural regionalism is always a contested topic of landscapes and the local resource use. They also identify the importance of local agents in forming regional institutions of both social and economic under the effect of external industries, maintaining social networking and securing the regional boundaries. Hence, this study delineates these two concepts of 'new' and 'ad-hoc' regionalism on the basis of globalisation and the role of agents which are not only limited to a specified region.

137. Harper, S. 1987. "A humanistic approach to the study of rural populations." ***Journal of Rural Studies*, *3*(4), 309-319.**

The spatial and demographic features of rural units are usually on a state of transformation in the form of either development or adversity. By taking cases from rural England, this study stands critical to two existing approaches in describing rurality. These two approaches are the positivist technique and the traditional approach. The positivist technique does not adequately explain the relationship between rural space to its contrasting inhabitants whereas the traditional approach ignores the subjectivity of the relationship. Through the theory of symbolic interactionism and the method of participant observations, the author emphasises the humanistic approach in studying the rurality both on the ground of realism and the theoretical construct.

138. Hawley, L. R., N. A. Koziol, J. A. Bovaird, C. M. McCormick, G. W. Welch, A. M. Arthur, & K. Bash, 2016. "Defining and Describing Rural: Implications for Rural Special Education Research and Policy", ***Rural Special Education Quarterly*, *35*(3), 3–11.**

The authors in this paper make an attempt to define and describe the particular rural concept with a specific attention to rural special education research. To conduct the study, they have taken the geographical units of U.S. However, this article is not applicable to the countries where geographical units are not properly classified through coding system.

139. Hayden et.al. 2021. "Sensemaking and the influencing factors on farmer decision-making" *Journal of Rural Studies*: pp. 31-44.

This article is contextualised in Ireland with a sample size of 27 farmers. The authors use semi-structured interview tools to observe strategic farm expansion decision process in the country. The researcher observes that various financial and non-financial factors have major impact on the strategic farm expansion decision-making process of farmers. However, the author suggests that for future studies the selection of farmers can be expanded in number and random selection process to engage samples can be adopted.

140. Herbert-Cheshire, L. 2000. "Contemporary strategies for rural community development in Australia: A governmentality perspective." *Journal of Rural Studies, 16*, 203-215.

In this article, the author basically speaks about governance through community and elaborately describes the bottom-up approach that is taking momentum in rural governance in Australia. Much of the literature drawn upon for this paper is based in Britain and Europe; however, the author links this to Australian (Queensland) examples as there is some evidence that Australia is following a similar rural development path. The author describes the bottom-up approach as a self-help approach to rural development within which partnerships and initiatives are key aspects. This is expected to empower the individual and community. The concluding comments emphasise that self-help is liable to bring extra burdens on the community and rural partnerships creates social divisions by handing power to a small local minority i.e., those with the resources and expertise to act.

141. Herbert-Cheshire, L., & V. Higgins, 2004. "From risky to responsible: expert knowledge and the governing of community-led rural development." ***Journal of Rural Studies, 20*****(3), 289-302.**

On both the grounds of policy and practice rural development in advanced western economies rely more on community participation in managing rural risks with minimum public interventions. Such people-led developmental strategies are generally acknowledged as means of empowerment which enables rural communities with skills and proficiencies. But this article delineates the development with expert knowledge and without it particularly when there is a need to transfer the rural risk to policy responsibilities. In reference to rural Australia, the paper elaborates how risk contributes in social transition through the adoption of self-governance and empowerment. It also finds that, strategies which are processed through an expert knowledge and supervision results in more efficient developmental outcomes whereas, other alternative methods end with enhanced inequalities while converting rural risk to responsibilities.

142. Hopcroft, Rosemary L. 2016. ***Local Institutions and Rural Development in European History*****, Cambridge University Press.**

This is a historical description of the rural development in Europe. The author tries to project that no doubt, class relations and state institutions have played an important role in rural development in European history. But they were not the only factors. Rural development through rising per capita incomes has a significant contribution towards industrialisation of Europe. But the author feels that when the dominant approaches to rural development in European history stress the role of local class relations and state institutions, they underplay and ignore the role of local institutions. Although class relations and state institutions were important in rural development in European history, the regional analysis presented by the author in this book establishes that institutional structure at the local level has equally an important role in shaping Europe's history.

143. Hunt, W., F. Vanclay, C. Birch, J. Coutts, N. Flittner, & B. Williams, 2011. "Agricultural extension: Building capacity and resilience in rural industries and communities." ***Rural Society, 20(2),*** **112-127.**

This article is based on an Australian study. The authors of this paper argue that agricultural extension can not only improve on-farm agricultural or natural resource management practices, but also can build capacity and resilience in rural industries and communities. The paper defines resilience as "the capacity of an individual or community to cope with stress, overcome adversity, or adapt positively to change". Extension is defined as a process of building capacity for change and resilience among individuals and communities through improved communication and information flow between stakeholders. Extension and resilience are thus conceptually linked. The authors cite the instances from Australian extension agents who operate outside their core areas of responsibility. They are found to have made notable contributions in recovering people from Severe Tropical Cyclone Larry; record pest outbreaks in the sugar industry between 1999 and 2002; and bushfire response efforts between 2005 and 2009.

144. Husain, A.M. Muazzam (ed.) 1996. ***Challenges of Rural Poverty by the Year 2010: Proceedings of the National Workshop of the Rural Social Science Network,*** **January, 1993." Dhaka: Rural Social Science Network.**

This is a compilation and a proceeding of the papers presented at the National Workshop on Challenges of Rural Poverty by the Year 2010 held in Bangladesh. The compilation explores different dimensions of rural poverty and development in Bangladesh. Major themes covered by the papers include socio-cultural dimensions of rural poverty, population and employment, gender dimensions in rural poverty, and issues of resource management. Papers in the first two sections provide a general overview of the rural situation in Bangladesh and pose some formidable issues that challenge rural development in the country. The papers on the gender dimensions of rural development look at gender disparities in poverty rates, women's work inside and outside the home, their coping strategies, evaluate the government programmes for alleviating poverty among women and their efficacy and suggest forward looking strategies to overcome the gendered character of poverty. The last section on resource management talks about low agricultural productivity contributing towards rural poverty, rural resource management, including agricultural resources as well as forests. The terminating chapter sums up the major recommendations that emerged from the workshop, focusing on understanding rural poverty, its causes, and possible approaches for alleviation of rural poverty.

145. Ibrahim, Saifullahai, HuseyinOzderser, Behiye Cavusoglu. 2021. ***Rural Migration and Relative Deprivation in Agro-Pastoral Communities Under the Threat of Cattle Rustling in Nigeria*****, Sage Open,Vol.11 Issue-1.**

This study examines the impact of cattle rustling and relative deprivation on shaping the patterns of migration in Nigeria. It has used the survey method and has sample coverage of 1,750 agro-pastoral households. The study results show that the loss of livestock, cattle rustling, income diversity, literacy, and herd size are significant determinants of migration patterns. These factors are instrumental in the households' decision to migrate transitorily or permanently. The study also indicates that relative deprivation is a significant push factor, migration in response to deprivation and cattle rustling may not necessarily decrease inequality due to weak social capital among the agro-pastoralists.

In this sense, increasing pastoral social and economic capital is critical to the reduction of inequality and competition for natural capital.

146. Jensen, Leif and M. Tienda, 1989. "Nonmetropolitan minority families in the United States: trends in racial and ethnic economic stratification, 1959-1986." ***Rural Sociology*****, Vol. 54, No. 4 (Winter 1989): 509-532.**

This article puts the search light on the economic status of rural black, Mexican and Native American families from the data retrieved and analysed from the U.S. Census and Current Population Survey data. The study is confined to a period of 27 years starting from 1959 to 1986. The article aims at making a trend analysis of economic change in the rural areas of America. The article makes a start with an introduction to the historical rural settlements and deprivation faced by the minority groups in the U.S. To the authors macro social changes have their repercussions on the U.S. rural settings. The study could note that on the whole the economic situations of rural minorities did improve in relative terms from 1959 to 1979. Contrastingly, data shows that family income deteriorated during the following seven years. Migration of minorities from rural to urban areas, stepping into new employment patterns had a better effect on minority family poverty which the public assistance system failed to cater to. The authors conclude that policies need to give precedence to job creation than to job training. The jobs of the minorities need protection through policies as they suffer from heavy job losses during the periods of economic downswing.

147. Johansen, Harley E. and Fuguitt, Glenn V. 1984. ***The Changing Rural Village in America: Demographic and Economic Trends since 1950.*** **Cambridge, Mass.: Ballinger Pub. Co.**

This book looks specifically at the "villages" in America. These are the places with populations of less than 2,500. The authors in this book have tried to depict the villages as small settlement systems within the larger social system and as the centers of trade the socio-economic changes that have taken places in the villages since 1950. The study is based on a sample of five percent of villages in the coterminous U.S., of 572 different incorporated places. Data has been derived from the U.S. censuses for 1950 through 1980 and Dun and Bradstreet reference books for 1950 through 1970, as well as from local public sources. The study also resorts to a telephone interview survey with mayors in 100 villages. The introductory chapter contains literature on the village and depicts the research design and methodology. The book begins with an analysis of recent trends in population patterns and analyses the determinants of population growth and decline. The following chapter outlines a detailed account of social characteristics of the villages and draws a comparison of the villages with the urban areas. The next three chapters focus on the economic engagements of the villages. In this connection, they project the rapid changes marked in the village economies since 1950. It makes an analysis of changes in the retail and service sectors, and an analysis of the relationship between village population and retail/service business that develops models of change in business, due to progressive urban accessibility and accessibility to basic economic activities. In the next chapter, the book looks at current village government and community group activities and their role in improving local infrastructure and promoting industrial growth and business development. The last chapter looks at issues of community attitudes toward growth and relations between newcomers and old-timers. It interestingly finds no evidence of possible community problems and heightened differences between newcomer-old-timer. Finally, the last chapter summarises the book's main findings on villages, including population growth, centralisation of economic trends, and acceptance of growth as good.

148. Jun Han (2020), "How to promote rural revitalisation via introducing skilled labor, deepening land reform and facilitating investment?" *China Agricultural Economic Review*, Vol. 12, No. 4, pp. 577-582.

The researcher through this article tries to find out the difficulties of implementation of the rural revitalisation strategy on the basis of three factors, namely, people, land and money in the rural areas of China. As per the researcher this problem can be solved by introducing skilled labour; managing the farmer–land relationships through deepening the land reform and facilitating multidimensional investment that includes fiscal, financial and social factors.

149. Kalantaryan et. al. 2021. "Immigration and integration in rural areas and the agricultural sector: An EU perspective" *Journal of Rural Studies*: pp. 10-11.

This study draws the insights from Italy and Spain. The authors link the different characteristics of agricultural production with migration. This study uses regression models and descriptive statistics for survey analysis of migration in European Union rural areas based mainly on two sources i.e., European Union Labour Force Survey and European Union Statistics on Income and Living Conditions. This article provides a quantitative overview of migrants in rural areas and in the agricultural sector for the entire EU. The study does not include irregularity, seasonality and vulnerability of migrants employed in agriculture.

150. Kearney, M. and C. Nagengast, 1989. "Anthropological perspectives on transnational communities in rural California", and Taylor, J. Edward, Illegal Immigrants, California Agriculture and the Mexican Economy. Davis: California Institute for Rural Studies.

This working paper combines two papers that are: one anthropological analysis of the Latinisation of rural agricultural towns in California's Central Valley, and another that looks at the links between the California agricultural economy and rural parts of Mexico where from the bulk of California's farm workers originate. The first paper generates an insight on community and its meaning with special reference to California's agricultural communities. It speaks on the creation of farm worker enclaves in rural California as well as the migrant networks responsible for their creation and perpetuation. The paper characterises Latino communities who experience problems resulting from structural and historical processes, relating to their own positions within the dominant society and its institutions. This perspective is contrasted with the assimilationist theory and cultural nationalist perspective. The paper also goes to the extent of discussing the conditions that are currently creating the enclave situation in California, nature of enclave communities including their demographic features, internationalisation of capital, socioeconomic conditions in Mexico, and conditions in Californian labour markets. The paper tries to bring into discussion different policy and research implications, spells out that the transnational community model is the most useful for future research. The second paper provides a glimpse of the role that illegal Mexico-to-U.S. migration plays in the Californian farm economy and the Mexican village economy. The first part comprises of a literature navigation on the subject, including the undocumented works on farmworkers by season and farm job. The second part explores the role of income remittances from illegal migrants to the Mexican village economy generating income inequality and changes in the economic structures. It concludes that remittances are vital to the Mexican village economy, and thus labour migration is unlikely to be stopped.

151. Kettler, T., J. S. Puryear, & D.R. Mullet, 2016. "Defining Rural in Gifted Education Research." ***Journal of Advanced Academics: Methodological Challenges and Paths Forward, 27(4)*****, 245-265.**

In this article the researchers analyse the difference in students' participation in rural and non-rural districts in advanced academic programmes. The data is collected from 1,029 schools of the district of Texas of which 685 are classified as rural according to NCES locale codes of Texas. The result indicates that the participation of students in non-rural areas are more as compared to rural areas. However, it needs to be mentioned here that this paper lacks concrete suggestive measures to improve the participation.

152. Kienzle, Josef, John E. Ashburner, G. Brian Sims, 2013. "Mechanisation for Rural Development: A review of patterns and progress from around the world." Integrated Crop Management, Vol. 20-2013, Plant Production and Protection Division Food and Agriculture Organisation of the United Nations Rome.

This publication presents a kaleidoscopic view of agricultural mechanisation experiences from around the globe. In this context, it has captured the situations from East, South, West and Central Africa, Bangladesh, Nepal, India, China, Brazil, Central Asia and East Europe. It offers a solid launching pad for the promotion of sustainable mechanisation technologies that are vital to sustain the planet's natural capital, the burgeoning world population both now and into the future.

153. Kiros, Fassil G. (ed.) 1985. *Challenging Rural Poverty*. New Jersey: Africa World Press.

This book contains the papers presented at the First Ossrea Congress held in June 1983 in Alemaya, Ethiopa. The papers are all related to rural development, institution building or popular participation in the African context, the bulk of papers pertaining to Tanzania or Kenya. The book is classified into three sections. The first section focuses on rural poverty in Africa. It presents both a pan African perspective as well as some typical local specific case studies. In this attempt, the papers included in this section take up a discussion on rural poverty and its components, famine-related mortality and the cycle of poverty, a review of the problems and conditions for rural women, and examinations of rural development pitfalls and the impact of population growth on food production and the approach for dealing with poverty in Africa. The second set of articles looks at problems of institution building in the African context. It focuses on the issue of 'center-locality' relations, the development of appropriate forms of rural development institutions, and the issues of grass roots participation. The problem of over centralisation is addressed in various forms throughout this section. The section also talks about the problem as well as of policies for decentralisation and the problems the Africans have encountered in this regard. This section banks mostly on case studies to illustrate the issues involved in various forms of institutional development. The third section consists of concluding remarks that summarise the main points of the book. The book suggests an integrated approach that takes multiple problems into consideration, and asserts that rural development and institution building need to include and stimulate local participation in order to attain real success.

154. Klauser F. & D. Pauschinger 2021. "Entrepreneurs of the air: Sprayer drones as mediators of volumetric agriculture" *Journal of Rural Studies:* pp. 55-62.

This study aims at examining the air-bound practices, expectations and imaginaries drone system managed by Agro Drone in Europe. For the study, 11 in-depth interviews are conducted with employees, pilots and representatives from public authorities between 2018-19. The researchers suggest that company, Agro Drone may come out to challenge the position of traditional decision-makers and farmers not only with regard to agricultural matters, but with also governance of rural life.

155. Krannich, Richard S., E. Helen Berry, and T. Greider, 1989. "Fear of crime in rapidly changing rural

communities: a longitudinal analysis." ***Rural Sociology*, Vol. 54, No. 2 (Summer 1989): 195-212.**

This article suggests that the fear of crime is escalating in rural areas. The growing population and the changing economy are bringing about such fear, whether or not there have been changes in actual crime rates. Based on the results of past studies, the article analyses the results of surveys done during three different years in four rural communities in the Intermountain West. Multiple regression analysis is used to link population changes and criminal victimisation experiences with fear of crime. The study concludes that the results point out that contextual change, individual social integration, and criminal victimisation influence increases the fear of crime.

156. Lazere, Edward B., Paul A. Leonard, and Linda L. Kravitz, 1989. "The Other Housing Crisis: Sheltering the Poor in Rural America. Washington, D.C." Center on Budget and Policy Priorities, Housing Assistance Council.

Based on the survey reports of the U.S. Census Bureau, this report looks at the availability and quality of housing in nonmetropolitan areas of the U.S. The report's first section looks at housing costs for poor rural homeowners and renters. It records that housing costs are increasing in rural areas and it is consuming a major portion of the household incomes in the rural settings.

This section also takes a look at housing costs for minorities versus whites and speaks about the shortage of housing and affordability issues. The second section compares poor housing situation in nonmetropolitan and metropolitan areas. It notes that housing costs are generally lower in nonmetropolitan areas depending on the lower average incomes in nonmetropolitan areas. The third section generates an insight into the quality of housing in nonmetropolitan areas, and concludes that nonmetropolitan households live in severely substandard conditions. The next section looks at housing assistance provisions for the poor. This housing support targets more toward homeowners than renters in rural areas. Homeowners also have very limited accessibility to these provisions. The fifth section analyses the demographic characteristics of poor households. Variable-wise analysis of the households is done in terms of income, race, age, marital status, employment, and geographic region. The sixth and seventh sections focus on housing affordability and conditions for black and elderly population. Finally, the report winds up by bringing forth the major findings and suggesting changes in the existing federal policies to better address the current the present housing crisis faced by the rural poor.

157. Lipton, M. 1985. "Land Assets and Rural Poverty." World Bank Staff Working Papers, No. 744. Washington, D.C.: The World Bank.

This World Bank report illustrates that poverty is a perennial problem of the rural space in India and Southeast Asia. It is exacerbated by the rising inequality. It points out the difference in calorie intake; asset ownership and labour use pattern still exist between the rich and poor. The paper also examines the access to land, land ownership and control pattern of the Third World's poor and ultra-poor, the various types of tenure systems and the extent to which returns from the land protect the poor from poverty and differ from the returns gained by the non-poor on the land asset. The author identifies that scarcity of land and their unequal distribution induces rural poverty. Even small land holdings play a significant role in poverty reduction. The final section of the report analyses the Indian large-sample data to test the relationship between lack of land assets and poverty, and brings up a comparison between India and Asia on the one hand and Latin America and Africa on the other. The report ends with some positive notes like landlessness and tenancy are not generally increasing; land distribution and the terms of tenancy are not in general worsening. It also discovers that redistribution of land has not been a complete failure; and inequality in access to land is not the sole correlate of poverty.

158. Lipton, M. 1988. "The Poor and the Poorest: Some Interim Findings." World Bank Discussion Papers. Washington D.C.: The World Bank.

This discussion paper brings into its fold some accepted correlates of poverty like nutrition, access to and control over land, returns to labour, human capital and demography. It draws the insights from the information furnished in four working papers on the characteristics of the poor and the ultra-poor. The paper findings emerge from the studies conducted in 30 villages in rain fed areas of western India and northern Nigeria, along with references to studies in many other developing areas. The paper elaborately discusses the measures of poverty and the characteristics of the poor. The paper concludes that measuring poverty is a difficult task. It suggests a modified scalar poverty indicator for dealing with the relationship between hunger, under-nutrition, and poverty. Subsequent chapters look at the relationships between work and poverty and assets and poverty for the poor and ultra-poor. It also explores the demographics of poverty. The paper ends with a number of policy implications based on these discussions.

159. Lipton, M. and M. Ravallion, 1993. "Poverty and Policy." Washington, D.C.: World Bank Policy Research Department.

This working paper is a beautiful combination of theory and application. It makes a historical analysis of economic thought on poverty and stresses on alleviating poverty through reducing biases against the rural sector and the urban informal sector. It also illustrates current economic analysis and policy. It then examines how consumption poverty is defined and measured and outlines several different methods for measuring poverty. The report discusses poverty in the context of the modern developing world and the units of analysis are the global, the village and household levels. Poverty is explored with respect to demographics (family size, age and gender), nutritional and labour-force characteristics. The paper discusses elaborately on the development issue, the impact of growth on poverty and inequality and the poor. It also brings into discussion the governmental attempts to reduce both transient and chronic poverty through direct intervention, including land, credit and public services interventions.

160. Little, J. 2002. "Rural geography: rural gender identity and the performance of masculinity and femininity in the countryside." Progress in Human Geography, 26(5), 665-670.

This review article illustrates 20 years of research in rural studies carried out by rural geographers and their adoption of the perspective of feminism. The author, however, finds this adoption to be 'half-hearted'. Amidst its own discipline centric disorientation, the recent rural geographers try to enculture the line of feminist geography to explain rurality. The author also extends the analytical framework even to Foucauldian approach of knowledge and power to verify the role of gender in rural livelihood practices and in the wider sense to establish the interlinkages between gender, community and the rural environment.

161. Luloff, A. E. and Louis E. Swanson, (eds.) 1990. *American Rural Communities*. Boulder: Westview Press.

This book is a collection of essays. These essays aim at describing the prevailing situation of rural America, the policies implemented to change the situation of these areas, identify the policy gaps and to make prescriptions for further research and action. The book puts forth the argument that a partnership between state government, local government and communities can bring economic prospects to rural America. The prescriptions made in the book call for revisiting the present actions undertaken, developing leadership on the part of local citizens and civic leaders. Most of the essays placed in the edited volume overstress the need of community interaction approach. To the authors contributing to this volume, financial development of the rural areas needs to be connected to social wellbeing of the rural dwellers. The book also contains chapter on timber dependent communities which point out to the significance of forest management. Similarly, some chapters spell out the significance of community relations and revival of communal associations. Separate essays on religion and crime in communities contribute interesting perspectives to the many facets of community in rural areas. The book's conclusion, written by the editors, calls for "a renaissance of the community literature that sheds assumptions about communities based upon times past, acknowledges the obvious importance of local societies and their community fields to its members, critically analyses the barriers to democratic participation and seeks innovative ways for helping people deal with the needs and take advantage of the opportunities offered by community action."

162. Maria, T. 2014. "Approaching rural firm growth: a literature review", *Journal of Enterprising Communities: People and Places in the Global Economy*, Vol. 8, Issue 4, pp. 261-286.

This study investigates the extent and content of research into rural firm growth, and identifies and describes various approaches studying firm growth. This study focuses on the firm growth literature in rural settings. It contributes to the field by mapping the current state of knowledge and articulates and challenges the taken-for-granted assumptions in prior studies on firm growth. This review notes some differences between rural firms and firms in other contexts. But this study is silent about the suggestive measures to eradicate the gap between the farms.

163. Marsden, T., J. Murdoch, P. Lowe, R. Munton, and A. Flynn, 1993. *Constructing the Countryside*. Boulder: Westview Press.

This book carries the research findings of the authors on the changing positions of rural areas and 'rurality'. Most of the findings are the derivations from the impressions generated from the case study of the late 20th century U.K. Three major research questions are responded to by the book. They are:

- How are international processes of economic and social restructuring being expressed and mediated within one nation state?
- How is the state 'regulating' rural change and to what extent does the late 20th century represent a break with the past?
- How can conceptual advances in mainstream social theory be applied to rural areas, and, conversely, how can locally base social action be effectively incorporated into our understanding of uneven development?

The book establishes an observation that differentials in the restructuring process are bringing diversities in rural areas. The authors also talk on the process of conceptualisation of these new rural formations that are being created and about the methods of their analysis. Thus, the primarily brings an understanding into rural change. The rest of the book discusses and analyses these changes through the case study of rural Britain. In this connection, it pays attention to agricultural development, property rights and land tenure, planning and land development, and power structure which are in a process of transition due to the new restructuring process. On the whole, the book makes an in-depth analysis of the socio-political and economic processes that are shaping and changing rural areas at the end of the 20th century.

164. Mayer, Leo V. 1993. "Agricultural change and rural America." ***Annals of the American Academy of Political and Social Science,*** **Vol. 529 (September 1993): 80-91.**

This article relates the changing agricultural scenario of rural settlements with the decline of rural areas in America and recommends possible policies for expanding economic activity in rural communities. It sketches out the processes of massive outmigration, increased farm productivity with the mechanisation of the farms contributing to rapid rural decline in the country and the barriers to economic development in rural areas including the barriers to new investments and businesses. Basically, it talks about the reluctance to restructure economic activity on farms, and a lack of support for strong measures to gain a share of the new jobs and new economic activity that are generated by the national economy. It also proposes possible solutions to rural growth and expansion and recommends some legislative reforms to develop rural business and including rural groups to actively take up them. Finally, it foresees that technical assistance to rural communities through rural educational systems, including land-grant universities and community colleges can bring real agricultural change leading to overall changes in rural America.

165. McManus, P., J. Walmsley, N. Argent, S. Baum, L. Bourke, J. Martin, & T. Sorensen, (2012). "Rural community and rural resilience: What is important to farmers in keeping their country towns alive?" ***Journal of Rural Studies, 28*****(1), 20-29.**

McManus et al., used the concepts of interactional rural community of place and rural resilience to study the phenomenon of rural decline in Australia. Rural decline is defined as loss of agricultural employment, a phenomenon observed in many developed countries, including New Zealand. The aim of the research was to determine farmer's perceptions of their interactions with their local town and how this may relate to rural resilience. In Australia, as with New Zealand, many small towns remote from major urban centres have gradually declining populations in response to economic changes. Such changes are often assumed to inevitably lead to negative outcomes. However, it has been suggested that social factors such as a sense of belonging and social engagement can mitigate against changes. The researchers interviewed 115 farmers in two rural regions of New South Wales, Lachlan and Northern Tablelands about their formal and informal interactions and sense of belonging within their local community. The farmers were asked for their perceptions regarding changes over time in a range of 'social fields', including education, health, recreational leisure facilities, employment opportunities, belonging, safety and crime, local environment and housing. A perception that any of these fields is being eroded may lead to a reduction in positive feelings about the community. Overall, despite experiencing a severe drought, farmers generally did not feel that social and community life was deteriorating. A regression analysis was performed to determine which factors significantly relate to community spirit. The analysis found that in both study areas Rural Community Resilience: Research Stock take 2015 35 perceptions regarding the environment were important for resilience, as were feelings of belonging, the local economy and community spirit. Despite population loss, economic difficulties and a severe drought, social cohesion in the both regions had not been adversely affected. This can be considered to be a form of stable adaptation to change. Farmers in these two areas participate formally and informally (through socialising) in community activities, including those in nearby towns. Informal socialisation is critical to the community as a whole but also to the individual farmers as a source of support through difficult times. Social connection with the nearest town is also important to farmers: "It is the primary place where they connect with others, offer and seek support, and build up feelings of affiliation and belonging" (p.28).

The implication of this research for rural policy-makers is that economic, environmental and social factors are inter-related and policies cannot focus solely on economic or environmental factors: "Resilience is an outcome of people's perceptions of the physical environment, their sense of belonging and job opportunities. Paying careful attention to farmers' perceptions of these factors, and particularly how they may be changing over time, is the first step to identifying the potential of small rural towns to be resilient in the face of major, inter-related economic, social and environmental challenges" (p.28).

166. Murdoch, J. and T. Marsden, 1994. *Reconstituting Rurality: Class, Community and Power in the Development Process.* London: University College London.

This book brings into elaboration several ideal typical forms of rural development in England. These types of development are, preserved countryside characterised by anti-development and preservationist attitudes; contested countryside that lies outside of commuter regions and is of no special environmental interest, where farm and development interests are opposed by in-migrants; paternalistic countryside dominated by large farms and established landowners; and clientelist countryside where farms are dependent upon state support and aid, and politics are dominated by employment concerns and the welfare of the community. The book focuses mostly on the preserved countryside characterised by anti-development and preservationist attitudes approach to establish how one English locality is constituted and reconstituted by struggles around development issues. It begins by exploring the role of the middle class in countryside change. It also acknowledges the role of planning systems in initiating and facilitating change in rural space. The second chapter puts light on regional context of the locality and the emerging tensions between urban growth and rural preservation. The third chapter explores housing and land development issues and elaborates the need and significance of rural housing. This chapter includes a case study of barn conversion, which is the most common form of "new" housing in rural areas. Issues of development are explored in Chapter Four. This chapter delineates three contrasting rural settlements in the study area. Subsequent chapters examine the growing influence of the middle class in countryside land use. Chapter Five deals with the upcoming agricultural crisis and its local manifestations. Chapters Six, Seven and Eight present case studies of farmers who are exploiting their land for non-agricultural purposes including golf courses, quarries and landfills, and the reactions of the local communities. Chapter Nine looks at new uses for surplus buildings. The book ends with a concluding chapter that is vocal on class issues and the ways in which the middle class manipulates rural ideologies and structures.

167. Murray, M. and L. Dunn, 1996. ***Revitalizing Rural America: A Perspective on Collaboration and Community.*** **New York: John Wiley & Sons.**

This book's main concern lies in emphasising the role of community collaborative efforts in bringing rural community change. It makes significant contributions to policy debates on rural development by correlating the roles of federal, state and local participants. To the authors, the relationship between community and governance is vital in designing rural development policy and converting them into practice. In this attempt, the book makes a number of critical case studies of rural development programmes. The book provides background information on rural America and brings forth the significance of community, community development, capacity building and collaboration. It then spells out the role of institutions and their practices in rural development. This chapter includes theoretical discussions along with the case-study examples of rural development policies. The next two chapters are programme specific analysis. They try to analyse WK Kellogg Foundation's Rural America Program and the Colorado Rural Revitalisation Project, and a third chapter looks directly at six communities that participated in the Colorado project. The book's conclusion reiterates the conceptual framework. It also gives a gist of the discussions on the meaning and implementation of institutional collaboration, and sums up the main arguments from the case study findings. The book recommends ensuring local involvement, linkages and facilitating collaboration as the most important ingredients for the revitalisation of rural America.

168. Nord, M. and A.E. Luloff, 1995. "Homeless children and their families in New Hampshire: a rural perspective." ***Social Service Review*, Vol. 69, No. 3 (September 1995): 461-478.**

This article ascertains that homelessness is not only an urban issue, but a rural problem too. It brings into its fold results of twenty case studies of homeless students and their families in New Hampshire. Data was gathered through interviews with school personnel, social service personnel, homeless children and their families in five selected school districts in New Hampshire. The study establishes that homelessness occurs across families, the causes being different. It notes that for two parent families generally came about because of reverses in their economic situations, while for single-parent family's disruption of the family precipitate homelessness. The article also explores the setbacks and problems faced by homeless children in schools, due to excessive mobility, inability to study properly and stigmatisation. It also proposes that the problems associated with homelessness are present not only during the period of literal homelessness, but also during the longer residential crisis period during which shelter may be found, but may be insecure, inadequate and short-term. The authors suggest to guarantee greater assistance to homeless people, the need to include rural areas in policies to eradicate homelessness, the need to pay attention to the specific needs of homeless school-age children, and the need to expand the concept of homelessness to include the full residential crisis period.

169. Okello et.al. 2012. "Drivers of Use of Information and Communication Technologies by Farm Households: The Case of Smallholder Farmers in Kenya." ***Journal of Agricultural Science*, Vol. 4, No. 2, 2012. 111-124.**

The researcher here uses the Transaction Cost Economics (TCE) theory, which is part of the New Institutional Economics. The concept of transaction costs was first introduced by Coase (1937) and has since been widely used in studies in agricultural economics and related fields in developing countries. The respondents are smallholder farmers located in Kirinyaga, Bungoma and Migori districts. This study assesses the conditioners of the use of ICT tools in general and mobile phones in particular by smallholder farmers for agricultural transactions. The study finds that several farmer, farm and capital endowment factors affect the use of ICT tools and mobile phones. Specifically, age, occupation, nearness to output market, number of crop enterprises, farming experience literacy and crop income explain the use of tools while gender, nearness to output market, household size, owning a phone, level of literacy, crop income and value of assets explain the intensity of use of the mobile for agricultural transaction purposes. This study is relevant for decision-making and policy formulations.

170. Omotesho, K. F., I. O. Ogunlade, and L. Muhammad (2012). "Assessment of Access to Information and Communication Technology among Agricultural Extension Officers in Kwara State, Nigeria", ***Asian Journal Agriculture and Rural Development*, Vol. 2, No. 2, pp. 220-225.**

This study is a Nigerian study. Here the authors have resorted to data collection through structured questionnaire tools from seventy-nine (79) Extension Agents (EAs) and twenty (20) Subject Matter Specialists (SMSs) of the Kwara State Agricultural Development Project (KWADP) of Nigeria. Income of the respondents is found to be significant and positively related to access to ICT. The numbers of years on the job and the age of the respondents have negative but significant relationship with access. The researcher uses Simple descriptive statistics and Pearson Product Moment Correlation (PPMC) tools to compile the data. As per the observations of the researcher's education is the only factor which plays a significant role in creating awareness and interest in innovations. But there is lack of Government support till date.

171. Oncescu, J. 2014. "The impact of a rural school's closure on community resiliency." ***Leisure/Loisir*****, 38(1), 35-52.**

The author quotes the study he made on the effect of closure of the local school in the rural village of Limerick, Saskatchewanon, Canada. His study resorted to semi-structured interviews and focus groups and interviewed 22 adult residents of the village. The author sees that with the social and economic changes in many resource-based rural communities in Canada bring declining populations, particularly in the younger age groups in the rural settlements. When there is a shortfall in the younger population, school are coming to closures in rural Canada. This affects the quality of life of rural communities. Analysis of the data obtained by the author shows that Limerick's school had strengthened the community's resilience due to the community interactions facilitated by the school's community recreation activities and other events, helped to develop community cohesiveness, a sense of belongingness, trust and sense of community. The school also generated local leadership and creative problem solving which are missing due to school closure. (Kulig et al.'s second component). The author has adopted the Kulig et al model to look at community resilience. However, the author concludes that after the school was closed the community was able to collectively develop a new, alternative recreation facility using the old school building. This facility and its associated recreational activities helped to maintain community resources and social cohesion and connectedness, demonstrating the community's resilience.

172. Peake, W. and M.I. Marshall, 2017. "Women's management practices and performance in rural female-owned family businesses." ***Journal of Family Business Management*****, Vol. 7, No. 2, pp. 134-150.**

This study is based on convenient sampling of 736 sample respondents. Among the 736 samples, the researchers have taken complete interviews for 721 samples and partial complete interviews for 15 samples. Usable partial complete interviews. The data has been collected from the 2012 Intergenerational Farm and Non-Farm Family Business Survey of Indiana, USA. Objective of this paper is to analyze the performance effects of management controls and goals for the business across both male and female-controlled farm and rural family businesses. But this paper is silent about importance of strategic management practices via monitoring and control mechanisms.

173. Peck, S. 1989. "California Farm Worker Housing." Davis: California Institute for Rural Studies.

This working paper presents an overview on the factors that lead to substandard housing for California's farm workers, including low incomes, inadequate supply of housing, limited English abilities, and fear of transportation and changing government policies. The paper reviews the available sources of information on housing conditions and needs from the state and national sources. It brings out the deficit of data. It also highlights on the Regulation and enforcement of farm worker housing in detail. The final section discusses the Immigration Reform and Control Act of 1986 (IRCA), and its implications for farm worker housing.

174. Roberts, E. & L. Townsend, 2015. "The contribution of the creative economy to the resilience of rural communities: Exploring cultural and digital capital." ***Sociologia Ruralis*****, Online advance publication.**

This paper assesses the contributions of creative practitioners in Scotland to rural community resilience. To be more specific, the study investigates how creatives are using internet-enabled digital technology and how this affects cultural capital and rural community resilience. The rural creative economy combines the features of craft-based and traditional local culture and new creative industries such as web design. Rural areas in Scotland attract creative individuals and businesses by their unique lifestyles and their strong regional cultural networks and economies. Rural creatives build cultural capital and become a powerful force in rural community development. It is often noted that when the contributions of social, economic and natural capitals to resilience is overstressed, the value of cultural and digital capitals is unduly underestimated. In the present study the researchers conducted 15 semi-structured interviews with 15 creatives in rural Scotland on four pertinent themes from previous resilience i.e. Adaptive capacity; cultural capital; leadership and resourcefulness; and ripple effects. The major findings revealed from his study are:

- Rural creatives are often dependent on information and communication technologies for survival of their businesses. But rural broadband often suffers from poor quality which the creatives try to overcome by using a variety of strategies to compensate, to allow them to continue to live and work in rural areas.
- Rural creatives formally and informally add to their community's cultural capital by establishing tourist trails, community arts centres, creative hubs and clusters.
- Rural creatives demonstrate leadership through their organisational capacity, sense of responsibility toward their rural community, and entrepreneurial skills.
- Rural creatives contribute to social capital by extensive networking; increasing economic and socio-demographic diversification; acting as community leaders; by developing a strong sense of place.

175. Rodgers, Harrell R. and G. Weiher, (eds.) 1989. *Rural Poverty: Special Causes and Policy Reforms*. New York: Greenwood Press.

This edited volume seeks to locate the causes of rural and urban poverty and whether the causes are common or not and whether special programmes are needed to address rural poverty. Most of the essays compiled in the volume unanimously agree that though rural and urban poverty have some common causes, there are some unique causes that trigger rural poverty. The typical causative factors of rural poverty are: inadequate employment compensation, rising unemployment, depression in the agricultural sector, and welfare eligibility rules that exclude significant proportions of the deserving poor. The book's chapters also explore the reasons of unresponsiveness of welfare programmes to the causal and demographic differences between rural and urban poverty, and suggest alternative reforms to mitigate rural poverty. Most of the essays focus on the impacts of structural forces on poverty, including welfare utilisation, labour force participation, the farm crisis, farm programmes, and the negative income tax. Two chapters of the volume examine the economic development policies, one with reference to income transfers, the other looking specifically at development in Midwestern states.

176. Rosset, P. & Maria Elena Martínez-Torres, 2012. "Rural Social Movements and Agroecology: Context, Theory, and Process" *Ecology and Society 17*(3).

These authors in this write up try to project that in the recent years rural social movements have adopted agroecology and diversified farming systems as part of their discourse and practice. They try to situate this phenomenon in the evolving context of rural spaces that are increasingly disputed between agribusiness, together with other corporate land-grabbers, and peasants and their organisations and movements. They use the theoretical frameworks of disputed material and immaterial territories and of re-peasantisation to explain the increased emphasis on agroecology by movements in this context. They provide examples from the farmer-to-farmer movement, the agroecology networking process and the transnational peasant and family farmer movement La Vía Campesina.

177. Rotz et.al. 2019. "Automated pastures and the digital divide: How agricultural technologies are shaping labour and rural communities" *Journal of Research Studies*, pp. 112-122.

This article addresses the issues like the rising land costs and automation, the development of a high-skill or low-skilled bifurcated labour market and issues around the control of digital data in North America. The paper tries to locate the impact of agricultural digitalisation on agri-food, and its impact on marginalised agricultural labourers and the rural communities. The review is drawn from a workshop conducted at the University of Guelph with 20 scholars from diverse disciplines who are working across the fields of agri-food, digitalisation and rurality. Further to make the study more reliable, five interviews with farmers who employ migrant labourers as well as interview and focus group data with 20 food activists and representatives of labour and agri-food organisations have been brought into picture. The author concludes that digitalisation can be used to build transparency around labour treatment, fairness and care.

178. Rubio, V. S. & F. R. Mas 2020. "From Smart Farming towards Agriculture 5.0: A Review on Crop Data Management" *Agronomy* 2020, 10, 207, pp. 1-21.

This paper studies about the recent trends of advanced farm management systems by reviewing the procedures from data acquisition in crop fields to variable rate applications by which smart farmers can make optimised decisions to save money while protecting the environment and transforming food production into a sustainable one to match the needs of growing population. The study finds that small and young farmers consistently learn and use modern technology in agricultural field whereas large farmers invest with advanced resources. The farmers need to have proper knowledge about the latest technology for taking appropriate decisions as and when required.

179. *Rural Sociological Society Task Force on Persistent Rural Poverty*. 1993. Persistent Poverty in Rural America. Boulder: Westview Press.

This book gives a critical evaluation of the theories that explain persistent rural poverty. It details out three conventional theories on poverty, used over a long period of time and tries to point out their limitations. They are the theory of culture of poverty, human capital theory and economic organisation theories. Added to these it also has reflected upon the social embeddedness theory, feminist critiques, linking biography with history, community theory, institutional theory, rational underinvestment, dependency theory, moral exclusion theory, global economic restructuring theory, and nation-state theories. The book begins with a chapter that talks on the trends and characteristics of rural poverty. The next chapter concentrates on giving an overview and critique of human capital theory and explores the linkage between human capital and poverty. The rest of the chapters look at work structures and rural poverty, theories of poverty in relation to the spatial location of economic activities with regard to lopsided development, theories related to natural resource dependency and persistent rural poverty, and persistent rural poverty among racial and ethnic minorities, women, families and children, and the elderly.

180. Sachs, Carolyn. 1996. *Gendered Fields: Rural Women, Agriculture, and Environment*. Boulder: Westview Press.

This book is a critique to the rural social theories which fail to address the conceptions of gender in rural social theories. It is based on a wide range of referencing and views developed by various authors on rural women. The book draws information from historical research as well as other contemporary studies of rural women, writings by rural women, and is based on the information captured by the author through her in-depth interviews. The book is enriched through the geographical diversity it addresses and by the multifaceted perspectives with which it looks into the rural issues. The author, Sachs analyses women's connections to nature and the land, their work with plants and animals, their roles on family farms, and the local outcomes of global restructuring from a pan global perspective. She tries to analyse rural women's issues from multiple points like race, class, age, nationality, ethnicity, and even sexual orientation. The plethora of points of view result in a complex set of arguments.

181. Salamon, S. and J. B. Tornatore, 1994. "Territory contested through property in a Midwestern post-agricultural community." ***Rural Sociology*, Vol. 59, No. 4 (Winter 1994) 636-654.**

This article is basically on contested territory and divided community. The authors present the study results of a 9-month field study done during 1989-1990 in a central Illinois community with surveys, participant observation, semi structured interviews and in-depth interviews. The article elaborates the history of the community, the cultural and economic factors that led to its decline and the rise of surplus housing, and the in-migration that changed its social construct and landscape. The changes in the village includes the clash between the old guards and the newcomers, the rise of public and private property. Open conflicts occur over the old guard's enforcement of property ordinances and newcomers' acts of vandalism in retaliation. This makes the territory contested and the community divided.

182. Schendel, Willem van. 1991. ***Three Deltas: Accumulation and Poverty in Rural Burma, Bengal and South India.*** **New Delhi; Newbury Park, CA: Sage Publication**

This book presents results of a comparative historical study of three areas situated in important river deltas in Asia: Lower Burma, Bengal, and the Kaveri delta in South India. The book describes poverty as a structural problem and ascertains that it is the by product of unequal development relationships. Factors like incapability to expand production and productivity, flexible systems of surplus extraction, inability to resist claims of accumulators, and the inability of primary producers to collect accumulated surplus are the main drivers to poverty. The book has five chapters. It begins with an introduction, then analyses the scenario of surplus in the three studied societies prior to colonisation. The next three chapters talk about the situation of three time periods i.e. the late nineteenth century, the mid-twentieth century, and the 1980s. A final chapter summarises and draws conclusions, focussing on uneven development and peripheralisation as contributing to the spread of mass poverty.

183. Sheridan, Thomas E. 1988. ***Where the Dove Calls: The Political Ecology of a Peasant Corporate Community in North western Mexico.*** **Tucson: University of Arizona Press.**

This ethnographic work is contextualised to the town of Cucurpe in northern Sonora, Mexico. It tries to make a theoretical combination of a political economy approach and the cultural ecology approach. The political economy approach focuses on a society's place in the world system and the cultural ecology approach examines adaptations to local environmental and demographic factors. With the household as the unit of analysis, the book gives a note on the history of Cucurpe. It examines the ecological and economic constraints arising out of scarce necessary resources in Cucurpe, the role of corporate communities in ensuring their access to resources, the class differences and competition that are noted in the space. It also explores the land use and water control process, livestock raising and other subsistence activities, and their contributions to community and inequality in Cucurpe. The book looks at class and competition in Cucurpe, breaking the town up into four competing class groups. It discovers that privately held agricultural land and communal grazing land is a major source of inequality. Free riding by large herds that degrade the resource, as well as to poor decisions on land use due to inexperience becomes an emanating point of inequality. The book end with a strong note that peasants are both exploited and responsible for their exploitation, constrained by resources as well as by their own societal structures.

184. Sideridis et.al 2010. "ICT and farmers: lessons learned and future developments." ***Journal of Agricultural Informatics,*** **Vol. 1, No. 2: 35-41.**

The researcher here uses the experience gained in the field of ICT in Agriculture over the last thirty years. This is done to evaluate and reason the poor performance in the area of applicability of ICT innovations and tools by the vast majority of farmers throughout the world. The researcher discovers that change of farmers profile through appropriately designed training courses like more business-like model will certainly improve his income and keep his farm going. Digital literacy, adaptive capability of farmers can bring increase food production and reduce starvation induces mortality in the world.

185. Singh, I. 1990. ***The Great Ascent: The Rural Poor in South Asia.*** **Baltimore: The Johns Hopkins University Press.**

The main argument of this book is that economic growth in South Asia (India, Pakistan and Bangladesh) has ameliorated poverty, despite also increasing inequality. The book poses two cardinal questions. They are: whether the antipoverty programmes and the Green Revolution have really failed to help the rural poor, and whether growth has benefited both rich and poor or it is at the cost of the poor. Secondly, the book tries to imagine what South Asia would look like without these changes. The book explores a host of issues which include: both farm and non-farm issues, the incidence and trends of rural poverty, agrarian structure and rural employment, strategies for increasing agricultural output, the impact of the Green Revolution on the rural poor, provisions of non-agricultural employment for the rural poor, rural industrialisation and antipoverty programmes, and land reforms. The book recommends for both agriculture-based development as well as policies favourable to non-farm industries and employment, particularly in areas marked with labour surpluses. The author notes that land reform is to be taken as a major consideration in designing poverty related policies, but it alone is not sufficient to reduce poverty. The book ends up with the summoning for developing a more complex theoretical paradigm to replace earlier simplistic concepts of rural poverty and its amelioration.

186. Steiner, A., & J. Atterton, 2014. "The contribution of rural business to community resilience." ***Local Economy*, *29*(3), 228-244.**

This article is the outcome of secondary data analysis and two case studies contextualised in rural Scotland. The article basically aims at exploring the role of private sector enterprises in the building of resilience in rural communities in Scotland. Through his analysis the authors land up at the conclusion that rural enterprises contribute to economic and social development in communities and play a major role in the building of resilience in rural locations. Private enterprises, both small and medium enterprises through their investments are noted to be having a major role in generating diversity of employment in rural Scotland. The case data provides the impression on the role of the private sector in bringing social and economic resilience of small rural towns in Scotland. They do so by enhancing the quality of life of residents and communities.

187. Steiner et. al. 2021. "Rurality and Social Innovation Processes and Outcomes: A realist evaluation of rural social enterprise activities" *Journal of Rural Studies*: pp. 1-9.

This study conducts 42 in-depth semi-structured interviews with beneficiaries, service providers, and external stakeholders of a rural social enterprise in Scotland. The study aims to examine how rurality affects the social innovation process. The data is collected through interviews and observations. The researchers observe that the positive outcomes of a social innovative intervention are also potentially rooted in rural peculiarity and problematic rural contexts.

188. Summers, Gene F. 1991. "Minorities in rural society." *Rural Sociology*, Vol. 56, No. 2 (Summer 1991): 177-188.

In this essay, the author tries to explore the dynamics behind the poverty class and the reasons for the disproportionate burden borne by the minorities. The author feels that the identification of the barriers that prevent rural minorities from achieving economic success can best explain the dynamics. To him rural poverty is structural in nature. However, the misconceptions about the nature of structural problems hinder the alleviation of poverty. He identifies seven misconceptions as barriers to understanding persistent rural poverty. These are:

- The belief that poverty can be reduced by merely improving the marketable skills of minorities.
- The belief that persistent unemployment and poverty can be reduced by making American industries more competitive in world product markets.
- The belief that the creation of a peripheral labour force affects urban minorities but not rural minorities.
- The belief that the informal labour market is largely a Third World phenomenon.
- The belief that labour market participation will eliminate poverty.

- The belief that the problems of rural minorities are due to failures of rural social institutions and inferior human resources; and
- The belief that merely the good will and social conscience of the powerful will overcome poverty.

So, he concludes that these misconceptions need to be eliminated and alternatives need to be thought of to alleviate poverty in rural areas.

189. Tickamyer, Ann R. and C. M. Duncan, 1990. "Poverty and opportunity structure in rural America." ***Annual Review of Sociology*, Vol. 16 (1990): 67-86.**

This article presents an overview of research on rural poverty. It tries to give an account of rural poverty by historizing it in the context of social, political and economic inequality and current economic restructuring. It finds a strong nexus between the persistence and severity of rural poverty with the limited opportunity structures that are the outcome of past social and economic development policies as well as current economic transformations. Limited opportunity structures have resulted in the lack of stable employment, opportunities for mobility, investment in the community, and diversity in the economy and other social institutions. The article discusses the past neglect of rural poverty in Sociology, and then provides an overview of recent studies that have been done in areas related to rural poverty. Topics covered include community studies, migration and rural-urban linkages, spatial analyses of economic opportunity, economic restructuring, and labour market analyses. It concludes that there is a serious connection between rural poverty and opportunity structure in rural communities, which must be addressed through more community studies and longitudinal research that explores the dynamics of poverty, labour markets and political structures in rural America.

190. Wahab, F. R. 1993. "Rural Industries: Employment and Income Enhancement for the Working Poor." ***Bangladesh: Centre on Integrated Rural Development for Asia and the Pacific.***

This paper is bases on reviews on rural industry policies. It is the outcome of the nine case studies done in India, Indonesia, Malaysia, Pakistan, Philippines, Sri Lanka, Thailand, Vietnam, and Kenya. The paper aims to give a comparative picture of the situations, and policy prescriptions in the nine countries, as well as to make policy prescriptions. The common notions the paper tries to establish are that the agricultural sector is waning in Africa and Asia, the urban sector cannot accommodate all the rural workers who suffer from agricultural labour displacement, and thus that rural industrialisation is needed in order to combat rural poverty. The case studies are descriptive as well analytic. They focus on rural industries, and look at production arrangements, marketing, credit, and other constraints faced by rural industries. The paper also attempts to evaluate the impact of rural enterprises on the income and employment of the rural poor, and highlight the common features and problems pertaining to rural industries in the case study areas. The main findings of the paper are rural industries contribute significantly toward household income in rural areas, but that the full potential in this regard is not being realised. Income disparities are found to be significant between entrepreneurs and workers, and workers' earnings are much lower than those in larger scale industries. State support for rural industries is generally found to be insignificant. Policy suggestions in the paper's conclusion point out ways in which these types of common flaws can be improved.

191. Walford, J. C. Everitt & D. Napton. (Eds.), ***Reshaping the Countryside: Perceptions and Processes of Rural Change*** **(Chapter Seven). United Kingdom: CABI Publishing.**

The authors in this contributed chapter investigate the reasons for population growth in the eastern rural coastal region of North Carolina in the post 1970s. They begin by describing the pre 1970 scenario in this area. To them the growing agricultural mechanisation and the transition to industrial farming reduced the number of farms and farm workers after 1950 in this study area. During the 1960s and 1970s industrialisation and businesses penetrated into rural areas to get volumes of voluntary workers to lower their costs of production. Industries were trying to hire people prepared to work with higher wages for a rural lifestyle. Supplemented to these two factors, in-migration was spearheaded due to the availability of recreation, tourism and retirement of the people from their urban occupations. The scenario of country living changed in this eastern rural coastal region of North Carolina within a span of 50 years as the economy transited from an agricultural economy to a service and manufacturing economy.

192. Wilkinson, K. P. 1991. ***The Community in Rural America*. New York: Greenwood Press.**

This book pulls together insights generated from research on the community in rural America and outlines challenges for the future in rural sociology and rural policy. It takes an interactional approach to community and social wellbeing in rural communities. So, it elaborates the interactional theory approach to community in the initial chapter. The central theme it proposes is that community is a process of local social interaction. Its main thesis is that neither the community has disappeared nor has ceased to be an important factor in individual and social well-being, despite the complexity of local social life. The book in the second chapter examines the properties associated with rural location that affect community, drawing insight from theory and research in the sociological literature. In this attempt it addresses the major conceptual issues about community and rural life, using the interactional perspective and concepts. In the subsequent chapters, concepts like wellbeing, community development as a means to social wellbeing, the components of community development are analysed. The book ends up with the examination of the policy efforts to promote well-being in rural areas and suggesting ways that rural sociological research can support these efforts.

193. Wilson, R. 2006. "Collaboration in context: rural change and community forestry in the Four Corners." *Society and Natural Resources, 19*, 53-70.

In this article, the author examines rural change and the subsequent rise of the community-based collaboration through a comparative case study analysis of four community forest projects on national forests in the rural "New West". He points out to the dramatic socio-economic change; the rural American has witnessed over the years. This change is characterised by a loss of traditional primary based industries and with the rise of amenity-based service sector economies, increasingly urbanised landscapes and a steady influx of new ex-urban migrants. These rural regions have become known as the "New West". These changes have led to the reshaping of the relationship between rural communities and their local rural environment. The new relationship is highlighted by the emergence of a new approach to resource management and planning in these areas known as community-based collaboration. This approach targets at increasing the amount and quality of rural community involvement in public land management and planning by providing a forum for frequent and open dialogue between the rural/local community, entrepreneurs who use the land for business purposes, and the government agencies that ultimately shape rural land-use policy. By examining socio-economic data, the author establishes that all four case study regions experienced dramatic change in the 1990s including population growth, a decrease in primary industry, a rise in service sector employment, a marked decrease in farm income, and a clear increase in overall income from new forms of employment such as the service sector. The author notes, however, that these developments have not occurred evenly throughout the American west.

194. Woods, M. 1998. "Advocating rurality? The repositioning of rural local government." ***Journal of Rural Studies*, 14(1), 13-26.**

In this article the author indicates the way in which the Thatcherian restructuring of Britain has weakened the power of the rural elected local government. However, this decline has led to the emergence of a concurrently, a new system of local governance which is characterised by self-organising networks. These self-organising networks include the state, private and voluntary sectors. This type of governing has led many local governments to discover a new role and purpose for themselves. They have also relocated themselves by developing a new sense of legitimacy/power in local politics. Woods suggests that some councils in Britain have assumed the role of pressure groups, lobbying as external actors on behalf of local interests. The author argues, that in doing so, these local governments have also found themselves advocating particular discourses of rurality.

195. Woods, M. 2014. "Family farming in the global countryside." ***Anthropological notebooks*, *20*(3), 31-48.**

This is a study based on the author's reference to some past studies conducted in the United Kingdom, Australia and New Zealand. The author records that irrespective of a decline in their numbers with the sway of globalisation, many family farms have however survived by adapting to change. But the number of these farmers was countable while the greater majority transited to the new mode responding gradually to the changes brought by globalisation. Woods begins by describing that globalisation has posed many challenges and changes for the farmers. But they have tried to adapt innovative strategies to resist to these changes and tiding over these challenges. The author notes three principal adaptation strategies i.e., diversification; mobility and resistance. The major challenges put forth for family farmers by globalisation include: changing farm labour requirements, gender roles and financial viability. Increasing use of mechanisation and technologies, agrichemicals; and alternative career options for farm children pose a threat to farm inheritance. In response to these changes, the farmers diversified their farm activities solely from agriculture as an adaptation strategy. The author cites an example from New Zealand where the farmers moved from sheep production to dairying, or to farming more 'exotic' species such as deer. Such diversification was usually a survival strategy however some entrepreneurial farmers undertook diversification to grow their business by taking advantage of opportunities that globalisation offered. Such "globally-engaged" farmers adopted a more corporate approach however remained family firms at heart. Some farmer moved their farm business to another more profitable location, either in their own country or in another country as the second adaption strategy. The third type of adaptation strategy family farmers have used is resistance by joining protest groups such as the Family Farm Defenders in the US. But this resistance was hardly having any effect. Woods predicts that such actions may not continue to save such farms longer term.

196. World Bank. 2008. "The Welfare Impact of Rural Electrification: A Reassessment of the Cost and Benefits" *An IEG impact evaluation*, ch. 5, pp. 39–52.

This study of the World Bank for 11 countries reveals that rural electrification brings manifold benefits for the rural areas. These benefits include: improvements of health facilities, better health from cleaner air as household reduce use of polluting fuels for cooking, lighting and heating, improved knowledge through increase access to television and better nutrition from improved knowledge and storage facilities from refrigerator.

197. Yanua, F. 2016. "The Health Status Model in Urban and Rural Society in West Sumatera, Indonesia: An Approach of Structural Equation Modeling." ***Indian Journal of Science and Technology*****, Volume 9, Issue 4, Pages 1-8.**

This is a study undertaken in West Sumatera, Indonesia. Here the author applies the Structural Equation Modeling (SEM) approach to model the health status in rural and urban society of the region. The data used in the article are drawn from the Primary Health Research that was conducted in Indonesia in the year 2013.In this study, SEM is applied to 3677 respondents from urban area and 3134 respondents from rural area who lived in West Sumatera. The survey involves the gathering of information on the respondent's socio-demography, lifestyles, mental health condition, and biomarkers. The study concludes that the health status model for urban area and rural area are different. For urban area's model, socio-demography and mental health condition are found to have a significant direct effect on the health status. However, lifestyle has an indirect effect on the health status, as mediated by the socio-demography. On the other hand, for rural area's model, this study finds that socio-demography, lifestyle and mental health have significant direct effect on the health status.

Section-II
Rural Studies: A Snapshot From India

1. **Abraham, V. 2009. Employment growth in rural India: distress-driven?. *Economic and Political Weekly*, 97-104.** The National Sample Survey revealed that after jobless growth during the 1990s, there was a shift in employment growth in the rural areas of India. However, this was during the period of distress in the agricultural sector. There was low productivity, indebtedness among the farmers, price instability and stagnation. This paper uncovers that economic growth in rural areas was a reaction due to the income crisis associated with the farming sector. Normally when the income level of non-working populations goes below the sustenance level, the non-working population enters the labour force to add to the family income. Hence, along with the non-working population, the working population also joined the labour force leading to forced sectoral and regional mobility because of distress in the agricultural sector.

2. **Adelman, I., & Dalton, G. 1971. A factor analysis of modernisation in village India. *The Economic Journal*, *81*(323), 563-579.** It attempts to overcome the difficulties of studying the micro-development of villages in India. Firstly, the villages change, and the studies' conclusions cannot be generalised due to huge variation among them. Secondly, quantitative measurement of the rural economy is scantily available and often deceiving. Thirdly, there is a lack of theory generating models which can be used to analyse change and development and further used for policy development. It uses statistical methods to determine the most important factors that explain their operation and indicate their policy uses.

3. **Agarwal, B. 1990. Social security and the family: coping with seasonality and calamity in rural India. *The Journal of Peasant Studies*, *17*(3), 341-412.** This article examines how poor rural families in India cope with the food insecurity associated with seasonal troughs in the agricultural production cycle, and with calamities such as drought and famine; the effectiveness of the coping mechanisms they adopt; the

intrahousehold sharing of the burden of coping; and the appropriate state and nonstate interventions that would strengthen the survival mechanisms adopted by the families themselves. The family is seen here as a bargaining unit, the ability of different members to command food (among other resources) depending on their relative bargaining strengths, determined by their ownership endowments like land, labour, etc., exchange entitlements, and external endowments social and communal support systems. Gender and age both form the basis of intrafamily inequality in this respect. While seasonality reveals a face of the family which is one of cooperation, famine mirrors one of disintegration. In both contexts, the burden of coping falls disproportionately on female members within poor households, traceable to women's already weak and further weakened like during the calamity, bargaining position within the family. A reinterpretation of existing facts about the 1943 Bengal famine illustrates the process of family disintegration and the abandonment of wives and children during a severe calamity. Therefore, state efforts complemented by nonstate interventions need to be directed to programmes that 'empower' low-income families and the more vulnerable members within them.

4. **Agarwal, B. 1997. Gender, environment, and poverty interlinks: Regional variations and temporal shifts in rural India, 1971–1991. *World Development*, 25(1), 23-52.** This paper especially focuses on the interrelationships between gender, poverty and the environment in rural India since they vary regionally, and there has been a shift since 1971-1991. The paper identifies the major factors of environmental degradation in a quick manner. Then it analyzes how stabilisation and privatisation use natural resources by the state, and private individuals have an adverse impact on the female members of the rural households. This paper analyzes the interrelationships between gender, poverty and the environment in rural India, focusing especially on regional variations and temporal shifts

over 1971–1991. Briefly identifying the major factors underlying environmental degradation, it traces why and how this degradation, and the appropriation of natural resources by the state (statisation) and some individuals (privatisation), tend to have particularly adverse implications for the female members of poor rural households. Regional and temporal variations in the likely intensity of these effects are traced both by examining individual indicators and the specification of a set of aggregative indices, termed here as the GEP(V) indices. These indices measure differences between states in their gender-environment-poverty vulnerability (or what could be termed the "GEP-gap") at a point in time and over time. Governmental and community-initiated environmental protection and regeneration attempts are also examined, and the importance of gender-directed policies is highlighted.

5. **Ahluwalia, M. S. 1978. Rural poverty and agricultural performance in India.** ***The Journal of Development Studies*, *14*(3), 298-323.** This paper examines time-series evidence on rural poverty over the past two decades. The time series shows that the incidence of poverty fluctuates in response to variations in real agricultural output per head, but there is no significant time trend. There is a statistically significant inverse relationship between rural poverty and agricultural performance for India, suggesting that agricultural growth by itself tends to reduce the incidence of poverty. The analysis for individual states presents a somewhat different picture. The inverse relationship between output per head and rural poverty is observed in several states. Still, there is also evidence that there are processes at work that tend to increase the incidence of poverty, independently of variations in agricultural output per head.

6. **Aklin, M., Cheng, C. Y., Urpelainen, J., Ganesan, K., & Jain, A. 2016. Factors affecting household satisfaction with electricity supply in rural India.** ***Nature Energy*, *1*(11), 1-6.** Electricity is an important component of socio-economic development, but most studies of household electricity access

focus exclusively on the presence or absence of a connection. Here the authors move beyond connectivity. They examine the relationship between various dimensions of the quality of electricity supply and a household's subjective satisfaction with their electricity or lighting situation. Through the results from a survey of 8,568 households in six large, energy-poor states from northern, central and eastern India, they find that household satisfaction responds strongly to the average hours of electricity available on a typical day. The positive effect of increasing the number of hours per day by one standard deviation on satisfaction is almost as large as electrifying a non-electrified household. These findings underscore the importance of moving from counting electricity connections to enhancing the quality of electricity supply.

7. **Balasubramaniam, D., Chatterjee, S., & Mustard, D. 2014. Got Water? Social Divisions and Access to Public Goods in Rural India. *Economica, 81*(321), 140-160. Retrieved January 20, 2021.** In this article, data from the 2001 Census of India examines how social divisions are associated with access to tap water across rural India. Different types of social fragmentation are associated with different outcomes for tap water access. Communities that are heterogeneous in terms of caste have lower access to tap water, while communities fragmented across religions have higher access. This underscores the importance of heterogeneity both within and across religions. Aggregated measures of social fragmentation may thus conceal the differential effects of its component measures and obscure important information that may affect the design of public policies.

8. **Bandyopadhyay, M. 2003. Missing girls and son preference in rural India: looking beyond popular myth. *Healthcare for Women International, 24*(10), 910-926.** In South and East India, the survival of girls are filled with hurdles. Various issues like female foeticide, infanticide, abandonment,

under-reporting of female birth and neglect in caregiving have mounted to a higher death rate of the girl child. The paper discusses the skewed sex ratio in rural West Bengal and discusses female foeticide, infanticide, son preference, and abortion. The majority of women prefer to have a son. The author observes more boys were recorded at birth than girls. Negligence of daughters and discrimination is researched broadly. The limitation of the study is that female foeticide, and infanticide has been less examined.

9. **Banerjee, B. 1981. Rural Urban Migration and Family Ties: An Analysis of Family Considerations in Migration Behaviour in India. *Oxford Bulletin of Economics and Statistics*, *43*(4), 321-355.** Based on evidence from rural-urban ties, the article explores the importance of family consideration in migration. The survey was conducted in Delhi with the migrant head of the household. The study used 7 part typology and unit analysis as a methodology. Nearly 4/5th of the migrants visited their place of origin who had their families at their origin. Married migrants who left their wives at their place of origin visit their native places in the agricultural season. Most of the migrants maintained their connection with their villages through economic links. The migrants who want to settle in cities send fewer remittances to their villages.

10. **Bardhan, P. 1993. Analytics of the institutions of informal cooperation in rural development. *World Development*, *21*(4), 633-639.** Community-level water management at the local level is very crucial for rural development. In South Asia and Sub-Saharan Africa, cooperative institutions have played a successful role in water management. However, there are many cases of failure in water management. The paper discusses lessons from theoretical approaches on cooperation and evidence from the field study by anthropologists and others on the success and failure of local cooperation.

11. Barnes and Sen, 2004. 'The impact of energy on women's lives in rural India'. The World Bank (Energy Sector Management Assistance Programme). This joint UNDP/WB study includes more than 5000 households in 180 villages in 6 states of India. They find that women suffer from respiratory illness, eye problems are common among women who work on traditional chulhas. Women spend maximum time in their domestic work. They spend nearly 3 hours on cooking and nearly six hours on other household activities. The study support that women who have a very burdensome life use biofuel. They have suggested that improved rural energy services can benefit rural Indian women.

12. Basant, R., & Kumar, B. L. 1989. Rural non-agricultural activities in India: A review of available evidence. ***Social Scientist*, 13-71.** Diversification of the rural economy is one of the main strategies in the development policies. But there is not much knowledge regarding the nature, types and determinants of rural non-agricultural activities. The paper explores the nature of rural non-agricultural activities and the characteristics of rural non-agricultural workers. The paper defines the scope of rural non-agricultural activities in India. It assesses the quantitative importance of the rural non-agricultural sector in terms of employment and the number of enterprises. Finally, the sectoral composition of rural non-agriculture employment is analyzed.

13. Basole, A. 2017. What Does the Rural Economy Need. ***Economic and Political Weekly*, *52*(9), 40-43.** The article analyses the budget and the promises that hold for improving the economy of rural India. The agricultural sector is not performing well in comparison to the other sectors. Even after the diversification of sources of income, 70 percent of the agricultural household cannot meet their consumption demands. The budgets allocated for the rural economy show that they have not been adequate to address employment opportunities in rural areas. Analysis of the budget shows that improving the rural economy keeps employment generation as a target. The author says that the biggest challenge lies in generating livelihood in rural areas capable of providing regular income for every household in the rural area. The budget lays two major points to raise rural income and create non-farm employment and other essential public services.

14. Basu, P. 2009. ***Villages, women, and the success of dairy cooperatives in India: making place for rural development.*** **Cambria Press.** The Cooperative Dairy Program of India has been the symbol of rural development. The structure of the Dairy Development Programme involves village-level cooperatives and the involvement of rural women in production. The book shows the value of dairying to the rural communities while it captures the limitation of the participatory nature. It uses ethnographic approaches and comparative analysis as methodology using people's perspectives and rural geography to understand dairying as part of rural development.

15. Basu, P., & Srivastava, P. 2005. Exploring Possibilities: Microfinance and Rural Credit Access for the Poor in India. ***Economic and Political Weekly,*** **40(17), 1747-1756.** Rural formal credit access has been low despite efforts to improve rural finances through the systematic engagement of rural banking networks. But the popularity of informal lending is high. Therefore, new microfinance approaches are introduced to rural finance so that poor people can be benefited from it. Though it seems promising, there are relatively few empirical assessments of the extent of its reach and impact. The article tries to analyse the SHG-bank linkage model, which is the leading microfinance initiative. The authors survey 6000 rural households' access to microfinance initiatives. Drawing from the study and the experience from international practices tries to chalk out the area of concern and steps that the government should take up to improve access to finance by the rural poor.

16. Batra, A. K. 2003. Burn mortality: recent trends and sociocultural determinants in rural India. *Burns*, *29*(3), 270-275. The higher mortality rate of younger married women due to burns is an alarming medical issue in rural India. The age, sex, residence, marital status, reasons for burn and their patterns have been less reported from rural India. The article discusses the trends wising 4042 medicolegal deaths from rural India over five years. It is found that 23.3 percent of deaths were due to burns. Out of the burnt death cases, 80.8 percent were female, 82.4 percent were married women. Nearly 72 percent of the dead were from the younger age group, and 75 percent were from rural India. It was found that 50 percent of the deaths were accidental, 47.8 percent was suicidal, and 1.5 percent were homicidal deaths. Burn was the most common method for 60 percent of female suicide, and torture by in-laws is a common reason for suicide by married women. The article tries to identify the high-risk groups in rural India and the reasons for burn mortality in rural India.

17. Baviskar, B. S., & Mathew, G. 2009. ***Inclusion and exclusion in local governance: Field studies from rural India.*** **Sage Publications.** This article provides valuable insights into the process of decentralisation in rural India from a micro-level perspective. It is a unique study that has considered 42 panchayats of twelve states to analyse the socio-political variations and commonality between them. The cases of stories of empowerment and discrimination of the marginalised group. It shows the inclusion and exclusion of the people in the rural power structure. The qualitative methodology used for the study is unique and hold promises from further studies like this.

18. Baviskar, B. S., Attwood, D. W. 2013. ***Inside-Outside: Two Views of Social Change in Rural India.*** **India: Sage Publications.** Villages are stereotyped commonly as passive, stagnant and pessimism. This book is an effort of two researchers, Baviskar, one from the village (insider) where the study is done and another Attwood (outsider) who has grown up in Chicago. They have tried to gain a complete view of the village by looking from different angles. Through stories, they have been looking for social change by rapid innovation and institution building in the village. These stories narrate grassroots change and innovation.

19. Behera, M. C. (Ed.). 2006. *Globalizing rural development: Competing paradigms and emerging realities.* Sage Publications India. The changes in perspectives in the field of rural development are affecting policies, programmes. With the advent of globalisation, it has become important to understand the most appropriate rural development approach. The fundamental argument of the book is that the new paradigm of rural development reflects the core-periphery dichotomy. This results in the top to bottom approaches in implementing the programmes in the rural area. It examines the impact of the changing paradigm of rural development on poverty alleviation, equity, gender, food security, employment and sustainability.

20. Behrman, J. R., & Deolalikar, A. B. 1987. "Will developing country nutrition improve with income? A case study for rural South India". *Journal of Political Economy,* 95(3), 492-507. International Institutions like World Bank and others believe that to increase nutrition, the major mechanism is increasing income. Food expenditure is relatively consistent with the income of the people. A case study of rural south Indian sample indicates that this bias is considerable and that the true nutrient elasticities concerning income may be close to zero.

21. Bhandari, L., & Dutta, S. 2007. Health infrastructure in rural India. *India Infrastructure Report, 2007,* 265-85. Health infrastructure does not refer to only physical infrastructure. Along with health centers, dispensaries, medical staff, doctors and services are also included under health infrastructure. The situation of health infrastructure is identified to find out the gaps and requirements in health infrastructure and services. The chapter discusses how to fill up the critical need of health structure in villages with policy, finances, and institutions. It also explores the possible role of the involvement of the private sector in improving health infrastructure in the village.

22. Bhandari, P. B. 2013. Rural livelihood change? Household capital, community resources and livelihood transition. *Journal of Rural Studies*, *32*, 126-136. It aims to determine how various capitals influence livelihood transition by using a sustainable livelihood framework to understand the household livelihood transition from farm to non-farming activities in a rural agricultural setting. The study area is the western Chitwan valley of south-central Nepal. The findings of the study reveal that households' livelihood assets determine the livelihood transition. Families having working-age children encourages the continuation of farming. Natural or economic capital are also inhibited transition from farming to non-farm activities. If government policies encourage small peasants to exit farming, then alternative jobs should be created in the non-farming sector to absorb the farmers who leave farming.

23. Bhattacharya, S., 1989. *Rural Poverty in India*. New Delhi: Ashish Pub. House. This book concentrates on the study of poverty and poverty alleviation programmes in India. The book discusses the conceptual aspects of poverty and poverty measurement yardsticks like the monetary and caloric measures. The author perceives that rural India suffers from acute poverty linked to unemployment in the rural sector. The book discusses different strategies to increase employment and reduce poverty. Among such strategies, Integrated Rural Development Strategy is an important strategy. The Indian planners and policy-makers have often adopted it as the most popular strategy for rural poverty alleviation. The development of small-scale rural industries have often been overstressed for rural livelihood generation and thereby poverty reduction. The book evaluates its efficacy by citing case studies. The book also looks at block level planning for rural economic growth. The block-level planning units are integrally connected to the district and state-level plans. Merits of this type of planning are discussed with several case studies. In the subsequent chapters, agricultural enterprise, community development projects, Panchayati Raj, and cooperatives in rural development have been highlighted. The book also clarifies that no less significant is the role of rural banks, the role of the village and small-scale industries, and the role of financial institutions in fighting rural poverty. Subsequently, a long chapter is devoted to assessing the successes and failures of the fight against poverty across states throughout India. The book makes many valuable suggestions to improve the existing poverty alleviation measures and end rural poverty.

24. Bhattarai, M. at al. 2018. ***Employment Guarantee Programme and Dynamics of Rural Transformation in India: Challenges and Opportunities.*** **Germany: Springer Singapore.** The edited book assesses MGNREGA programme of the Government of India through the performance, impact and welfare implications measures. The book presents the outcomes of the programmes and discussed critical insight from the author's experiences received from different part of rural areas of India, and compare with other similar schemes of Africa, Latin America and South and South-East Asian countries.

25. Bloch, F., & Rao, V. 2002. Terror as a bargaining instrument: A case study of dowry violence in rural India. ***American Economic Review*, *92*(4), 1029-1043.** Dowry related violence does not mean only payments during the marriage but also refers to abuse as a form of bargaining instrument used by groom and family to get larger transfers. The paper is a case study of rural India where domestic violence is used as a bargaining instrument. The study employs ethnographic information with open-ended interviews conducted in three villages of rural south India to infer the non-cooperative bargaining and signally development. The prediction from the surveys is econometrically tested. It finds that women who gave the smaller amount of dowry are at more risk of domestic violence. Similarly, those women who come from rich families are also at risk as more money can be extracted from them. A large amount of dowry and satisfaction in the marriage with a greater number of male children lessens the risk factor.

26. Borooah, V. K., & Iyer, S. 2005. Vidya, Veda, and Varna: The influence of religion and caste on education in rural India. *The Journal of Development Studies*, *41*(8), 1369-1404. This paper discusses how education is related to caste and religion in India. It tries to find out whether and up to what extent these two factors influence education. The study uses econometrics estimates from a survey of 33,000 rural households, in 1765 villages, from 16 states of India. The study's main findings show that the caste and religion effect depends on the non-community circumstances in which children are grown up. If the circumstances are favourable, then community, for instance, in literate parents, the size of community effect is negligible. However, under unfavourable circumstances, the size of the community matters.

27. Breman, J. 2007. *The poverty regime in village India* (Vol. 13). New Delhi: Oxford University Press. This book is an in-depth account of changing poverty of the landless peasants in four villages of South Gujarat. His ethnographic study engages the macroeconomic debate of poverty in India. It is a longitudinal study covering four villages. The fourth village he included because other economists pointed out that his cases were uniquely deviating from overall growth and economic development. This anthropological research work and publication stretches beyond nearly half a century. The author has been consistent in visiting the field and factories every year to collect data.

28. Brule, R. 2015. Accountability in Rural India: Local Government and Social Equality. *Asian Survey*, 55(5), 909-941. The paper intends to view recent research on the accountability of local and state governments in India. The article uses the Downsian theory of electoral competition as a methodology to classify different sources of government accountability failures. It deals with sources like limited voter participation and awareness; ideology, honesty and competence of political parties and electoral candidates; capture by elites; clientelism and vote-buying. Finally, it summarises the lessons learnt, and they raise questions at the end. The paper describes a range of possible reasons that limit the effectiveness of elections as a mechanism inducing governments to be accountable to their citizens and reviews the evidence available from the Indian context concerning each of these.

29. Burgess, R., & Pande, R. 2005. Do rural banks matter? Evidence from the Indian social banking experiment. *American Economic Review*, 95(3), 780-795. This article tries to answer how state-led credit and saving expansion facilities in rural areas helps in reducing poverty. The paper used state-level panel data of bank branches in rural areas, rural credit and saving shares and poverty outcomes. In analysis, it discusses how the 1977 and 1990 licensing policy helps in the extension of commercial bank branches in rural areas of less financial developed districts and states. This policy helped in equalising and increases the bank branches across the state. The study finds that poverty reductions in rural areas are linked to an increase in rural saving and credit, which is happened due to the extensive presence of rural bank networks. So this formal institutional structure helps in the growth of the economy as well as reducing rural poverty.

30. Byres, T. J., Kapadia, K., & Lerche, J. (Eds.). 2013. *Rural Labour Relations in India* (No. 18). Routledge. This edited volume is all about the rural labour relation and its development trajectory in India. This book comprises nine chapters written by eminent scholars. The first chapter introduces the theme of the book. The second chapter discusses persistent themes, common processes and differential outcomes of labour relations in India. The third chapter narrates the story of the Haryana issue in the context of India. The fourth chapter deliberates on the issue of feminisation of agricultural labour in the context of Andhra Pradesh. The fifth chapter brings notice of the dilemmas of a social transforming labour force in India. The sixth chapter highlights the agricultural labourers and political transformation in the state of Uttar Pradesh. The seventh chapter analyses the agrarian power and unfree labour in India. The eight chapters are on emerging features of contradiction and resistance in rural labour relations in India. The nine chapters highlighted the changes in the agrarian relation in central Bihar in the all India context.

31. Cabalion, J., & Thivet, D. 2019. Who Speaks for the Village? Representing and Practicing the "Rural" in India from the Colonial to the Post-Colonial. *South Asia Multidisciplinary Academic Journal*, (21). The village concept has been a focal issue in Indian history as it is believed that India resides in its village. Indian villages were pictured as small republics from colonial times. The villages are considered to be representatives of Indian society. The paper investigates the representations of rural society. The actors may be internal or external to the rural community. These are the actors who claim to represent the village and how the internal social differentiation is addressed. It also discusses who communicates for or against the village. The representation of the rural and its social space is discussed from a range of disciplinary perspectives, from history to literary theory. Lastly, the paper aims to underscore the importance of village and rural studies and allied research work to understand various dynamics that have marked the course of Indian society.

32. Calì, M., & Menon, C. 2013. Does Urbanisation Affect Rural Poverty? Evidence from Indian Districts. *The World Bank Economic Review, 27*(2), 171-201. This article explores the relationship between urbanisation and rural poverty in India. To reveals the relationship, the article uses large district-level data of India from 1983 to 1999. The finding reveals that urbanisation affects reducing poverty in surrounding rural areas.

The poverty reduction in rural areas due to urbanisation is the increased demand for rural agricultural products in these areas. This also results from rural-urban remittances, rural nonfarm employment, and rural land and population ratio.

33. Chacko, E. 2004. Positionality and praxis: fieldwork experiences in rural India. ***Singapore Journal of Tropical Geography*, *25*(1), 51-63.** This paper provides an account of the personal fieldwork experience of the author in the rural areas of India. The author highlights the power relation and the research process between the researcher and those who researched. It also discussed the multiple identities of scholars and the subject in the field setting. While doing fieldwork, the author uses self-reflexivity to inform, measure and activity in the field setting.

34. Chadha, G.K. and A. N. Sharma, (eds.) 1997. ***Growth, Employment and Poverty: Change and Continuity in Rural India*. New Delhi: Vikas Pub. House.** This volume contains twenty papers presented at the Indian Society of Labour Economics' 1995 national seminar on Agricultural Growth, Employment and Rural Poverty: Emerging Issues in the Context of Structural Adjustment Programme. All the papers revolve around the discussions on the positive and the negative impacts of structural adjustment programmes on Indian rural society. The book comprises five sections. The thrust areas of the book are economic liberalisation and Indian agriculture; agricultural growth, employment and rural poverty; changing non-farm scenarios; regional development experience; and policy concerns for the poor. All the papers talk about rural poverty, growth and employment in the context of the structural adjustment of the Indian economy. The sub-topics are land reforms, agro-climatic regional planning; people's participation in local development; common property issues, social forestry and livestock development; social security for the rural poor; workforce diversification; and structure and pace non-farm employment expansion. The book establishes that growth in agriculture is a necessary precondition for rural employment generation in the farm sector. Added to the themes described above, the book also focuses on the importance of economic growth for rural communities, tragedies of the commons, participatory development, and social security issues.

35. Chambers, R. 1981. Rapid rural appraisal: rationale and repertoire. *Public administration and development*, *1*(2), 95-106. The author reveals that lack of available information and higher expenditure in gathering the information makes it difficult for discussion makers to avail right information. To understand rural areas in a cost-effective manner, the author proposes a rapid rural appraisal method. This method or form to understand rural condition helps in quick information gathering by ignoring inappropriate professional standards. The author suggests optimal ignorance and proportionate accuracy to be used while doing the rapid rural appraisal. This method also helps in reducing bias against the rural poor people in rural development promotion.

36. Chambers, R. 1994. Participatory rural appraisal (PRA): Analysis of experience. *World development*, *22*(9), 1253-1268. From experience, it is revealed that participatory rural appraisal shows higher reliability and validity of information shared by rural people than long practices of the traditional method. The explanations include both shifts and reversals of emphasis in closed to open, etic to emic, individual to group, measuring to comparing, verbal to visual, and extracting information to empower local analysts in using the method.

37. Chambers, R. 1994. Participatory rural appraisal (PRA): Challenges, potentials and paradigm. *World development*, *22*(10), 1437-1454. The popularity of Participatory Rural Appraisal is accelerating in the research field work. The article tends to review the theoretical and the practical issues raised internationally along with its growth. The author has demarcated the difference between PRA and RRA and the difference in their training methods. The three basic components have been identified as methods, behaviour and attitudes and sharing. The PRA model has been lateral more than vertical, personally more than official and experiential more than didactic. The author expresses four dangers as instant fashion, rushing, formalism, routinisation and rut as concerns for PRA and suggests measures for dealing with it.

38. Chambers, R. 1994. The origins and practice of participatory rural appraisal. ***World development*****, *22*(7), 953-969.** There has been a shift in the approach to rural development from a top-down to a bottom-up approach. PRA has its source from activist participatory research, agroecosystem analysis, applied anthropology, field research on farming systems, and rapid rural appraisal (RRA). The changes in research method to Participatory Rural Appraisal (PRA) is seen where local people share, enhance and analyse their knowledge. In Rapid Rural Appraisal (RRA), information is extracted by the outsider, whereas PRA involves more local people. It is the dominant behaviour of the outsiders which explains our past ignorance in recognizing the importance of people in participating in research till the 1990s.

39. Chambers, R. 2014. ***Rural development: Putting the last first.*** **Routledge.** Rural poor get external support from the people who are neither rural nor poor. Chamber interestingly divides these outsiders into two groups with two polarised cultures. One is a negative academic culture, mainly of social scientists, engaged in unhurried analysis and criticism, and a more positive culture of practitioners engaged in time-bounded action. Pluralism has a third leg in rural development, which include rural people too. Conventional and professional research methods for rural studies used by outsiders is insufficient. Rural people's knowledge about their problems is more than the outsiders. The book explains to know about the micro-details of poverty which is multidimensional rather than one dimensional. To enable rural poor, it is important to understand how are at present and conduct research in their environment.

40. Chandran, K., Balaji, N., & Mani, M. 2015. Understanding transitions in a rural Indian building typology in the context of well-being. ***Current Science*, 109(9), 1610-1621.** Traditional dwellings in Karnataka in rural areas are made of local resources and are built by villagers or local masons. The authors explore how the traditional dwellings are changing into modern ones and change in people's lifestyles. The study areas are three villages Bommanahalli, Bommanahalli 1, and Pallerayanahalli in Karnataka. It focuses on the observed changes in architecture, building typologies and lifestyle in rural areas. The article finally recommends sustainable rural designs. Waste Management, educating design practitioners on environmental design, promoting renewable resources, community awareness and participation in rural design are some key recommendations for administrators and policy-makers for sustainable well-being.

41. Chauhan, B. R., & Satyanarayana, A. (Eds.). 2012. ***Changing Village India*. Rawat Publications.** Village studies are important to understand the pluralities of society. This edited volume is thematically divided into five sections. It is a compendium of studies on the themes of development administration, political events, constitutional amendments, empowerment of marginalised groups, and socio-psychological probing of villages. This book represents the changing nature of village India along with social change.

42. Chen, M., & Drèze, J. 1992. Widows and health in rural north India. ***Economic and Political Weekly*, WS81-WS92.** Widows are socially disadvantaged groups, particularly the widows of north India. She has a weak support system and is mostly supported by her son, who is more vulnerable to neglect. Patriarchal norms in patrilineal inheritance and gender division of labour lower her ability to engage in income-earning activities. As a result of which it leads to economic marginalisation, which affects her health and increases the mortality rate. The paper uses empirical data from two Dreze (1990), and Chen (1991) studies on widows in rural areas through intensive field work. It tries to find out the situation of widows in north India and how it impacts their health and well-being. The article also focuses on the aspect of the social support system for widows.

43. Chudgar, A. 2011. Female headship and schooling outcomes in rural India. *World development*, *39*(4), 550-560. The study aims to find out the study outcomes of the female-headed household. This study separately analyses data from two types of the household of the widow and the other household of married women. It compares the schooling outcomes in both types of households. It also quantifies the improvement of schooling outcomes of children with an increase in economic and financial status. It finds the children in the widow headed household are no worse off than men headed households. The household headed by married female children has better study outcomes. When the economic condition of a widow headed family increases, then it positively affects the schooling outcomes. Moreover, it finds that these households do not discriminate on the basis of gender.

44. Connell, J. et al. 1976. *Migration from rural areas: The evidence from village studies*. Delhi: Oxford University Press. The book analyses the issues of migration from rural areas by studying the villages of developing countries. The book focuses on the Todaro hypothesis and rural causes that effects migration. It analyses the attributes of migrant villages, its accesses of economic, educational and opportunist available, the impact of migration on villages and households. The study findings revealed that migration is both cause and contributor to rural inequality. The study suggests redirection of resources towards the rural sector instead of urban bias development policy.

45. Das, A., & Usami, Y. 2017. Wage rates in rural India, 1998–99 to 2016–17. ***Review of Agrarian Studies*****, 7(2369-2020-2016).** The article examines the trend of labour wage rates in rural India over the last two decades. The paper used and compiled the Wage Rates in rural India reported in the Indian Journal Labour Journal. The paper examines all Indian and State wise trends in the growth of wage rates in two periods – 1998-99 to 2006-07 and 2007-08 to 2014-15. The first-period wage rate is in stagnation, whereas the second rapid growth is marked in the wage rate.

46. Das, N. 2012. Impact of Participatory Forestry Program on Sustainable Rural Livelihoods: Lessons From an Indian Province. Applied Economic Perspectives and Policy, 34(3), 428-453. The paper analyses the rural livelihood policy interventions through community-based forest management in West Bengal. The study found that the rural livelihood of poor people who are participated in the programme are improved and sustainable. It also finds that feminine units attained positive livelihood outcomes than others. The paper suggests expanding the participatory forestry management programme for the sustainable livelihood of poor households in the forest periphery of rural areas.

47. Dasgupta, B. 1975. A typology of village socio-economic systems: from Indian village studies. ***Economic and Political Weekly*****, 1395-1414.** The paper tried to fill the gap in research in rural areas of India. The paper develops a typology of village socio-economic system based on the study of 126 villages of India. The paper study the variables like demography, occupation, workforce participation, availability and productivity of land, occupation pattern, land holding, agricultural input, wage, consumption, education, access, and socio-cultural aspects. These variables described how they helped develop a dynamic theory of village job situations in the socio-political context of villages.

48. Dasgupta, P., & Goldar, B. 2006. Female labour supply in rural India: An econometric analysis. *Indian Journal of Labour Economics*, *49*(2), 293-310. The paper analysed the female labour supply in rural areas of India by using 1999-00 year NSS data. The analysis results revealed that female labour supply from poor rural households is oppositely related to the number of earning members in their family and wage rate. The paper suggests greater attention should be given to female labour supply while framing rural employment schemes to avoid any difficulties.

49. Datar, A., Mukherji, A., & Sood, N. 2007. Health infrastructure & immunisation coverage in rural India. *Indian Journal of Medical Research*, *125*(1), 31. The paper investigated the role of community health workers and health infrastructures in escalating immunisation coverage in rural areas. The paper used 1993 and 1998 NFHS children data aged between 2-35 months living in rural areas. The paper estimated multinomial logit regression models for polio and non-polio vaccines, which evaluated the possibility of receiving full cover, some cover, and no cover. The result reveals that the availability of health infrastructure has only a modest consequence on coverage of immunisation. It also finds out that large and better health infrastructure facilities had bigger impacts on coverage. In comparison, community health workers in the village have not associated with an increase in coverage. The paper suggests expanding better rural health infrastructure and community outreach programmes for universal immunisation coverage.

50. Datt, G., & Ravallion, M. 1998. Farm productivity and rural poverty in India. *The Journal of Development Studies*, *34*(4), 62-85. To answer the question, 'to what extent do India's rural poor share in agriculture growth?', the paper used 24 household data across 35 years of a longitudinal study and estimate a model of consumption poverty measures, food price and agricultural wages. The paper finds that the poor rural household gains both relatively and terms when farm production is higher. The gains are not confined to the poverty line, but the wages and price help a large in the gain.

51. Desai, A. R. 1987. Rural development and human rights in independent India. ***Economic and Political Weekly*****, 1291-1296.** In analysing the concept of rural development has changed in India since the 1950s. Though the government aims to reduce poverty, it found poor people sliding into declining in their purchasing power. In contrast, the government have been strategically engaged in the rural development programmes and policies for the selected groups and propertied class and diffuses the increasing upsurge of the rural people. These rural development activities are the political will of the ruling class and favoured propertied class, who are a small section of people. It brings adverse impacts on the rural people and their human rights.

52. Desai, A. R. 1994. ***Rural sociology in India*****. Popular Prakashan.** This book makes a summary of the village and describes different aspects of village life in India. In the first part, the book highlighted the different concepts, ideas, approaches and problems of rural society in India and conceptualised rural sociology in India. The second part of the book is the collection of readings in rural sociology in India. This part describes by different thinkers on regional, historical, village community, tribes, rural stratification, agrarian unrest, land reforms, rural and village industries, panchayat raj, community development, rural movements, rural transition, list of village studies, and theories on agricultural development.

53. Desai, R., & Joshi, S. 2014. Collective Action and Community Development: Evidence from Self-Help Groups in Rural India. ***The World Bank Economic Review*****, 28(3), 492-524.** The paper gathers evidence from rural self help groups on women's collective action and community development. The paper finds that SHGs programmes increased women's participation in group savings and non-agricultural labour force in rural areas. The study further found that women participated more in household decisions and engaged in civic activities compared to the control village under study. At the same time, there is no evidence of the increase in income or the negative impact of the socio-economic status of the women members. The government programmes like National Rural Livelihood Mission needs to be expanded SHGs development in rural areas.

54. Desai, S., & Jain, D. 1994. Maternal employment and changes in family dynamics: The social context of women's work in rural South India. ***Population and Development Review*****, 115-136.** The paper examines the gender role inequality within the economic-political context in shaping intrafamily dynamics associated with the employment of women's. The paper analysed maternal employment and child welfare within the background of gender inequality in the labour market, poverty and lack of access to rural infrastructure in south India. The paper has identified two broad dimensions of gender inequality in the rural setup of India that are directly influenced the material condition of women's participation in non-domestic work and allocation of time in different activities. These two gender inequalities are discrimination in the labour market and the burden of domestic activities of women.

55. Dev, S. M. 2004. How to make rural India shine. ***Economic and Political Weekly*****, 4415-4422.** The paper examines selected important rural indicators in the pre and post-liberalisation period to make rural India shine. The paper finds that rural India is not shining. The paper suggests making a broad-based and balanced approach through investment, technology, and setting up appropriate institutions for rural development. The paper suggests investment in ten areas, which includes increasing public investment, create employment, agriculture development, water management, reforms in rural institutions, development in rural non-farm sectors, investment in health and education, reduction in social, economic and gender disparities, and decentralisation governance, which will make India shine.

56. Dhanagare, D. N. 1974. Social origins of the peasant insurrection in Telangana (1946-51). ***Contributions to Indian Sociology*, *8*(1), 109-134.** The paper examines both the general and specific features of the Telangana Peasant Revolt. The focus is mainly on the structural setting and the class character of the revolt, and the specific historical conditions are shaping its character.

57. Dhanagare, D. N. 1975. The Politics of Survival: Peasant Organisations and the Left-Wing in India, 1925-46. ***Sociological Bulletin*, *24*(1), 29-54.** It traces the formation, growth, decline, formal organisational features, leadership and class characters, programmes and ideology. Their character as a peasant organisation and their contribution to the peasant movement in India are examined systematically.

58. Dhanagare, D. N. 1979. Prosperity and Debt in Rural Punjab. ***Sociological Bulletin*, *28*(1-2), 120-130.** Through this review, article Dhanagare has highlighted the importance of Darling's work. The issue of rural credit and cooperative institutions' role in agrarian society is of much interest for the students and researchers in Sociology. Darling has concluded that cooperation is a viable alternative mean for the upliftment of the rural mass. Dhanagare writes that though Darling knew that the cooperatives were making the strong more powerful, he also recommended establishing cooperatives in every village. However, without adequate support to the rural poor or curbing the landholding class's growing economic and political power, measures like cooperative institutions will be futile.

59. Dhanagare, D. N. 1985. Rural development, poverty and protest. ***Contributions to Indian Sociology*, *19*(2), 349-**

358. In particular, the nature of rural transformation, poverty, agrarian protest of South Asia in general and India, in particular, is under study. It ties to find the linkages between rural development policies and the interest of the rural dominant class, whether there are contradictions within the ruling class, how the interest of the periphery aligned with the core and finally how the poor rural response to these changes over which they have little or no control.

60. Dhanagare, D. N. 1987. Green revolution and social inequalities in rural India. *Economic and Political Weekly*, AN137-AN144. The paper examines the available extensive literature on the green revolution and its impact on the development strategy of different rural society sections. Answering whether the green revolution reduced socio-economic inequalities and help poor people out of poverty in rural India or not, the author added that the green revolution failed to raise the income of rural poor. In some parts, it was getting lower. The paper suggests rethinking the development strategy for basic changes in the system to reduce the inequality in rural society.

61. Dhanagare, D. N. 2015. *Populism and Power: Farmers' movement in western India, 1980–2014*. Routledge. The book has traced the peasant movement in Western India, particularly in Maharashtra, for over three decades. It explains the rise and fall of the peasant movement in Maharashtra. Populism as ideology and as political power are contradictory to each other. The book highlights the ideology of the movement, its emergence during the agrarian crisis, the intermixing of economics and populism in a democratic setup. The role of leadership and grassroots agitation from the masses. All of this is eventually leading to the formation of a separate political party and its consequences. Dhanagare views that the movement's effectiveness lies in addressing the class and gender equation in the region. The book is an excellent source of researchers and students of rural sociology focusing on gender, power and social movement.

62. Drèze, J., & Kingdon, G. G. 2001. School participation in rural India. ***Review of Development Economics*****, 5(1), 1-24.** The paper analyzes the determinants of school participation based on household surveys in the rural north, including school characteristics as one of the parameters. The study reveals that school participation among girls depends on a different variable: parent's motivation and education, social background, village development, work opportunity, mid-day meals, teacher postings, and infrastructure quality. Among all, mid-day meals play a major role in dividing the proportion of girls excluded from schooling. Besides all, school quality and infrastructure also matter in schooling participation.

63. Dreze, J., & Srinivasan, P. V. 1997. Widowhood and poverty in rural India: Some inferences from household survey data. ***Journal of Development Economics*****, 54(2), 217-234.** The paper analyses the relationship between poverty and widowhood in rural India based on the consumer expenditure data of the National Sample Survey. The study findings suggest that there is no evidence that widows benign concentrated in poor households or female-headed households are poorer than male-headed. The paper further reveals that poverty indices of households are more associated with economic scale. It highlights that the incidence of poverty is higher those widows who live in small economies, and these are single widows, widows living with unmarried children and female households.

64. Dreze, J., Lanjouw, P. F., & Sharma, N. 1997. Credit in rural India: a case study. This paper is a case study of the credit transaction of a village in north India. Based on lenders and borrowers information in the studied village, it examines the issues attached with the credit market in rural areas. The examined issues are achievement and failure of public lending institutions, segmentation of rural credits, the lending strategy of moneylenders, role of interest-free lending, social inequality access to credit, and the politics of rural credits. The study finds that the credit market in rural India is heavily segmented, leading to a wider interest rate. Interest-free credits are limited and governed by social norms, institutional credits associated with the un-manageable procedure. Due to lack of retail buying, slow pace of technological change, low educational investment, in-active land market, absence of landless tenants, lower non-agricultural self-employment, implicit credits, and lack of proper economic insecurity are problematic nature of credit arrangements in rural India. Drought-proofing of agriculture has made little headway. The conditions of the rural poor in dry and remote areas have not changed much. They continue to suffer from fluctuations in the food supply, employment and income. Environmental degradation exacerbates the drought trends. The book suggests bringing about biotechnological advances to avert the food crisis under unfavourable environments. The next section talks about the poor purchasing ability of the rural poor, paralysing them to access food despite increases in food availability. A highly centralised poverty programme fails to cater to the needs of the underdeveloped areas. Against this backdrop, the book suggests expediting poverty alleviation by expanding the land base of the rural poor and women. For this, land reforms and provisions of capital supply in the form of land loans are to be given priority. The other suggestions include developing the infrastructure of remote areas. The book also makes a recommendation to improve the standards of living of rural dwellers. The book also recommends strengthening the rural poor's human capital and healthcare and educating the rural household for family planning. The next section discusses environmental degradation leading to rural poverty. This section talks about rapid defor estation, which poses a threat to agricultural development in India. Population explosion contributes significantly to environmental degradation, bringing scarcities of drinking water, fuelwood, and fodder for the rural people. In this context, the author visualises technological changes should be combined with environmentally sound irrigation practices. Environmental conservation strategies must be integrated with agricultural development and poverty alleviation programmes and plan to arrest rapid deforestation in the rural sites. The section on decentralising rural development stresses the need to integrate centralised planning goals with local-level planning, awareness-raising, and support for local leadership. The last section on economic reforms and agriculture suggests that restrictions on the lease market for agricultural land would help improve land use. The positive effects of subsidies are found to be outweighed by their negative effects.

65. Dube, S. C. 2017. *Indian village.* Routledge. This book is an ethnographic account and descriptive study of the village life of Shamirpet village of Hyderabad. The book describes the village composition through setting, social structure, economic structure, ritual structure, family ties, levels of living, living together and the changing scene of the studied village. He highlighted accounts of government authority in villages, reciprocal relationships between castes, a feature of the caste system, economic activities and methods, ritual purity, and marriage system.

66. Dubhashi, P. R. 1970. Rural development administration in India. *Rural development administration in India.*Popular Prakashan. The book identified the changes in rural administration in India since the beginning of community development and Panchayati raj for rural development. The book highlighted the evolution and principal features of community development in India and its administrative achievements in rural India. The book also discussed how the local planning approach came up with the community development programme and raised the issue of centralised and decentralised approach in delivering rural development programmes. The book also tries to capture the lacunas and challenges faced by rural development administrations, limiting the community development in India.

67. Dutta, V.R. (ed.) 1992. *Rural Poverty and Economic Change in India*. New Delhi: Radiant Publishers. This book contains a collection of papers from a 1987 seminar organised by the Gandhian Institute of Studies in Varanasi, India. It focuses on the rural poor and anti-poverty programmes. The book contains papers falling into the following themes. The broad themes are theoretical perspectives, evaluation of anti-poverty programmes, economic dimensions, non-economic factors, the effectiveness of administration and people's participation, and voluntary action. The theoretical papers contain the Gandhian perspective, including a confirmation of Gandhi's faith in 'rurality', a Gandhian critique of rural development programmes, decentralised micro-level planning at the village level. There is a paper dedicated to the evaluation of anti-poverty programmes. It suggests the need to change people's attitudes and reorient the traditional caste structure to uplift the lower castes and contribute to the betterment of the whole rural society. This also contains the strains of Gandhian philosophy. This paper sees development and anti-poverty programmes as a means not just for ending economic exploitation but also social oppression in the rural space of the country. The section on economic issues contains essays on the dimensions of rural poverty among agricultural laborers and the critiques of the framework of poverty alleviation programmes. Perhaps one of the most interesting essays in the book is under the 'non-economic factors' theme. This paper highlights the social and psychological deprivations experienced by poor people. It argues that these non-economic factors become the determinants of poverty in economic terms. This paper asserts that values, attitudes and perceptions have a strong influence on economic development. The essays suggest that education, motivation, development, and leadership training may help alleviate the non-economic dimensions of poverty and are the drivers for poverty alleviation in rural areas. The last chapters of the book critique anti-poverty programmes from the perspective of people's participation. However, it is worth noting that the book ends without a concluding chapter to draw together the implications of the many different perspectives and focuses ingrained in different articles.

68. Dutta, P., Ghatak, N., Mahendiran, S., Jha, J., Menon, N. 2019. ***Women's Education and Empowerment in Rural India.*** **India: Taylor & Francis.** The book is all about understanding women empowerment, pathway and obstructions in accessing economic empowerment in rural areas. This is a product of evaluation based research on the impact assessment of the Mahila Samakhya programme on the empowerment of marginalised communities women in Bihar. This book conceptualises the context of women empowerment programmes, their deprivation and struggle, the inter-generational impact of the empowerment programme, their negotiations and adjustments for empowerment and in conclusion raise certain important issues based on finding pertaining to the planning, policy and implementation strategy of women education and empowerment programmes and discussed what alternative pathways are.

69. Ellis, F. 2000. The determinants of rural livelihood diversification in developing countries. ***Journal of agricultural economics, 51*****(2), 289-302.** The paper analyses the reason for households to adopt multiple livelihood strategies in low income developing countries. The paper makes a distinction between necessary and choice of diversification. For survival strategy in rural areas of lower-income countries, diversification plays a major role and positive attributes in livelihood security. It also helps in balancing the negative aspects it possesses. Instead of slow down, policy needs to facilitate diverse rural livelihood options because diversified livelihood is less vulnerable.

70. Eswaran, M., Ramaswami, B., & Wadhwa, W. 2013. Status, Caste, and the Time Allocation of Women in Rural

India. ***Economic Development and Cultural Change, 61*(2), 311-333.** The paper argued that women in rural India might be reluctant to participate in the work market due to concern over family status and culture that stigmatises work by married women. The book developed a theoretical framework for the forecasts of caste-based status on women's time allocation for market work. The study used all India NSS data of the year 2004-05 and Time use Survey 1998-99 data of six states to test the hypothesis. The study finds that ratio of women's market work decline as increased in caste hierarchy compared to men market work. This ratio also rises with rises in wealth and decline with a move up in higher caste. The findings support the initial assumptions and view that family status and caste play an important role in market work and undermine women's freedom and autonomy in rural areas. The article also suggests how to reduce the cultural encroach of poverty among women in rural India.

71. **Fan, S., Hazell, P. B., & Thorat, S. 1999.** ***Linkages between government spending, growth, and poverty in rural India*** **(Vol. 110). Intl Food Policy Res Inst.** This report addresses the issues attached to government policies faced by policymakers. In particular, it discussed public fund allocations, expenditure, productivity growth and poverty reduction goals in rural areas. The study finds that investment in agriculture research and development and rural roads have a greater impact. Whereas modest effects received from specific poverty reduction programmes such as employment and rural development projects. The paper suggests that policy-makers increase spending on agriculture research and extension and rural road construction to get a larger impact on poverty reduction and create new employment sources.

72. **Fan, S., Hazell, P., & Thorat, S. 2000. Government spending, growth and poverty in rural India.** ***American journal of agricultural economics, 82*(4), 1038-1051.** The paper examines the direct and indirect impact of different government

programmes expenditure on productivity growth and rural poverty in India. The paper developed a simultaneous equation model using state-level data for the years 1970 to 1993. The paper finds that the government needs to prioritise agriculture research and the construction of rural roads to reduce poverty in rural areas. Besides poverty reduction, it also brings higher productivity growth in the rural agriculture sector.

73. Fraser, A. G. 1986. *Village Education in India.* Mittal Publications. This book is a compilation of a report of a commission supported by the Missionary Societies in Great Britain on education in Indian Villages. The book highlights the initiation of education in villages, mode of teaching, medium of instruction, curriculum, female education, problems, and prospects of students. The book mostly discussed missionary education and found a way to spread Christianity in Indian villages through education. The book started with the origin and purpose of the commission and then factors in missionary education. This background highlighted the problem of literacy and village schools, vocational schools, education for girls, community centre, teacher, training, supervision, and physical welfare. It stressed the need for Christian literature, economic improvement, administration, co-operation with government, and financial demands in contextualising.

74. Fremantle, S. H. 1937. Village Government in India. *Journal of the Royal Society of Arts*, *85*(4399), 385-401. The village opinion and proper representation have a crucial role in the stable government in India. The paper highlights the pivotal role of the traditional representation of spokesperson of the village such as Mukhia or mouthpieces. This paper analyses the illiteracy and role of village finance for the employment of labour and other activities in villages. The author highlighted the issues, experiences, and experiments of village governance and government in rural India's northern and southern parts. The paper suggests reviving the traditional institutions of the village with the efforts of the government. The author extends that small villages need to be grouped for development purposes; self-government and decentralisation must be established at the village level.

75. Friedland, W. H. 1982. The end of rural society and the future of rural sociology. *Rural Sociology*, *47*(4), 589. Rural sociology confronts a continuing crisis of identity because it fails to develop a sociology of agriculture. Historically, despite an initial focus on agriculture, rural sociology became deflected to the analysis of rurality. The recent emphasis of rural sociologists on the turnaround phenomenon is symptomatic. Still, it fails to deal with the fact that such turnaround represents the penetration of previously rural space by urban-based economic functions. Rural sociology has increased its irrelevance by failing to locate itself appropriately in the productionist oriented land grant system. It could resolve its problems, as has agricultural economics, by providing the ideological justification for production. It could also seek to develop a new constituency for its production. This would probably jeopardize its location in the land grant system but probably represents the only way out of a closed and limited paradigm. Several new developments in the sociology of agriculture involving neo-populist and neo-marxist paradigms hold promise for revised rural sociology.

76. G. Niranjan Rao, & Nair, K. 2003. Change and Transformation in Rural South India: Findings from Village Studies. *Economic and Political Weekly*, *38*(32), 3349-3354. The paper analyses the aspects of transformation and change in rural economies and societies of southern states in India. The findings state that different patterns of transformation and directions of change are found in different villages, regions, and states. The paper suggests emphasising the decentralisation of planning and micro-level development plan for villages for rural transformation and change.

77. Gang, I. N., Sen, K., & Yun, M. S. 2008. Poverty in rural India: Caste and tribe. *Review of Income and Wealth*,

54(1), 50-70. The paper examines the determinants of rural poverty and how it differs from scheduled caste and scheduled tribal households to non-scheduled households in India. The incidence of poverty is higher among the scheduled caste and scheduled tribal population than in other communities. To answer why the difference persists in the incidence of poverty, the paper used regression analysis of per capita expenditure ratio to the poverty line and decomposition analysis. The findings reveal from the decomposition that the gap persists due to different attributes of households and occupational structure.

78. Garg, P., & Thawani, M. 2011. The Role of Panchayati Raj in Watershed Development Programme Myth or Reality. ***The Indian Journal of Political Science, 72*****(1), 165-171.** The paper access the role of Panchayati Raj institutions in watershed development programmes regarding Gujarat state. The paper highlights the institutions set up for implementing watershed development programmes, function and role of DRDA, project implementing agency, village-level committee, watershed association and watershed secretary. The paper finds that panchayat raj institution involvement is limited in the implementation and monitoring of the programme. The paper suggests that institutions carry out their assigned roles and duties, and permanent qualified staff must be appointed to implement the watershed development programme better.

79. Gaurav Nayyar. 2005. Growth and Poverty in Rural India: An Analysis of Inter-State Differences. ***Economic and Political Weekly, 40*****(16), 1631-1639.** The paper aims at analysing the differentiation in poverty level across different states of rural areas of India. The paper analyses the poverty level during the period 1983-2000. The paper explains interstate economic growth and its differences to analyse the impact of policies and institutions on the poverty-reducing effects of growth. The study finds that though economic growth plays an important role and determinant in the reduction of poverty in rural, but fails in providing a complete explanation.

Whereas expenditure on the anti-poverty welfare programme positively impacts poverty reduction and brings democratic decentralisation and gender equality in rural societies.

80. Gautham, M., & Shyamprasad, K. 2010. The 'Basic' Doctor for Rural India: A Failed Promise? *Economic and Political Weekly*, 45(38), 25-29. This article is a commentary to the present healthcare system in rural India on the 1946 Bhore committee report on Health Servey and Development in India. This commentary argued that most of India's population is neglected, and the major reason may be that vested interests may have shaped the Indian Health Care system after independence. Rural areas are facing a serious shortage of healthcare professionals and human resources in India. The paper questions the time duration of health professional courses in India. It suggests that the government needs to implement and regulate shorter courses so that the human resources gap could be fulfilled on time.

81. Ghosh, B. N. 1990. *Political Economy of Rural Poverty in India: Lipton Thesis Revisited*. New Delhi: Deep & Deep Publications. This book reviews the Lipton thesis in the context of the Indian economy. The Lipton thesis suggests that basically resource transfer from rural to urban direction causes and aggravates rural poverty. Particularly, taxation, unfavourable terms of trade for agriculture, and skill and cash drain from rural areas escalate the existing level of rural poverty. Thus, urban development strategies bring rural underdevelop-ment and worsen rural poverty. With this hypothesis in the context, the present book looks at the validity of this argument; the book analyses the development strategy designed and implemented by the Government of India. The author pinpoints the determinants of rural poverty and analyses the difference in rural and urban incomes. In chapter two it highlights the urban bias of investment in India. In the next chapter, the author looks into the rural savings pattern in India and discards the conventional idea that urban areas have higher saving per unit of investment. The next two chapters talk about price distortion and agricultural taxation. In this context, the author has captured that unfavourable trade and high taxes have contributed to prolonged rural poverty and have been major drivers for transferring rural resources to urban areas. Chapter Six discusses rural transfer resources in general and the brain drain problem in particular. The data are collected from ten villages in West Bengal and are vocal on rural skill migration and the monetary loss involved in such skill drain. The final chapter is a conclusion chapter that brings forth the major study outcomes and suggests some policy implications. The study finds that the Lipton thesis holds good in the Indian rural context and recommends taking up some immediate steps like redistribution of urban resources and their investment in rural areas, more development investment into the rural sector, rural savings to be utilised for the rural space, limiting additional taxation for the rural sector, and improving rural education and wage and restructuring rural employment to prevent brain drain.

82. Ghosh, B., & Kumar, G. 2003. ***State politics and panchayats in India*****. Manohar Publication.** The book highlighted the condition and nature of state politics and the Panchayats system in India. The book consists of six chapters. The first chapter traced the evolution and development of panchayats as a local institution of decentralisation of power and responsibility. This chapter also highlighted the question of political leadership and links it with the character of state government and its role to govern these local bodies. Chapter two to five analysed four state-specific panchayat systems their strength and weakness and made a compared description. The states are Maharashtra, Gujarat, Bihar and West Bengal. The last chapter discussed the value system of democracy in India and how it can be a deliberative democracy through rural local institutions. It concludes that political parties are not involved in actual decentralisation; they involve in vote politics. He suggests democratic decentralisation needs to be a mass movement for policy reform to deliver better services and participation of local peoples in the decentralisation process.

83. Gough, K. 2008. ***Rural society in southeast India.*** **Cambridge University Press.** The book is a study of the economic and political structure of two villages of Thanjavur district of Tamil Nadu state in India. With the changing structure of the nation, state and district at large, the book brings notice of the changing internal class and caste relation in villages of southeast India. The book is divided into three parts on the name of district and villages, namely Thanjavur, Kumbapettai and Kirippur. The book defines the rural class, caste relation, agrarian structure, peasant movements, mode of production, demographic profile, power structure, and religion, but also tried to answer whether Indian pastoral relations are still pre-capitalists or not.

84. Gulati, A., Jain, S., & Satija, N. 2014. Rising farm wages in India–The 'pull' and 'push' factors. ***Journal of Land and Rural Studies*****, 2(2), 261-286.** The paper tries to answer what factors influence farm wages and what needs to be done to control the rising of agricultural labour costs with a view to moderate the cost of push factor in food prices. The paper visualises that growth of overall GDP, GDP-construction, and GDP-agriculture brings growth in pull factors. In contrast, MGNREGA's push factors are measured by the employment generated through MGNREGA programme. Economic analysis is carried out with panel data from 1990-91 to 2011-12 among 16 major states. The results reveal that growth pull factors influenced the rise in farm wages than push factor of MGNREGA since 1990-91. Further, it showed growth in overall construction, and agriculture GSDP leads to increased wage rates of farms. The construction sector GDP has a greater influence on farm wage than other sector GDP. However, MGNREGA impact is significant but found less effective. Overall the finding suggests that the pull strategy works better in raise farm wages than the push strategy in the long term.

85. Gupta, D. 2005. Whither the Indian Village: Culture and Agriculture in 'Rural' India. ***Economic and Political Weekly*, 40(8), 751-758.** The paper highlights the profound changes that happen in the unchanging and idyllic lifestyle of village India. Indian villages lost their stronghold on the exercise of caste and agriculture. Village people are marching towards urban areas for employment choice due to a break in their caste rigidity. The caste identity and system gradually brought several changes in the cultural level of village society. Village India is witnessing the disappearance of specific kinds of jobs in the rural community. Agitations are shifted against landlords to the government for not providing better amenities. The author rightly put 'if the village is bloodless as the rural economy is lifeless'. If everyone from villages is to leave the village for better employment choice, then its time to understand the culture. Though this is not a stable culture, policymakers need to understand its importance and economy in the present society.

86. Gupta, D. 2005. Whither the Indian Village?: Culture and Agriculture in 'Rural' India. ***Review of Development and Change*, *10*(1), 1-20.** Villages in India were represented as idle places that are rigid and unchanging. In recent times it is found that villages have gone through various changes. Caste and Agriculture, which were the hallmarks of Indian villages, do not hold the same importance that earlier it had. The weakening of caste rigidities has helped in occupational diversification among the rural people; however, stagnation in agriculture has led to the migration of employable rural populations to the urban areas. Due to the prominence of vote bank politics, the politicians seldom address the real issues of the villagers. They pay lip services to woo the farmers, mostly the poor farmers, for getting votes. The culture and the agriculture of the villages need to be seen through these changes in the rural areas. This culture of the Indian villages is not a stable one, and these changes are to be studied by the policy-makers and the people.

87. Gupta, R., Gupta, V. P., & Ahluwalia, N. S. 1994. Educational status, coronary heart disease, and coronary risk factor prevalence in a rural population of India. *Bmj*, *309*(6965), 1332-1336. The paper tries to find the relationship between coronary heart disease, coronary risk factors and educational level in rural India. The study is carried out a cross-sectional survey at three villages of rural Rajasthan. The study reveals that the prevalence of coronary heart disease and coronary risk factors of smoking and hypertension is significantly higher among less educated and uneducated people.

88. Haan, A. D. 1997. Rural-urban migration and poverty: The case of India. *IDS Bulletin*, *28*(2), 35-47. The paper explained the relationship between poverty and rural-urban migration in India, particularly in Kolkata. The paper discussed the inequality in migration versus the role of poverty, the socio-economic background of migrants; income and expenditures of migrants; origin of migrants; and the migrants' data with non-migrants to find out whether migrants can improve their income time or not. The paper reveals most migrants are from north-eastern rural areas with an increase in industrialisation in urban areas moved to urban areas searching for employment. Findings show that poverty and inequality play a significant role for migrants; migrants come from different districts that are not necessarily poor only; they come from diverse backgrounds and choose an other occupation in the urban areas, and migrants are found better off in income and expenditure.

89. Haberfeld, Y., Menaria, R. K., Sahoo, B. B., & Vyas, R. N. 1999. Seasonal migration of rural labour in India. *Population Research and Policy Review*, *18*(5), 471-487. This article talked about the impact and determinants of seasonal migration on rural labour in India. The paper did a household survey of 624 in the Dungarpur district of Rajasthan, India. The findings of the paper disclose that seasonal migration is widespread among rural labour individuals and households. The labour use migrant as a strategy to overcome the difficulties and improve households' wellbeing by raising income. It also highlighted that migrant families are characterised by lower income from agriculture, low education, and live in inferior geographical regions. The household income is better off of migrant labour than non-migrants households. Further, it describes that out of total family income, 60% income comes from migrant labour if one of the households' members is migrant labour.

90. Hanumantha Rao, C. H. 1994. ***Agricultural Growth, Rural Poverty, and Environmental Degradation in India.*** **Delhi; New York: Oxford University Press.** This book establishes the interrelationships between agricultural growth, rural poverty, environmental degradation, and development policy, taking the experiences from India. Five major facets are under discussion in the book. They are agricultural growth, rural poverty, environmental degradation, participatory rural development, and economic reforms and agriculture. The section that deals with agricultural growth and technology suggests that it is obvious that growing this penetrating into the rural regions failed to reap the benefits from the green revolution. The income disparities marked in the country are on the decline. But the author notes that agricultural investment is taking a downward turn.

91. Harper, E. B. 1959. Two systems of economic exchange in village India. ***American Anthropologist, 61*****(5), 760-778.** This article describes the economic exchange system in the villages of rural India. It talked about two systems of economic exchange, first based upon the growing of subsistence crops, and second is upon a crop sold for cash. These two types of Jajmani systems regulated the rural economy and its interdependence within various caste groups present in the village. The paper describes these two systems of exchange between occupational groups fund in rural areas of South India. In these two Jajmani systems, the land is considered the major source of wealth, and the dominant crop is a subsistence crop main in the Jajmani system village. In these villages, crops viewed as a medium of exchange for gods and services. Whereas, in the Malnad system, major crops are sold outside of the village. The crop value concerning human needs is constant, where production and population remain stable, where wage, prices if given in-kind, stay the same. The value of cash or cash crop does not hold this constant relationship. One is here a stable medium of exchange other one fluctuates in value. The substantial crop is used only for the medium of exchange rather than stable the long relationship between different occupation groups in villages of rural India.

92. Harriss-White, B., & Janalakarâjanal, E. 2004. ***Rural India facing the 21st century*** **(Vol. 1). Anthem Press.** This edited volume is a collection of essays on the issues of rural India in the 21st century and highlighted recent changes in village and development policy. The book is divided into three parts – Long Term Changes, Production Policy and Village Perspective, and Social Welfare in the Villages. The book highlighted the issues on agriculture, green revolution, irrigation, gender and rural economy, rural credit, rural infrastructure, differentiation and inequality, resistance to reform, fertiliser reform and ecological crisis, corruption, village institution and structural reform, and state interventions in rural development.

93. Harriss-White, B., & Janalakarâjanal, E. 2004. ***Rural India facing the 21st century*** **(Vol. 1). Anthem Press.** This book is a unique study of the rural society of South India, which has been done over 20 years. The book is divided into three parts. The first part focuses on the long-term changes. It introduces the part with heavy agriculture and light weight industries in South India, Irrigation as a result of the agrometeorological crisis.

It discusses social institutions, stratification of rural households, labour and gender issues in the economy. The second part of the book deals with production policies and village perspectives covering policy, rural infrastructure and rural credit. The third part covers social welfare in the villages, including the anti-poverty policies, disability issues, food and nutrition in Northern Tamil Nadu.

94. Hathi, P., Spears, D., & Coffey, D. 2016. Can collective action strategies motivate behaviour change to reduce open defecation in rural India? *Waterlines, 35*(2), 118-135. The paper argued that as a community-led strategy to end open defecation free proven effective in different developing countries, a similar method would work in rural India. The social hierarchies in rural areas obstruct the spirit of collective action, which further goes with the caste-based notion of purity and pollution, make latrines used unattractive in rural India. The paper reveals that the idea of 'community in a geographical area is missing in rural villages instead of people believe in caste and religious groups. The paper suggests, besides community-led methodology, other strategies need to have experimented with for better implementation of the open defecation programme in rural India.

95. Hazell, P. B., & Haggblade, S. 1990. *Rural-urban growth linkages in India* (Vol. 430). World Bank Publications. The importance of rural-urban growth linkage and how agricultural growth impacts the national demand for the non-farm product, income, and employment in India is examined. The article divided into four sections firstly, describes the non-farm activities in India; secondly, highlights the relationship between agriculture and non-farm activities; thirdly, it discusses and estimates the volume of non-farm income and employment generated in rural areas through agricultural growth; and last, highlights the demand for non-farm goods emanating from alternative agricultural growth scenarios.

96. Hillyard, S. 2007. ***Sociology of rural life*** **(p. 224). Berg Publishers.** In this book, the author views that rural areas have overturned the development in farming, organic food movement has revived the rural population that is already politicised. Although urban studies flourished with urban areas, rural studies have not gained enough momentum and have become outdated sociological concepts. Hence, the author calls for the reappraisal of rural studies in the light of new changes, development and challenges in the countryside. The book discusses the issues in Rural sociology and Rural Studies. Through case studies like 2001 Foot and Mouth disease in UK, Game Shooting in UK, the authors try to show the need to reinvigorate rural sociology to tackle the new range of changes and issues pertaining to the rural areas. Hillyard suggests new methods and approaches for representing rural sociology. It concludes with the future of Rural Societies and Rural Sociology.

97. Hirway, I., & Roy, A. K. 1999. Women in rural economy: The case of India. ***Indian Journal of Agricultural Economics*****, *54*(3), 251-271.** The paper discusses two important issues like how the role of rural women in the economy can be measured, why rural women have been vulnerable and what can be done to reduce the vulnerability. The study uses two stages of stratified sampling. The inferences drawn from the study shows that the survey methodology for netting women's work through census population and NSS data are not adequate and have limitations. These methods underestimate women's participation in economic activities. Secondly, it suggests policy inferences for strengthening rural women's position in the rural economy. It suggests gender centric development approach that gives importance to gender equity at the centre of the development process and the margin.

98. Hope, R. A. 2007. Evaluating social impacts of watershed development in India. ***World Development*****, *35*(8), 1436-1449.** The paper analyses the distribution and magnitude of the social impact of the watershed intervention in the state of Madhya Pradesh, India. The paper used the propensity score matching method to estimate the social impact on the domestic water collection times and gross agricultural returns from the state's control and treatment watershed data. The study results illustrate how the matching method can objectively estimate the social impact of watershed development among the beneficiaries. A positive social impact recorded by a significant reduction in domestic water collection times for households with the highest collection of times. The study emphasis on the early evaluation needs to carry out for better implementation and project execution. The paper suggests inputs based on the result for the appropriate design for rural development interventions.

99. Iqbal, F. 1988. The determinants of moneylender interest rates: evidence from rural India. *The Journal of Development Studies*, 24(3), 364-378. This paper looks at the determinants of the interest rate of moneylenders in rural areas of India. The paper examines the determinants on the background of the introduction of the green revolution and the spread of government-sponsored rural credit through banks. The study finds that the money lenders interest is lower among farmers residing in the geographical area which uses Green Revolution technology. The paper also reveals that the monopoly of moneylenders' power reduces after the initiation of formal lending stakeholders. The paper concludes that informal credit is a sensitive mechanism, and changes in agricultural technology influence the supply of loans.

100. Ishwaran, K. 2003. *Tradition and economy in village India* (Vol. 74). Taylor & Francis US. This book is a field study conducted by the author in a village in northern Mysore. The study village is the largest in the district of Dharwar comprises different caste groups. The book is divided into eight parts. The book introduces the village with the scene, then analyses the social structure, Jajmani system and the caste, the rights and responsibility, strength and values, conflict and tensions, changing scene in the village and evaluation. The village differs from other villages in its interaction pattern and dynamics. The book highlights the traditional structure of the Jajmani system - Aya, and how it has linked to caste and dharma. It highlights the exchange system and elements of reciprocity in the village. The book also recorded the evidence of economic motivation that how men's keep their traditional occupation so simply and avoid alternative occupation due to uncertainty.

101. Iversen, V., Kalwij, A., Verschoor, A., & Dubey, A. 2014. Caste Dominance and Economic Performance in Rural India. ***Economic Development and Cultural Change, 62*(3), 423-457.** The paper examines whether the minority groups perform better or worst about their income when the village dominated by their own or upper caste group. The paper uses rural household panel data of the Indian Human Development Survey of 1993-94 and 2004-04. The study reveals that the gap between upper caste and other minority social groups widened considerably between these two panel round data. The minority groups perform better economically in their own dominated villages than dominated by upper castes. As same upper caste groups also perform better in their own dominated villages than others.

102. Jacoby, H. G. 2013. ***Food prices, wages, and welfare in rural India.*** **The World Bank.** This policy paper examines the welfare and distributional consequences of higher relative food prices in rural India. The findings show that rural manual labour wages rise faster in rural districts growing more than those with significant price run-ups over 2004-09. The study also highlights that adjustment of rural wages plays an essential role in protecting the welfare of the poor in rural areas than the public distribution system. The policy also points out that the export ban on agricultural products insults both producers and consumers and harms the poor rural producers in India.

103. Jain, A. K. 1985. Determinants of regional variations in infant mortality in rural India. *Population studies*, *39*(3), 407-424. The present paper analyses the determinants of infant mortality and its regional variations in rural India. The paper also distinguishes infant mortality from three levels of factors – individual, household and village. The paper finds from the state-level data that both medical and non-medical factors play an essential role in determining the regional difference in rural infant mortality. In the neonatal mortality rate, poverty and percentage of birth attended by trained medical personnel are two determinants of regional variations. Whereas, the post-neo-natal mortality triple vaccination and medical facilities at the village level are two significant determinants. Besides all these, adult women's literacy helps in better medical care both at birth and post-neo-natal period. Medical factors play an important role over non-medical factors, so the paper suggests the intervention of medical facilities to reduce the infant mortality rate in rural India.

104. Jayaraman, R., & Lanjouw, P. 1999. The evolution of poverty and inequality in Indian villages. *The World Bank Research Observer*, *14*(1), 1-30. This article tries to draw the evolution of inequality and poverty in rural India. The authors review the village's studies on a longitudinal basis to arrive at the answer. The article analyses the important forces of economic change in rural areas from a multi disciplinary perspective. It also highlights the importance of various institutional supports in channelising the change. The village studies also show that rural poverty declined has been slow and irregular, and inequalities persisted in villages during the 1970s to 1980s. The paper suggests if the inequalities persist in the long run, they may be constrained in the scope of poverty reduction from policy intervention impacts and economic growth.

105. Jejeebhoy, S. J. 1998. Associations between wife-beating and fetal and infant death: impressions from a survey

in rural India. ***Studies in Family Planning*****, 300-308.** This paper examines the linkage between wife-beating and fetal and infant death in rural areas of India. The paper used community-based data collected from surveyed women from rural sites of Uttar Pradesh and Tamil Nadu. The results revealed that wife-beating is deeply rooted in the patriarchal system and consequence of considerable pregnancy loss and fetal mortality. The article suggests addressing the urgent need and attacking root causes of women violence and recommended fulfilling the immediate need for healthcare, shelter, economic support, and legal assistance for women's. To tackle domestic violence, the paper suggests addressing it in multiple ways.

106. Jejeebhoy, S. J. 2002. Convergence and divergence in spouses' perspectives on women's autonomy in rural India. ***Studies in Family Planning*****, *33*(4), 299-308.** The paper describes the perception of rural women and their husbands about women's autonomy in India and highlighted the similarities and differences in their opinion. The paper investigates the women's autonomy over various reproductive outcomes of women's and partners views of women autonomy. From a community-based study of women's in 1993-94 at Tamil Nadu and Uttar Pradesh, most of the households are more and less patriarchal. Findings suggest that there is no losses agreement between partners concerning women's autonomy within the home. There is a disagreement between partners where husband projects liberal view than their wives. The results also pointed out that cultural context influences the partner's perception.

107. Jha, P. & R. Gerry 2016. ***The changing village in India: Insights from longitudinal research*****. Oxford University Press.** This edited book represents the changing aspects of rural India and the revival of village studies through longitudinal village studies' evidence. This book is the compilation of seventeen articles by eminent scholars on different issues of villages across other states. The highlighted villages issues include agrarian change; change in rural life; changes in land distribution;

labour market and employment; work and wellbeing; changing aspects of non-farm activities, diversification and inequality; changes in migration pattern; changes in gender and social relation; reform in public services; changes in caste structure; and changes in rural-urban economic relation.

108. Jodha, N. S. 1986. Common property resources and rural poor in dry regions of India. *Economic and Political Weekly*, 1169-1181. The paper attempts to analyse the benefits of common property resources to the poor rural farmers in dry regions of India. The study is conducted in 80 villages of seven states and reveals how common property resources helps rural poor in their employment and income generation. The data reveals that per year household income from common property resources is higher than the income generated from anti-poverty programmes. The study also revealed that household with the higher income is less dependent on common property resources. Though common property resources play an important role in India's dry rural regions, their productivity and area are declining. The introduction of privatisation in the control of common property resources lost the collectivity of rural poor and retained or given land for collection of common property resources never compensated them. The paper calls for a larger consideration of common property resources as a part of poverty mitigating strategy in the rural dry regions of India.

109. Jodhka, S. S. 1998. From "book view" to "field view": Social anthropological constructions of the Indian village. *Oxford Development Studies*, *26*(3), 311-331. "Book view" of rural India was adopted by Indologists and Orientalists, taking insights from scriptures and historical records. The "book view" was eventually replaced by the "field view" promoted by sociologists and anthropologists in the post-independence period. This "field view" involves participant observation. The researchers were concerned regarding the characteristics of rural communities through the framework of caste, gender and political faction. As traditional societies are in a state of flux, the field view reflects the mobility that is very important for studying development. Villages are not isolated communities; rather, they are well integrated into the broader economy and society. The paper recognises this contribution of the field view. However, it points out certain issues of participant observation. That includes the researcher's bias from particular socio-economic groups; those who are part of the investigation can affect the output. Even prominent researchers have accepted this issue as a limitation to the writings.

110. Jodhka, S. S. 2002. Caste and untouchability in rural Punjab. ***Economic and Political Weekly*, 1813-1823.** Despite having the largest proportion of the caste population in India, Punjab has rarely been seen as a relevant case for conceptualising the caste system and the changes taking place therein. Though some aspects of caste in Punjab have been studied, there has virtually been no detailed empirical documentation of the practice of untouchability in rural Punjab. This paper provides a broad mapping of the prevailing caste relations and the practice of untouchability in rural Punjab based on an extensive field study. The study focuses specifically on the process of change, particularly in the context of rural transformations that the Punjab countryside has experienced in the wake of the success of green revolution technology. The paper also argues that change processes could be meaningfully captured through the categories of 'dissociation', 'distancing' and 'autonomy'.

111. Jodhka, S. S. 2002. Nation and village: Images of rural India in Gandhi, Nehru and Ambedkar. ***Economic and Political Weekly*, 3343-3353.** In this special article of Economic Review and Political Weekly, the author tries to picture the images of rural India from the nationalist's point of view. The colonial construct has left its influence on Indian society as per modern historians. Villages are considered to depict the continuity of Indian society. Here, the author has taken village as a central concept for capturing realities characterising rural India. Though there is an agreement that villages represent

India's traditional social order, three leaders had different opinions regarding it. While Gandhi views the village as the site of authenticity, for Nehru, it was the place of backwardness. Ambedkar considered villages as the site of oppression for the people belonging to the lower rungs of the society.

112. Jodhka, S. S. 2006. Caste and democracy: Assertion and identity among the Dalits of rural Punjab. ***Sociological Bulletin*, 55(1), 4-23.** Caste mobilisation and democracy have been a part of sociological enquiry for political sociologists in the macro analysis of electoral politics and caste association. The analysis of caste and politics have been empirically dominated by data from dominant caste or landowning castes. In this paper, the author has taken three caste-related conflicts and Dalit assertions in rural Punjab. The author tries to say that the politicisation of caste identities significantly varies among different caste groups. A member of the Dalit caste and the members of dominant or upper castes do not share similar experiences. Therefore, there is a need for a segregated understanding of their experiences in the micro settings where changing caste relations can be assessed.

113. Jodhka, S. S. 2014. Emergent ruralities: Revisiting village life and agrarian change in Haryana. ***Economic and Political Weekly*, 5-17.** This article is an outcome of revisiting the village setting in Haryana after twenty years. The paper has tried to give a historical overview of development and change in a rural society in a micro setting. It locates socio-economic transformation in two villages post green revolution and introduction of industrial projects in the area. Along with exploring the nature of changes taking place in the internal structure, which includes caste and class of the agricultural economy. It also views the changing equations of the village with nearby urban settlements in terms of employment, engagements and political relations in the local political equation. Along with the physical commons, social and emotional commons are disappearing from the rural landscape. Has weakened the sense of collective identity, and there is the growth of individualism. Neo-religiosity through cults is gaining popularity. Lastly, the disintegration of community and growth of individualism is creating neo-liberal sensibility. The penetration of urban middle-class lifestyles to the village has its socio-economic implications.

114. Jodhka, S. S., & D'Souza, P. 2009. Rural and Agrarian Studies. ***Sociology and Social Anthropology in India*, 118-84.** Rural society and 'agrarian change' has been rather fluid areas of research in Indian social science. Besides sociologists and social anthropologists, valuable studies on rural India have also been produced by economists, historians, public administration specialists and political scientists. Diverse disciplinary orientations and different conceptual frameworks and research techniques have enriched the studies on rural India and agrarian change. For example, many of the social anthropologists who carried out 'village studies' during the 1950s and 1960s were influenced by the British tradition of social anthropology. These scholars confined their fieldwork mostly to a single village and used mainly the method of participant observation. Their interest was to understand and document the structure of the "traditional Indian village society". Their effort was to provide a 'field-view' of the village, in contrast to the 'book-view' that the Indologists had popularised. On the other hand, the economists mostly used the survey method. They focused on documenting the processes of social and economic change being experienced in micro settings, usually covering more than one village.

115. Johnson, K. 2001. Media and social change: the modernising influences of television in rural India. ***Media, Culture & Society*, *23*(2), 147-169.** The paper analyses the role of television and its impact on rural areas' socio-economic and political processes in India. The paper used ethnographic data collected from two villages of western Maharashtra. The paper makes a framework out of the television characteristics to analyse the recent cultural changes in rural areas. The villagers view the changing social process of consumerism, restructuring human relations, urban modelling, migration, and linguistic hegemony both positively and negatively. The study revealed that villagers are active in media use, which results in the development of the villages.

116. Johnson, K. 2005. Globalisation at the Crossroads of Tradition and Modernity in Rural India. *Sociological Bulletin*, 54(1), 40-58. The article explores the continuing cultural and structural changes in the rural mountainous areas of India in the background of liberalisation and globalisation model of development that forces materialism and consumerism. With the introduction of these two forces, village life significantly found reorientation in its activities, amenities, services in culture. This research suggests three vital processes of rural life in India. First, consumerism has reached rural society at a timely high. Second, mass communication and information technology facilities are connecting villages to another world. Third, the impact of western lifestyle and relationships are taking hold in rural societies.

117. Jose, A. V. (Ed.). 1989. *Limited options: women workers in rural India*. International Labour Organisation. The edited volume is the assemble of works aimed at analysing the structure of women's labour force participation in rural India. The book also tried to address the issues of factors, forces, and consequences of rural women and their entry into the labour force. This book is a collection of six chapters by eminent scholars. The first chapter discusses the female labour force participation in India and its issues and problems. The second chapter analyses the interstate variations in women work force participation in India. The third chapter discussed the work participation of women in female agricultural labourers in India. The fourth chapter makes analyses of rural female workers in Tamil Nadu state. The fifth chapter makes analyses of rural labour force participation in Maharashtra. Whereas the last chapter of the book analyzes the state of Panjab and Haryana's rural labour markets and employment of women.

118. Kanodia, K. 2013. Rural Local Governance: A Comparative Study of India, Australia and The US. World Affairs: *The Journal of International Issues, 17*(3), 94-105. The paper compares the system of rural governance in India, the United States, and Australia. The author conducted first-hand studies at three villages of three countries and gathered primary and secondary information on the rural governance system. It analyses find that the constitutional recognitions, functions, structure and funding of local governance are different in nature and type.

119. Kapur, R. L. 1979. The role of traditional healers in mental healthcare in rural India. *Social Science & Medicine. Part B: Medical Anthropology, 13*(1), 27-31. This article analyses the role of indigenous healers in mental illness care in rural India. Over one year, the study carried out in western India and 26 healers' concepts, and mental healthcare practices have been analysed. The findings show an agreement between healers and patients with psychiatrists in diagnosing the problem of mental illness. The patients in rural areas preferred to consult more than one traditional healer for their mental illness. There is no relationship between the choice of healer and their age or level of education and wealth.

120. Karmakar, K. G. 1999. *Rural credit and self-help groups: micro-finance needs and concepts in India*. Sage Publications India Pvt Ltd. This book reviews and analyses the strengths and weaknesses of the rural credit system in India. The book is divided into three parts. The author reviewed the problem and prospects of rural credit in the context of rural development. Here the author also highlighted the history and evolution of rural credit and discussed recommendations of different committees. The second part of the book addresses the need for micro-finance among different groups of people, including tribal, rural women, non-farm sectors, and micro finance entrepreneurs. The third part of the book discusses self-help groups and their functions in Thailand and Bangladesh system of micro credits. The author recommended these countries systems of micro credit to ensure that rural poor in India don't remain marginalised. The concluding pages prescribed different innovations and strategies for the sustainability of the rural credit delivery system and how to make them stronger and viable in rural India.

121. Kesterton, A. J., Cleland, J., Sloggett, A., & Ronsmans, C. 2010. Institutional delivery in rural India: the relative importance of accessibility and economic status. *BMC Pregnancy and Childbirth*, *10*(1), 30. The paper analyses role of economic status and accessibility of rural people to institutional delivery in India. The paper uses descriptive analysis of the delivery trend in rural areas from the data gathered from a national sample survey in 1992 and 1998. The findings suggest that economic categories play a crucial role in determining access to institutional care. It also determines the choice between to avail public or private instructional care. The paper suggests financial constraints need to be addressed in rural areas to achieve maximum institutional delivery.

122. Khan, A. H. 1978. *Ten Decades of Rural Development: Lessons from India*. Department of State Washington DC Office of External Research. This policy report analyses India's historical and current rural development programmes and analyses Africa, Latin America, Asia, and the near East countries. The paper starts with the colonial connection of rural development programmes and how new and rival ideology has emerged to address the distress in rural society. The paper further analyses the impact of World War II and American Leadership and Aid on the community development programmes. After then it highlights the origin of cooperatives, the green revolution and local governance and administration in managing different welfare programmes.

Finally, the report brings the Chinese rural development model and compares it with the Indian rural development model.

123. Khanna, T., & Das, M. 2016. Why gender matters in the solution towards safe sanitation? Reflections from rural India. ***Global Public Health*****,** ***11*****(10), 1185-1201.** They make a descriptive analysis of women role in finding the solution for safe sanitation and hygiene. This paper is part of a study conducted in rural Uttar Pradesh. The study findings suggest that women still practising unsafe sanitation despite the demand for a safe toilet. Poverty, inadequate sanitation policy and implementation, and gender-based power dynamic are three structural constraints determining the use of toilets and their construction at the household level. The paper concludes that emphases need to be given to women and girls in the planning process of the programmes and policies for a gender-sensitive approach.

124. Kinra, S., Bowen, L. J., Lyngdoh, T., Prabhakaran, D., Reddy, K. S., Ramakrishnan, L., ... & Ebrahim, S. 2010. Sociodemographic patterning of non-communicable disease risk factors in rural India: a cross-sectional study. ***Bmj*****,** ***341*****, c4974.** This article aims to investigate the socio-demographic pattering of non-communicable disease risk factors in rural areas of India. The paper used cross-sectional analysis of data gathered from the 1600 villages of 18 states in India using the convenience sampling method. The significant risk factors among the rural participants are prevalence of tobacco use, low fruit and vegetable intake, obesity, alcohol use, low physical activity, hypertension, diabetics, central adiposity, underweight and dyslipidaemia for non-communicable diseases. It also revealed from the data that risk factors increase with age. The paper suggests the need for careful monitor and control of non-communicable disease risk factors in rural India.

125. Koski, A. D., Stephenson, R., & Koenig, M. R. 2011. Physical violence by partner during pregnancy and use of

prenatal care in rural India. ***Journal of Health, Population, and Nutrition*****, *29*(3), 245.** The paper analyses the effects of physical violence by partners on prenatal care in rural India. The study used 1998-99 National Family Health Survey of India data and a follow-up study in 2002-03 by re-interviewing women of four Indian states. The study finds that those who experienced violence in pregnancy were received less parental care and less visit from health workers to their homes for a prenatal check-up. The study also revealed that they were less likely to receive at least three visits from health workers and less likely to initiates early pregnancy prenatal care. The study highlights the hindering effects of domestic violence experienced by women during pregnancy in taking up prenatal care in rural areas of India. The study concludes that mental healthcare is a unique need for women experiencing violence.

126. Kumar, A. V. A. 1997. ***Rural Industrialisation in India: Aspects of Policy, Technology, and Employment with Special Reference to Kerala. India:*** **M.D. Publications.** This book discussed policy, technology and employment aspects of rural industrialisation in India regarding the state of Kerala. The book divided into eight chapters. The first chapter introduces and defines the topic and highlights the importance of rural non-farm sectors and employment in India. This section also introduces the study area and objectives of the study. The second chapter discusses the rural manufacturing sector in Kerala. It highlights the pattern and growth of rural non-farm employment and different forms of rural industries in Kerala. The third chapter analyses the general characteristics of all the rural industries. The fourth chapter highlights major government policies and programmes towards rural industries in Kerala. The fifth and sixth chapter discusses different conditions of production and technological aspects of rural industrialisation in Kerala. The seventh chapter deals with the employment aspects of rural industries in Kerala. The last chapter concludes the findings of the study.

127. Kumbhar, V. M. 2013. Some critical issues of women entrepreneurship in rural India. ***European Academic Research, 1***(2). This paper highlights the critical issues women entrepreneurs face in establishing their entrepreneurship in rural India. The paper finds that the traditional mindset among community members and negligence of the state is a prime obstacle for women entrepreneurship. Besides this, lack of financial freedom, absence between career and family life, lack of ownership of property, no awareness about their capabilities, problem to work with male members, low ability to bear risk, lack of self-confidence, negligence of financial institutions, mobility constrains, lack of professional education and lack of interaction with other successful entrepreneurs are the problems of rural entrepreneur women in India. The paper suggests creating awareness among rural women entrepreneurs through motivating, inspiring, encouraging and co-operating them to various aspects of entrepreneurship.

128. Kurosaki, T., Ito, S., Fuwa, N., Kubo, K., & Sawada, Y. 2006. Child labour and school enrollment in rural India: Whose education matters?. ***The Developing Economies, 44***(4), **440-464.** This article analyses the determinants of school enrollment and child labour in rural areas of Andhra Pradesh. The study used a village fixed-effect logit model for each child in the village to determine the incidence of school enrollment and child labour as a dependent variable to determine the characteristics associated with practices among individual and household levels. The paper uses regression analysis, and it found that child's mother education is crucial in reducing child labour and increasing enrollment in school than the household head, child's father or other spouses. The mothers' education effects also similar among boys and girls, whereas the child's father favourable for boys only.

129. Lahiri Dutt, K. U. N. T. A. L. A., & Samanta, G. 2006. Constructing social capital: Selfhelp groups and rural women's development in India. ***Geographical Research,***

44(3), **285-295.** The paper tries to answer and examines why few self-help groups failed in bringing women's and development in rural areas of India through the programme of Development of Women and Children in Rural Areas. The study conducted over two years among rural women of Burdwan areas in eastern India. The study finds that most self-help groups experienced in decline membership and younger women involved in fewer activities. The groups are more involved in short term activity and then long-term engagement as seen as not worthwhile. Lack of resources and capital make them further vulnerable to access the market for their products. The production and technology, raw material, organisation, infrastructure, finance, and market problems led to the closure of self-help groups in rural areas. Among most, lack of proper coordination and communication between the group members is the primary reason for their failures. The paper suggests government and its programme officials need to listen to the voice of group women than imposing a government target of action. The government policies must respect and recognise the self-help group members work efforts and need to help them for their enhancement.

130. Lanjouw, P., & Murgai, R. 2009. ***Poverty decline, agricultural wages, and non-farm employment in rural India: 1983-2004.* The World Bank.** This paper examines the relationship between poverty and rural diversification in India. The paper used five rounds (1983-2004) of National Sample Survey data of India to explore the relationship. The study finds that poverty declined in rural India during this study period. While correlating with agricultural wage and labour, it found that there is a change in wage rates. The growth of the non-farm sector found reasonably and non-farm employment closely associated with social status and level of their education. The econometric estimation reveals that the falling of poverty is related to the rise in non-farm sector employment in rural areas. The other determinates behind the falling of poverty in rural areas are agricultural productivity, availability of land and consumption pattern in nearby urban areas.

131. Lanjouw, P., & Shariff, A. 2004. Rural non-farm employment in India: Access, incomes and poverty impact. *Economic and Political Weekly*, 4429-4446. This article analyzes the impact of rural non-farm employment on access, income and poverty in rural areas of India. It also correlates non-farm employment with the effect on agricultural wage rates in rural areas. The study examines the National Council of Applied Economic Research data in 1993-94, from 1765 villages across India. The study finds that non-farm income contributes a significant percentage in rural households across major Indian states. The rural non-farm sector employment is determined mainly by wealth, education, caste, agricultural condition, and population density. It also revealed that due to poor households' lack of access to assets, the poverty rate remains stagnated in India's rural areas. It has also found that growth in the specific non-farm sector is firmly linked with increased agricultural wage rates in rural areas. The study suggests expanding the non-farm sector to reduce the poverty rate in rural areas by removing obstacles in accessing non-farm sectors by increasing the education level of the poor.

132. Lindberg, S. 2012. Rural India 1970–2005: An Arduous Transition to What?. *The Indian Journal of Labour Economics*, *55*(1), 61-75. This paper questions the present form of transition and transformation in rural India. To answer the question, the paper used the Additional Rural Income Survey of 1969-71 and Rural Economic and Demographic Survey of 1982 & 1999 of rural Tamil Nadu. It analysed the data through a panel study. It discussed the changing aspects of rural India, increases in non-farm sector income and activities and state interventions. The study found that non-farm income is an essential source of income among rural areas and helps reduce poverty. It also reveals that there is an increase in inequality in the productive assets and ownership of land. The paper concludes that the changes and transformations in Indian rural areas are not the same as in other countries, but the differences are unique.

133. Lobao, L. 1996. A Sociology of the Periphery Versus a Peripheral Sociology: Rural Sociology and the Dimension of Space. *Rural Sociology*, *61*(1), 77-102. Rural sociology is intrinsically concerned with the spatial dimensions of social life. However, this underlying research tradition, particularly the use of space as a research strategy, has been insufficiently addressed and its contributions to general sociology are little recognised. I outline how a concern with space, uneven development, and the social relationships of peripheral settings have provided substantive boundary and conceptual meaning to rural sociology propelled its evolution and left it with a legacy of strengths, weaknesses, and challenges. A willingness to tackle the dimension of space and the thorny problems it raises often sets rural sociologists apart from other sociologists. This research tradition contrasted with general sociology's concern with developing generalisation, a spatial covering laws, and prototypical relationships of modern or Fordist development settings. Conceptual openings have left sociologists questioning their past agenda. Coupled with the "creative marginality" inherent in the questions and contexts addressed by rural sociologists, this makes the subfield central to contemporary sociology.

134. Madan, G. R. 1959. *Changing pattern of Indian villages*. S. Chand & Co. The book attempts to present a systematic view of various rural development programmes and projects in India. It is the collection of lectures delivered by the author for rural welfare and community development. The book comprises ten chapters. It highlights the list of reports, five-year plans, community development programmes, extension service programmes, agriculture and irrigation development, soil conservation programme, development of animal husbandry, land reforms, co-operatives, panchayats and social welfare programmes for health, education, housing etc. The book also covered various development programmes concerning different physical challenges, class, caste, and gender. The book assesses the programmes and their progress and provides deep insights into the programmes.

135. Mahadevan, R., & Suardi, S. 2013. "Is there a role for caste and religion in food security policy? A look at rural India." *Economic Modelling*, 31, 58-69. This paper finds that factors like caste and religion influence food security at the religious level. It criticised the 'one size fits all' policy of the central government. It lacks the region-specific analysis within the rural areas. Evidence shows that socio-economic factors and social assistance programmes had different impacts on the calorie gap depending on one's nutritional status. This nonlinear relationship has been neglected in most studies on food security while raising doubts on past assessments.

136. Mahapatra, S. 2007. Livelihood pattern of agricultural labour households in rural India: Evidence from Orissa. *South Asia Research*, 27(1), 79-103. The present paper analyses the livelihood pattern of rural landless labourers and agricultural families in rural Odisha of India. It discusses the income of labourers, employment generation, and extent of earning indebtedness among the labour households. The paper analyses the variable using available published data. The paper reveals that one-third of rural households are landless labour and depend on wage employment for daily livelihood. Whereas another 60 percent constitutes small and marginal farmers, they failed to generate adequate income from their land. These households marked a decline in employment for both female and male labour. The paper also reveals the decline of earning members per household in rural areas. While characterising these labour households, the author highlights declining income, low earning, high debt, low consumption, and difficulty getting employment and income.

137. Maheshwari, S. 1985. ***Rural development in India: a public policy approach.*** **Sage Publications.** The book is all about rural development efforts in India. The book comprises 14 chapters with a prologue in the first and an epilogue in the last. The prologue conceptualises the concept of rural development and explains rural life in India. The book's initial six chapters are devoted to the administrative rural development efforts after the Bengal Famine of 1858. These chapters discuses rural development programmes like Agricultural Experiments, Community Development Programmes, Panchayti Raj, Intensive Agricultural District Programmes, Drought Prone Areas Programme, and Integrated Rural Development Programmes. These chapters also highlight major failures of the programmes. There is another four-chapter on rural credit, land reform, technology for rural development, and agrarian unrest. These chapters discuses the administrative theories of these above concepts and their progress and concerns. Besides these chapters, there are another two chapters on the evaluative measures and bureaucracy in rural development. These chapters give a lucid description of the administrative mechanisms and problems at the district, state, and centre levels. The epilogue section discusses different aspects of rural societies like the rehabilitation programme in rural areas and research in the rural sectors.

138. Maheswari, S. R. 1995. "Rural development in India: a public policy approach." ***Asia-Pacific Journal of Rural Development.*** The book attempts to analyze the rural development policies and programmes of India. Commencing with the conceptual, historical and constitutional background of rural development in India. He critically evaluated the major rural development programmes initiated in the country since independence. It is organised into 16 sections.

139. Marriott, M. 1952. Social Change in an Indian Village. ***Economic Development and Cultural Change, 1*****(2), 145-155.** Marriott has written this piece of article while doing his fieldwork in Uttar Prdesh state of India. The author tries to capture the changing aspects of the studied village in the last thirty years. The paper analyses kinship grouping, rank groupings, economic groupings, associational social structure of the village prior to thirty years of the study, and how these structures have changed during the last thirty years. The paper discusses the economic developments in the regions and different government policy measures that help alter the structure. The study finds that the development of autonomous tenants and broader distribution of power, wider integration of local groups, increasing solidary grouping, and development of formal associations are some of the alternation marked in the village.

140. Marriott, M. 1955. ***Village India; studies in the little community.*** **Rawat Publication.** This book is an edited volume by McKim Marriott. This volume analyses the details of caste, religion, social structure, community, the personality of the village in India and highlights the changes. This edited book has complied of eight chapters contributed by eminent scholars from the social science field. Professor M N Srinivas writes the first chapter of the book on the social system of the village Mysore. The second chapter discusses the social structure of Tanjora Village, written by Dr E. Kathleen. B S Cohn writes the third chapter on changing status of a depressed caste in the village of Uttar Pradesh. The fourth chapter contributed by Alan R Beals on the interplay between change factors in the village of Mysore. The fifth chapter is on studying personality formation in a Hindu village written by Gitel P Steed in a Gujarat village. The next chapter is written by Oscar Lewis on the peasant culture of India and Mexico. Marriott writes the seventh on the theme of the book that is little communities in an indigenous civilisation. The last chapter is on the world and world view of the Kota village studied by David G Mandelbaum.

141. Marsden, T., Murdoch, J., Lowe, P., Munton, R. C., & Flynn, A. 2005. ***Constructuring the countryside: An approach to rural development.*** **Routledge.** The book is a product of the work done at the London countryside research center by the Economic and Social Research Council. The book focuses on the social and political forces for change in rural areas and how these relate to the rapid alterations in national economic circumstances and public policies affecting the countryside. The book provides a set of insights into the trends that will guide rural change in advanced economies. It intended for students and researchers in rural planning and environmental studies.

142. Mascarenhas, R. C. 1988. ***A strategy for rural development: dairy cooperatives in India*****. Sage Publications.** This book is on developing the dairy cooperatives in India and how it has developed as an alternative strategy for rural development. This book evaluates the operation flood strategy of the National Dairy Development Board in extending the cooperative model for other areas of India. The book discussed the issues like role dairying for rural development strategy, the problem of small scale projects for dairy cooperatives, and the role of NDDB's in developing and implementing the programme.

143. Mehta, B. C. 1993. ***Rural poverty in India*****. New Delhi: Concept Pub. Co.** This book is based on a quantitative approach. It concentrates on measuring the extent of rural poverty in India and making the mapping of poverty for different countries' regions. The author overwhelmingly clings upon a structural approach to poverty and adds other approaches and measures to counter poverty. The first part of the book conceptualises poverty and chooses its measures, and compares the results of different poverty measures of poverty. This endeavour considers the head-count ratio, poverty gap, Sen's Index, per capita expenditure, resource deprivation, inequality in the distribution of expenditure, calorie intake and assets, and quality of life measures. These multiple indicators are then used to create poverty profiles for each region of India and are analysed subsequently. Chapter six of the book pinpoints regional variations in agrarian relations. It establishes a connection between land use and rural poverty in India. The book suggests adopting multiple indexes of poverty by policy-makers and an understanding of rural economic structures and agrarian relations.

144. Mishra, Anand Prasad. 1988. ***Rural Poverty in India: Problems in Planning and Strategy for Poverty Alleviation.*** **New Delhi: Deep & Deep Publications.** This book on rural poverty illustrates social, economic and cultural dimensions of poverty. It is based on a field study of the Deoria district of Uttar Pradesh in Northern India, which houses around 71% of the population below the poverty line in 1988. The author observes that the immobility of human, agricultural, and industrial resources has contributed to this abject poverty. The author introduces the concept of poverty and poverty measures at the beginning of the book. The second chapter makes a resource profile mapping of Deoria's, including water sources, soil types and climate and discusses their impacts on poverty. The next chapter analyses the cultural practices of the area attributing to poverty. In this context, it takes up the issues like population growth, population characteristics like easy gratification, acceptance of a lower standard of living, lethargies, resource use pattern, land distribution system, demographic variables, and assess their impact on poverty and under-development. The follow-up chapter looks at poverty from the angles of inequality generated through caste, land, labour, agriculture, literacy, infrastructure, geography and income. The book also deals with climatic issues, social, economic and political issues as the preconditions of poverty. The book's beauty lies with the suggestion to promote "people's development councils" consisting of the poor themselves, the small farmers, artisans and landless labourers to eradicate poverty.

145. Mistry, R., Galal, O., & Lu, M. 2009. "Women's autonomy and pregnancy care in rural India: a contextual analysis." ***Social Science & Medicine*****, *69*(6), 926-933.** The study explores women's autonomy that influences several reproductive health and child health outcomes, including the use of pregnancy care services. It also analyzes data on women and their villages from the cross-sectional population based on the national Family Health Survey (1998-1999) of rural India to investigate women's autonomy with the association of prenatal, delivery and postnatal care. Village level factors suggest that public investment in rural economic development, primary healthcare access, social cohesion and basic infrastructures such as electrification and paved roads were associated with pregnancy care use.

146. Mitra, A., & Murayama, M. 2009. "Rural to Urban Migration: A District Level Analysis for India." ***International Journal of Migration, Health and Social Care*****.** This paper analyses district-level rural to urban migration rates among males and females separately in India. The social networks effects are prevalent among short-distance migrants. Place of destination and prospects for better job opportunities are major determinants of male migration whereas low caste, minority group, and women show network effect. It also discusses the effect of migration on health.

147. Mohanty, B. B. 2018. ***Agrarian Transformation in Western India: Economic Gains and Social Costs*****. Taylor & Francis.** Here the author examines the economic gains and social costs of agricultural transformation in India in three phases: colonial, post-colonial and neo-liberal. The book combines macro and micro economic data into economic and non-economic phenomena and engages with qualitative and quantitative aspects to explore the plot of historical and contemporary changes. The author has taken Maharashtra of Western India as a reference to explain it. The author deliberates regional disparities in agricultural development, issues of modernisation and social inequality land-owning among scheduled castes and tribes, women in agriculture, the pattern of labour migration and farmer's suicides, and documents the experiences and conditions of the rural poor and socially weaker sections to provide a comprehensive understanding of significant changes in the rural agricultural economy of western India. It discusses the impact of current development policies and practices.

148. Mohanty, B. B. ***Agrarian Relations and Social Structure in India.*** Sociology and Social anthropology in India owe their development to the village studies in India. Though the village studies started during the colonial period, they dominated anthropological and sociological studies until the 1960s and beyond. In terms of style and temper, village studies in India do not have a uniform tradition. Due to the changes in global, national and global scenarios, significant changes can be seen over decades. Colonialism and Planning have influenced the interest in village studies in India.

149. Mooney, P. H. 2004. Democratizing rural economy: Institutional friction, sustainable struggle and the cooperative movement. ***Rural Sociology*, *69*(1), 76-98.** Sustainable development demands institutions manage the conflicts and struggles that inevitably arise over material and ideal interests. While current cooperative theory privileges the economic element, a political economy of cooperation emphasises cooperatives' tentative bridging of economic and political spheres with a democratic ethos. The cooperatives democratic political structure exists in tension with a capitalist economic structure and other sites of friction. These contradictions are: in the realm of social relations, between production and consumption; in the realm of spatial relations, between the local and the global; and in the realm of collective action, between cooperatives as both traditional and new social movements. Where neo-classical economic models seek to eliminate or reduce these tensions, the political economy views these tensions as functional to sustainability by creating an "institutional friction" that facilitates innovation, flexibility and long-term adaptability. This political economy of cooperation is intended as a step toward the development of multi-dimensional sociology of cooperation.

150. Mukherjee, A., & Zhang, X. 2007. "Rural industrialisation in China and India: role of policies and institutions." ***World Development, 35*****(10), 1621-1634.** This paper argues that the patterns in the rural nonfarm development are the results of institutional differences between the two countries, especially in their political systems, ownership structure and credit institutions. A review of the strengths and weaknesses of the rural nonfarm economy in China and India highlights the potentials and challenges of growth in the sector.

151. Mukherjee, R. 1963. "On village studies in India." ***Indian Journal of Social Research.*** The trend of "village studies" in India from 1920-60 suggests the existence of virtually two different worlds of concepts and models of analysis and interpretation concerning the social economy and social anthropology. He gives importance to the culmination of the "economic" and "social" aspect to understand the composite form of village life and a balanced view of the dynamics of village society.

152. Murugan, M. 2011. "An analysis of Rural Household Energy Consumption in Kanyakumari district- Tamil Nadu" ***ZENITH International Journal of Multidisciplinary Research,*** **Vol.1 Issue 7 , 130-139.** The article studies the energy consumption pattern in the rural household of the Kanyakumari district of Tamil Nadu. In this article, the researcher projects that the energy consumption pattern depends on the income level and availability of energy services. He has also calculated the estimated carbon emission, which has negative impacts on the environment. He has suggested that renewable energy sources like biogas plants can help curb pollution to some extent.

153. Nahar, U.R. and Chandani, Mabika (eds.) 1995. ***Sociology of Rural Development.*** **New Delhi: Rawat**

Publications. This book is a collection of papers presented at a 1990 National Seminar on Rural Development at Jai Narain Vyas University in Jodhpur, India. The compilation evaluates the efficacy of the rural development efforts and their synchronisation with the goals targeted. The book analyses India's development from the two dominant paradigms that guided the planners in the post-independence era. The Gandhian view of self-reliant villages and the technological viewpoint insisted on utilising science and technology for planned social development through economic growth. Essays in the volume deal with different dimensions of rural development. The first two essays look at the 'crisis' in rural India. In this connection, they present the cardinal issues of rural India that include poverty, exploitation, and inequality and call forth the development process to address equality and distributive justice to tide over many rural problems. Other chapters look at theoretical issues, caste and class movements, the green revolution's effects on rural development and inequality, and rural demographics. Two chapters of the volume are devoted to the analysis of issues affecting rural women. They are the nutrition and health status of rural women and the marginalisation of women caused by the development process and technological advances in agriculture and reproduction. The book's chapters also highlight rural health service, cultural diffusion and reproduction, and the socio-cultural dimensions of drug addiction. On the whole, the book provides a multidimensional perspective of rural problems and development issues in India.

154. Narain, U., Gupta, S., & Van't Veld, K. 2008. "Poverty and resource dependence in rural India" ***Ecological Economics*, *66*(1), 161-176.** This paper shows that poorest and richest household depends more on common-pool resources than households with middle income. It also suggests that common-pool resources are abundant sources of income for the poor and for the rich. Improvement in the stocks of these resources can potentially form the basis of poverty reduction efforts in economies.

155. Narang, R. 2011. "Determining quality of public health care services in rural India." ***Clinical Governance: An International Journal.*** This paper aims to measure patients' perception of the quality of services in public healthcare centres in rural India. Negative opinions are drawn for "availability of adequate medical equipment" and "availability of doctors for women". Education, gender and income are found to be significantly associated with the user perception. The study is limited only to the state of Uttar Pradesh, and quality of health is only restricted to the public health centres.

156. Narasimhan, S. 1999. "*Empowering women: an alternative strategy from rural India.*" Sage Publication Pvt. Ltd. The book compares the effectiveness of state initiatives with the motivation and conscientisation strategy advocated by AWARE (Action for Welfare and Awakening in Rural Environment), a non-governmental organisation strategy of development and empowerment. Empowering women psychology with confidence and information rather than economic interventions can contribute to growth.

157. Nathan, H. 2014. "Solar Energy for Rural Electricity in India: A Misplaced Emphasis." ***Economic and Political Weekly, 49*(50), 60-67.** This paper questions the relevance of promoting solar photovoltaic systems for lighting in rural areas. A study shows that solar PV's failure in villages is primarily due to glitches in maintenance, arising from lack of money, materials and skilled human power.

158. Newby, H. 1983. The sociology of agriculture: Toward a new rural sociology. ***Annual Review of Sociology,*** **67-81.** Sociology of Agriculture is one of the new areas which has developed from Rural Sociology. Though there was a decline in the research in this area after the rural-urban continuum since the 1960s, the sociology of agriculture is gaining momentum.

There was a theoretical vacuum and failure on the part of rural sociology to make an impact since the 1970s. Sociology of agriculture has got the potential to overcome the crisis. However, there are certain difficulties that this approach has got. The paper observes the institutional setting of rural sociology. It also discusses if it is compatible along with the development of the sociology of agriculture.

159. Nielsen, B. K. and Oskarsson, P. 2017. ***Industrialising Rural India: Land, Policy and Resistance. United Kingdom*****: Taylor & Francis.** This edited volume examines important features of rural industrialisation in India. In broadly, this book discusses the evolution of the industry and its related policies, land transfer, destruction and disposition, and resistance against industrial projects. It also highlighted modern industrialisation in rural India and attached challenges. This edited book comprises ten articles and distributed into four parts. In the first part, the editors introduce the topic by highlight industrialising rural India. The second part of the book is on policy evolution in rural industrialisation. The scholars discuss large-scale development projects, industrial and social policies, state-led development and neoliberalism and resistance of framers. The third part of the book is all about governing nature and society. Here, the authors debate national development, industry, nature, power, tribal livelihood, and resource extraction. The last part of the book analyses the ambiguity of resistance. In this section, the authors bring the issues of the forest right act, rural industry and resistance debate.

160. Ojha, S., & Mohapatra, B. 2017. State of livelihood capitals in rural India: a concern towards its development. ***Odisha journal of social science*****, 16.** In this paper, the authors have highlighted the present state of livelihood and its capitals in rural India. The paper used secondary sources of information from census 2011, Indian Rural Development Report of 2013-14 and NSSO data. The paper analyses human capital from educational attainment and poverty level, financial capital with reference to income sources, banking services, debt and saving in rural areas. Whereas for physical capital analysis, the paper took accessibility to basic services and infrastructure, for natural capital authors to land holding and forest dependency of rural people. To analyses, social capital the paper brings the discussion of self-help groups and migration. The paper argued though the structure of livelihood capital increasing in rural areas with the government policy and programmes for the livelihood capital developments, the effectiveness is lagged behind. The paper suggests that policy and programmes relating to livelihood activities must be implemented properly for livelihood capital enhancement and rural development in India.

161. Pal, S. 1999. "An analysis of childhood malnutrition in rural India: role of gender, income and other household characteristics." ***World Development*, *27*(7), 1151-1171.** This paper re-examines the issue of anthropometric indicators to measure childhood nutritional status. This focuses on a nutrition index based on the weight-for-age of children in rural India to know their health status. It is found that female literacy improves the nutritional status of girls at the cost of boys while higher per capita current income improves that of boys at the cost of girls. But more income and literacy give more ways to discriminate between boys and girls.

162. Pal, M. (2020). ***Rural Local Governance and Development*. India: SAGE Publications.** This book explores the political dynamics of the Panchayati Raj system and its role in rural development in India. This book is divided into two sections. The first section discusses rural local governance in India. In this section, the author conceptually the governance, rural local governance and rural development. It also discusses the evolution and working of Panchayati Raj in India, provision of the Panchayat (Extension to Scheduled Areas) Act (PESA), Nyaya Panchayats in India, Inclusiveness of Panchayats, and Civil Society Organisations and Rural Local Governance. The second section brings the discussion of rural development.

The author started with changing rural development strategies, major rural development programmes and their implementation, convergence and inter-sectoral linkage of programmes, decentralised planning, training and capacity development, delivery of health and educational services, and lastly, the author in the way forward analyses effective rural local governance.

163. Pandey, J. (2016). Structural and Psychological Empowerment in Rural India. ***Indian Journal of Industrial Relations, 51*****(4), 579-593.** The author deciphers the transformation of structural empowerment to psychological empowerment through the mediating mechanisms of self-efficacy and perceived resource adequacy. A questionnaire administered to 80 women gram pradhans from rural India.

164. Pandey, V. L., & Chaubal, A. 2011. "Comprehending household cooking energy choice in rural India." ***Biomass and Bioenergy, 35*****(11), 4724-4731.** This paper tries to understand the decision-making process in rural households regarding the choice of cooking fuels. Energy is an important aspect to attain the quality of life and economic prosperity. In the rural areas of India, cooking dominates the aggregate consumption of energy, i.e. biomass fuel. The logistic regression model is used to explain the determinants of clean fuel use for cooking purposes. Families with educated females aged between 10 to 50 years old, households with higher education index, regular salary and monthly per capita consumption expenditure have effective use of clean fuel for cooking whereas below poverty line ration cardholders belonging to reserved caste categories, large family size and size of farmland have a negative linkage with clean fuel.

165. Patel, B., & Chavda, K. 2013. "Rural entrepreneurship in India: Challenge and problems." ***International Journal of Advance Research in Computer Science and Management Studies, 1*****(2).** This paper tries to find out the problems and challenges for the potentiality of rural entrepreneurship. Lack of education, insufficient technical and conceptual ability, financial problem, unavailability of electricity, water supply and transport facilities act as hurdles to set up small industries in the Rural belt.

166. Pradhan, S., & Ranjan, A. 2011. "Corporate social responsibility in rural development sector: Evidences from India." ***School of Doctoral Studies (European Union) Journal*, 2, 139-147.** The paper attempts to explore Corporate Social Responsibility (CSR) practices, particularly in rural development. It evaluates the impacts of CSR on the socio-economic development of rural people. For the study, 14 public and private Indian companies and firms have been selected to study their CSR practices in the context of rural development.

167. Prasad, N. 2015. Agrarian Class and Caste Relations in 'United' Andhra Pradesh, 1956–2014. ***Economic and Political Weekly*, *50*(16), 77-83.** It tries to discover agrarian relations in terms of class and caste in Andhra Pradesh from 1956-2014. It shows that land remained in the control of the upper caste in coastal Andhra and Rayalseema in Telangana. Due to the peasant movements, the land ownership came into the hands of Other Backward Classes. The contradictions of agricultural workers, tenants, and the landless with the rich peasant class led to intense caste conflicts, violence and struggle against the state.

168. Rajvanshi, A. 2016. "Roadmap for rural India." ***Current Science*, *111*(1), 39-43.** This article talks about the importance of rural economy to create a sustainable development of rural India. It can also reduce and eventually stop rural migration to the urban centres. To achieve this, a three-step approach is proposed (i) to make modern devices available at reasonable prices for rural households (ii) to create rural livelihood via high-tech farming and (iii) to engage the best brains in the country for rural development.

169. Ramaswamy, N. 1998. "Rural transport in India." *Current Science, 75*(8), 800-803. The paper emphasises the role of rural roads and rural transport in the country's development. Drawing on the experience of Kerala, it explains how attention to these two matters could improve economic conditions in rural India and reduce migration to the cities.

170. Ramji, A. et al. 2012. "Rural Energy Access and Inequalities: An analysis of NSS Data from 1999-2000 to 2009-10". New Delhi: The Energy and Resource Institute. To find out the trends of energy use for cooking and lighting among rural households in India. Availability, distance, income occupations, price, education, religion, household size are important variables for determining the household energy consumption level and opting for certain fuels. These variables also pose barriers and bind them to use certain fuels. It is very critical to consider the role of gender when it comes to household energy transitions. Moreover, cleaner fuel choices reduce the fuel collection time, which has a positive impact on the health of women and children.

171. Rao, C. H. 1994. ***Agricultural growth, rural poverty and environmental degradation in India.*** **Oxford University Press.** This paper focuses on the interrelationships between agricultural growth, changes in rural poverty, environmental degradation and participatory processes in rural development. It also highlights the implication for development strategy and policy in India's ongoing economic reforms. It concludes that decentralisation of management through the active involvement of farmers and poor beneficiaries has become imperative. Factors like efficient management of infrastructure, recovery of water and electricity rates from the users, and effective design implementation of poverty alleviation programmes free from leakage play an important role.

172. Rao, V. 2001. "Celebrations as social investments: Festival expenditures, unit price variation and social status

in rural India." ***Journal of Development Studies, 38*****(1), 71-97.** This article tries to study the festival expenditure of rural India. It uses both qualitative and quantitative data from a case study of three south Indian villages. This shows that active participation in festivals generates private economic and social returns, which help resolve a potential free-rider problem. The evidence is consistent with the notion that festivals serve as mechanisms by which communities build social networks.

173. Rath, N. 1996. ***Women in rural society: A quest for development.*** **MD Publications Pvt. Ltd.** The book focuses on the role of women in the development of rural society. It is comprised of three parts. The first two parts are based on the micro-study. The first part makes a situation analysis of the women in India in past and present, describing their plight. The second part makes a policy analysis by discussing the planned proposals launched by the government for rural development and the women-specific programmes. The final part consists of role analysis of rural women in the development process. This role analysis embraces an assessment of their awareness, their perception of the rural development programmes, their participation in the planning and implementation of the programmes, and the benefits they receive from the programmes.

174. Ravallion, Martin. 1995. ***Growth and Poverty in Rural India.*** **Washington, DC: World Bank.** This World Bank working paper uses longitudinal consumption surveys from India to examine how much the rural poor in India have benefited from agricultural growth. It also examines the roles of the labour market and distributional biases in the generation of poverty. This working paper uses the data of research that used 20 household surveys from rural India during the years 1958-90 to measure the effects of agricultural growth on rural poverty and the rural labour market and determine the time it takes to impact the household economy. The working paper concludes that growth in farm yields and increased wages will bring gains to the rural poor in the long run.

175. Rawal, V. (2008). Ownership holdings of land in rural India: Putting the record straight. ***Economic and Political Weekly*, 43-47.** This paper finds that more than 40% of the households in rural India do not own land, as much as 15 million acres is in ownership holdings of more than 20 acres, and inequality in ownership has worsened between 1992 and 2003-04.

176. Retzlaff, R. H. (1962). ***Village government in India: a case study.*** **Asia Publication House.** This study discusses the retrospective and prospective views by presenting the traditional village society. This includes caste panchayats, the system of statutory village panchayats during the British rule set up to assist in civil administration and criminal justice. The author stresses state governments should give that village panchayat more power. It also states that the center and state authorities should educate villagers about their responsibilities, potentialities and development of local leadership.

177. Rutten, M. 1995. ***Farms and factories: Social profile of large farmers and rural industrialists in West India.*** **Delhi: Oxford University Press.** Rutten argues that small scale industry and large farmers are two different economic groups that need to be considered a single newly emerging class as the rural capitalist class. The book is the authors' analysis of the data collceted from field work on the social and economic changes in the Kheda district of Gujarat. They derived at the rural capitalist class, by studying the pattern of social, cultural and economic behaviour of the small scale industries and large farmers. The author identified similar behaviour among the two groups created the new class through the socio-economic transformation of rural Gujarat.

178. Saith, A. (1981). Production, prices and poverty in rural India. ***The Journal of Development Studies*, *17*(2),**

196-213. This paper challenges the view that increases in agricultural production have reduced poverty in rural India. Rural poverty is related directly to the consumer price index number for agricultural labourers and inversely to agricultural production.

179. Saxena, A. 2005. Village Studies in India: Old and New. Ethnic Rural and Gender Issues in Contemporary North-West, 131. The paper analyzed village studies in India. The author discusses the village study conducted during colonial times and how it has shifted to a new form. Earlier Indian village studies considered villages as a closed and isolated system. These static, isolated and homogenous identities of villages are changed with the contact with outsiders. Mostly the studies are conducted by sociologists and anthropologists. The first part of the article discusses and review the village studies 1950s, and the second part highlights the changes in the village and its social structure.

180. Sen, A. K. 2020. ***The Making of a Village: The Dynamics of Adivasi Rural Life in India*****. Taylor & Francis.** In this book, the author tries to reveal the vital aspects of the history relating to the Adivasi during the pre-colonial and colonial periods. It looks into the social and cultural facets of indigenous people. It looks into the village community's genesis, demographics, social bonding, migration, and dialects of the indigenous community. The data is collected from eastern India using oral data from archives and empirical data. It writes about the governance of a village and also about the changing rural landscape. It weaves the themes of the village community, indigeneity, migration, governance, colonialism, agency, subjecthood, rural change, environment and ecology.

181. Shah, G., Mander, H., Thorat, S., Baviskar, A., & Deshpande, S. (2006). ***Untouchability in rural India*****. Sage.** This book presents systematic evidence of the incidence and extent of the practice of untouchability in contemporary India. It is based on a very large survey covering 560 villages in 11 states, which found that untouchability persists in India. Data found that 80% of the villages still practice untouchability by discriminating against Dalits.

182. Shah, M., Rao, R., & Shankar, P. V. 2007. Rural credit in 20th century India: overview of history and perspectives. ***Economic and Political Weekly*****, 1351-1364.** This article examines the theoretical and historical case for the nationalisation of banks and provides evidence of its positive impact on rural credit and development. It also overviews the rural credit in 20th century India which finds a remarkable continuity in the problems faced by the poor throughout the period. These include dependence on usurious moneylenders and the operation of an exploitative market.

183. Sharma, A. 2014. The National Rural Health Mission: A Critique. ***Sociological Bulletin*****, 63(2), 287-301.** This paper examines the goals and strategies of NRHM and discusses its strengths and weaknesses. It suggests that to make health interventions effective, there is a need to strengthen the primary health care system in rural and urban areas.

184. Sharma, K. L. 2019. ***Caste, Social Inequality and Mobility in Rural India: Reconceptualizing the Indian Village.*** **SAGE Publishing India.** This book provides a holistic view of rural India and analyses different compositions of villages social structures like peasants, weavers, middle class, artisans, caste, mobility, migration, inequalities and education. This book comprises fifteen chapters into five parts, excluding the introduction and conclusion. The first part discusses the social consciousness of Indian villages, where the author introduces Indian villages and analyses caste, inequality, mobility, and individual and family. The second part of the book is on glimpses of the village economy. This sector analyses how peasants, artisans and weavers play a role in the village economy. The third section is on the rural power structure, where the author compares Indian polity with the village, and election and rural India. It also highlights the role of the Panchayati raj institution in the power structure and how it brings empowerment in rural India. The fourth part of the book discusses emerging patterns of stratification and changes in rural India. Here, the author analyses the formation of middle class in rural areas, education and social stratification in villages, and rural development in India. The last part is on the theoretical and empirical concerns in villages studies. The author analyses his revisit to few villages of Rajasthan and the rise of subaltern studies in the wake of globalisation. In conclusion, the author highlights the emerging matrix of social status and change in villages of India.

185. Sharma, M. 1978. ***The politics of inequality: Competition and control in an Indian village.*** **Honolulu: University Press of Hawaii.** This book is all about the existence of politics and inequality in rural India. This book consists of eleven chapters on various aspects of Indian villages. The first chapter introduces the politics in the village society of India, where the author brings the debate of politics in her study village, the dialectic and fieldwork and collection of data from the studied village. In the second chapter, the author started with a brief description and history of the study area. This section also discusses the village's land, water and labour cycle, the traditional mode of conflict resolutions, and the distribution of resources in the village. The third chapter compares the studied village with the outside world and discusses government administration's extension, alternative conflict resolutions strategy, new resources, and the political arena. The fourth chapter highlights the social relationship in the village among castes and kins. The fifth chapter analyses the conflict in their social relations like family, caste, and jajamani relation. The sixth chapter discusses the village leader in pre and post-independence of India. The seventh chapter analyses the political arena of the studied village and their factions and recruitment, and organisation and interaction. The author discusses the condition, disputes, factions and changes in the village's caste conflict in the eighth chapter. The ninth chapter is on water distribution, competition between class and individuals, and conflict structure. The tenth chapter analyses the village election politics, class tension and vote, perception on voting, and different poll types. And lastly compare between the village with regional politics. In the last and conclusion chapter, the author discusses the political arena of the village and its changes, alternative actions, competition for new resources, development class conflict, and role of caste and class in Indian politics.

186. Singer, M. B., & Cohn, B. S. (Eds.). 1970. ***Structure and change in Indian society*** **(Vol. 47). Transaction Publishers.** This edited book reports on twenty empirical studies of Indian society conducted by various scholars. The contributors demonstrate the adaptive changes experienced by the studied groups in particular villages, towns, cities and regions. The chapters in this book show that the study of Indian society reveals the dynamics of the structures.

187. Singh, B. 1961. ***Next step in village India.*** **Asia Publication House.** The publication presents the results of a research study of the impact of land reforms, particularly the abolition of zamindari on caste and class tensions. It also reflects the social status and mobility, group formation, factions, and feuds to visualise a future land reforms policy. Land reform, consolidation of holdings, irrigation, agricultural taxation, state trading in foodgrain and marketing, rural credits and cooperative are the central objectives of the study.

188. Singh, K. 2009. ***Rural development: principles, policies and management.*** **SAGE Publications India.** The book focuses on the basic concepts, policy instruments and the rural management of rural development. It emphasises the pivotal role of human resources as both a means and an end of developments. Some new pedagogical features are also included in the book.

189. Singh, K., & Pundir, R. S. 2000. Co-operatives and rural development in India. ***Institute of Rural Management.***

This research paper highlights the importance of cooperative organisations in the rural development of India. The paper distinguishes its different forms and pointed outs its importance in the rural economy. It examines how different forms of co-operatives help increase per capita income, income distribution, equitable access to employment opportunity, health, and education in rural areas of India. It brings to notice of the lack of professionalism, excessive interference of government, outdated co-operative laws, lack of efficient leaders, lack of financial viability due to small size business, not friendly work culture, and lack of reward system for growth, are the constraints of co-operative management in rural India. Looking into the lacunas, the paper suggests liberating the co-operatives from the interference of government, democratically governance of directors, and needing to be managed by professionals. Last, the paper comments that to survive and grow, the co-operatives need to be part of globalisation, privatisation, and deregulation.

190. Singh, Nirvikar 2006. ICTs and rural development in India, Working Paper, No. 06-11, University of California, ***Santa Cruz Institute for International Economics*** **(SCIIE), Santa Cruz, CA.** This working paper compares different information and communication technology models and their economic growth and development methodologies in India. The paper highlights the reforms made in the policies and administration of government, particularly in the rural economy. The rural economy needs the most significant support for development; simultaneously, the use of information and communication technology is also most confronting. It examines the role and benefits of information and communication technologies in health, education, democratic participation, efficiency in the market, and government policies and innovations.

191. Singh, P. K., Rai, R. K., Alagarajan, M., & Singh, L. 2012. Determinants of maternity care services utilisation among married adolescents in rural India. ***PloS one, 7*(2),**

e31666. The paper discusses the factors that determine the maternity healthcare services among married adolescents (15-19 aged) in rural sites of India. The paper uses National Family Health Survey data of the year 2005-06. Three components, including antenatal care, safe delivery and postnatal care, are analysed through the Thaddeus and Maine framework on the causes of maternal mortality. The findings suggest that women's education, economic status, and residency regions determine the use of maternal care. The marginalised community women's are less access to safe maternal care, and southern regions women's avail greatest maternal healthcare services in rural India, than other regions. The paper suggests targeting the marginalised community women in rural areas through different healthcare programmes to strengthen maternal healthcare services in rural India.

192. Srinivas, M. N. 1975. Village studies, participant observation and social science research in India. ***Economic and Political Weekly*****, 1387-1394.** In this paper, Srinivas discusses the tradition of fieldwork in social science research, particularly in sociology and social anthropology in India. He argues lack of proper fieldwork tradition has adversely affected the subject growth and development. This tradition alienated the subjects to find out the ground reality and resulted in a lack of proper social, economic and political forces in rural sites. The paper briefly discusses the importance of participant observation and field notes for social science research and how the field notes become historical material in the long run. The paper also highlights some common misconceptions and errors in village studies.

193. Srinivas, M. N. 1976. ***The remembered village (No. 26).*** **Univ of California Press.** This book of Srinivas is the study of a multicaste village known as Rampura in the Mysore district of the Karnataka state. The book starts with how the field study at Rampura began and reminded what and who motivated Srinivas to go for a village study. In describing the field situation of the villages, 0Srinivas started with the Bullock House and its Inhabitants, then the urban tenant, rapport building in the village, moving around the village, curiosity among the villagers, author as a Brahmin and outsider, and failures in encountering collection of field data. In the next section, the author highlighted the three key individual men and their role in understanding their village. These three men's are headman Kulle Gowda and Nadu Gowda. The fourth chapter highlights and discusses the agriculture activities of the village, dominant practices, land use, the need for water, the role of animals and trees in agricultural practices, and shows some pictures of agricultural practices in the village. The fifth chapter discusses the role of different sexes in the household. The sixth chapter brings the discussion of the relation between different caste groups in the village. The seventh chapter discusses the different forms of classes and their factions in the village. The eighth chapter analyses the changing aspects of the Rampura village, including technological, economic, political, cultural, and the changing role of the state. The ninth chapter discusses the social relation through reciprocity, hierarchy, face, friendship and enmity, gossip, envy, and sense of humour. Chapter tenth discusses different aspects of the religion in the village, including kinds of deities, character of deities, astrology, religious ideas, and the relation between man and god. In chapter eleventh, the author narrates the story of his farewell from the village.

194. Srivastava, J. 2015. Grassroots environmentalism as discursive contestation in India: narratives from the "chipko" and "save the Naramada" movements. *Rivista Degli Studi Orientali, 88*, nuova serie, 131-147. The paper analyses two grassroots environmental movements in India, namely Chipko and Save the Narmada, and how these movements bring the environment into the centre of national development. These grassroots environment movements start with the survival and livelihood of local communities and accelerate with the key question of justice and equity in society. It also highlights how the traditional knowledge system and man and nature relationship create an alternative pathway for the development and environment puzzle.

195. Srivastava, N., & Srivastava, R. 2010. Women, work, and employment outcomes in rural India. ***Economic and Political Weekly*****, 49-63.** This paper argues that though rural women's employment has grown, many women are still employed or self-employed as casual labour in agricultural activities. The rural working women face various discriminations, including low wage jobs in their work. Lack of access to higher education and assets leads to lower job participation, and education considered significant determinant among women to avail better quality of work. Rural women's autonomy enables them to choose their work and move for non-agricultural work. This autonomy based on the join self-help groups has mobility and control over the land. The paper recommended strategic policy intervention to enhance wages and opportunities among women workers in rural areas.

196. Srivastava, S., Dutt, C., Nagaraja, R., Bandyopadhayay, S., Rani, H., Hegde, V., & Jayaraman, V. 2004. Strategies for rural poverty alleviation in India: A perspective based on remote sensing and GIS-based nationwide wasteland mapping. ***Current Science, 87*****(7), 954-959.** The paper examines the anti-poverty programmes and interventions in rural areas and how it needs a database for both the socio-economic and natural resources indicators. The research carried out nationwide wasteland mapping by the National Remote Sensing Agency to highlight natural resource degradation problems. The survey reveals the dynamic relationship between natural resources degradation and incidence of poverty through statistics and maps in different parts of India. It also analyses different social and economic policies and institutional mechanisms for poverty eradication measures. Besides wasteland, the paper highlights the macroeconomic variables that determine the poverty dynamics and degradation of natural resources in rural India.

197. Stephenson, R., Koenig, M. A., Acharya, R., & Roy, T. K. 2008. Domestic violence, contraceptive use, and unwanted pregnancy in rural India. *Studies in Family Planning, 39*(3), 177-186. The paper examines the relationship between physical domestic violence, contraceptives, and unwanted pregnancy in selected rural India. The paper used the National Family Health Survey of 1998-99 and a follow-up survey in 2002-03 in four selected states. The study finds that women who experienced violence have less used contraception methods and faces an unwanted pregnancy. There is a clear relationship exists between women's fertility intention and experience of their physical violence. The paper suggests improving the pregnancy measurement and uses future actions for necessary interventions.

198. Sunil, B. C. 2013. Sociology, Village Studies and the Ford Foundation. Economic and Political Weekly, 113-118. The paper considered the village studies in India during the 1950s as a paradigm change in the history of Indian sociology. It accelerated with the essence of community development programmes, which the Ford Foundation funds. To oppose the spread of communism in India during that period, United States used its sentimental approach through Ford Foundation in this strategic location for community development and village studies. The paper discussed Ford Foundation ideology, its activities and growth in India, and India's foreign policy in this paper very lucidly. It highlights how Ford Foundation helps and funded villages studies and community development programmes and brings the benefits of its activities. In conclusion paper highlights that structural functionalism as a methodology become popular among Indian sociologists to study and understands the Indian villages.

199. Sunil, T. S., Rajaram, S., & Zottarelli, L. K. 2006. Do individual and program factors matter in the utilisation of maternal care services in rural India? A theoretical approach. *Social Science & Medicine*, *62*(8), 1943-1957. The present study is about the utilisation of programmes and individual factors relating to maternal care in rural sites of India. The paper used Andersen and Newman theoretical model of 1973 to analyse the individual and social determinants of medical care utilisation in rural India. The paper used the second National Family Health Survey to analyse the paper objectives. The paper finds that education awareness programme relating to maternal care helps increase in the use of healthcare services in rural places. It also reveals that private health facilities in nearby areas didn't help in increase of services utilisation. Whereas the increase in the access to health services marked with the visits of health workers to the households during the pregnancy period. For generalisation of the study, the paper suggests more state-specific studied on the utilisation of maternal healthcare services.

200. Suthar, S. 2011. Contaminated drinking water and rural health perspectives in Rajasthan, India: an overview of recent case studies. *Environmental Monitoring and Assessment*, *173*(1-4), 837-849. The paper reviews and highlights recent case studies on the quality of drinking water in rural areas of northern Rajasthan. From the reviews, the paper finds 95 percent of the region contain a higher level of fluoride than the maximum permissible limit in the groundwater. Nitrate and biological contamination of drinking water sources have created challenges for cultivating and safe drinking water in rural regions. However, the study concludes that water quality is not safe for drinking purposes and suggests running a safe drinking water supply programme in rural areas for better health of rural habitats.

201. Taylor, M. 2011. 'Freedom from poverty is not for free': rural development and the microfinance crisis in

Andhra Pradesh, India. *Journal of Agrarian Change, 11*(4), **484-504.** This article examines the microfinance crisis in Andhra Pradesh during 2010 and highlights the major faults of the crisis. It reveals that drought cycles, the impact of trade liberalisation, and changes in social relationships in rural areas are the three major contexts in which crises happened. The crises further exuberated with the influx of microfinance institutions into the rural areas to attract its rural customers. They boost consumption and continue under debt conditions with distress and uncertainty. These are certain factors that thrown the microfinance institutions to failure in rural Andhra Pradesh.

202. Thakur, M. K. 2013. Of 'Village Studies' and the 'Village': A disputed legacy. *Sociological Bulletin, 62*(1), **138-151.** Thakur has written this paper to understand the tradition of village studies, and it has helped in the development of Indian Sociology. The paper highlighted the theoretical impulses and methodological approaches to study villages and discussed M. N. Srinivas appraisal of village studies. With declining village studies in India and the author suggests recalibrating the village study tradition. This tradition can give us significant insights into the changing power structure, caste relation and economic disparities with the changing village structure, and how it has changed from time to time by adding new dimensions like migration, gender, ecology, movements, and breaking down structures. The paper suggests the necessity to study village societies to grasp the changing aspects of rural society.

203. Tiwari, M. 2013. The global financial crisis and self-help groups in rural India: Are there lessons from their micro savings model? *Development in Practice, 23(2)*, **278-291.** The paper reveals that communities may be benefited potentially if there will be a collective engagement. It argued that individual savings of the poorer are possible through partnership mechanisms. To cope with vulnerability and hardship, rural women's goes for such savings and especially to help their families strengthening their livelihood and better off in the future. The women considered the savings as a positive action, contributing to their families financial security when needed. The paper suggests integrating the mechanisms of saving with the budget for different income groups irrespective of economic hardship or booms for empowering and sustainable individuals.

204. Turton, C., & Farrington, J. 1998. Enhancing rural livelihoods through participatory watershed development in India. ***Natural Resource Perspectives, 34.*** As India implemented different watershed development programmes to reverse the wasteland degradation, link poverty reduction, and improve the local environment through these programmes. Looking into these programmes and its participatory approach of design and implementation, this paper reviews the government guidelines of the micro watershed programme of 1994. It discussed the policy recommendations, land degradation and public sector response, institutional structures, institutionalising participation, strengths and weaknesses of agencies, the problem faced by agencies, project implementation at the village level, and cutting issues. The paper concludes that this programme tries to mainstream the participatory approach and has a positive impression received from the local level on the programme.

205. Urban, F., Benders, R. M., & Moll, H. C. 2009. Energy for rural India. ***Applied Energy, 86*****, S47-S57.** This paper investigates how India could achieve rural electrification through different sources of energy. The paper uses Regional Energy Model to analyse and develop the context for electrification of rural areas for 2005-2030. It also analysis energy use and cost with assess the effects on emission of greenhouse gas. The paper compares different electrification contexts like diesel, grid, renewable energy with business-as-usual. The paper finds that the diesel electrification system has the highest emission of CO_2 and most expensive. It also reveals that renewable energy could save the emission of CO_2 up to 99 percent, primary energy up to 35 percent and cost-effective. Whereas renewable energy is more costly than grid systems. The paper suggests that renewable energy is a better option for rural areas' electrification and helps mitigate climate change.

206. Venkatesh, V., Sykes, T. A., & Venkatraman, S. 2014. Understanding e-Government portal use in rural India: role of demographic and personality characteristics. *Information Systems Journal, 24*(3), 249-269. Looking into the growing electronic government to bridge the digital divide gap, the paper develop a model of electronic government portal use. The study used different individual features like gender, age, education, income; personality characters like neuroticism, agreeableness, extraversion, conscientiousness and openness; and personal technological innovativeness to analyse the electronic government portal use. The study is conducted in a village and collected data from 300 sample households. The study finds that households supported the authors model. It also reveals that all the variables are significant, whereas only 40 percent variance is found in the portal's use.

207. Vlassoff, C. 1990. Fertility intentions and subsequent behavior: a longitudinal study in rural India. *Studies in Family Planning, 21*(4), 216-225. This paper is the outcome of longitudinal studies on the intentions of rural women infertility and family planning. The study is conducted between 1975 to 1987. The findings reveal a definite intention shifted among significant pertion of rural women regarding their fertility and use of the contraceptive method. It also reveals that women stopped childbearing when they reached their ideal number of sons, and sons considered reproductive success determinants. The intention and behaviour of rural women's needs to be changed significantly and can be achived through the official family planning programme of two child norms.

208. Vlassoff, M., & Vlassoff, C. 1980. Old age security and the utility of children in rural India. *Population Studies, 34*(3), 487-499. This article is a study of an Indian village through means of participant observation and questionnaires during 1975-76. The study investigates how old age security becomes a motivation for high fertility in rural areas. The findings indicate that social security programmes have little impact and motivations are weak in nature. A variety of evidence suggested that economic assets, particularly land, were more important than a large number of sons in ensuring security in old age. Furthermore, given the low expectation of life, the need to provide assistance to the elderly was infrequent, a fact that the villagers questioned seemed to recognise.

209. Wade, R. 1989. ***Village republics (No. 40).*** **Cambridge University Press.** Robert Wade gives an informative overview of collective action at the village level in South India. This book contributes significantly to the study of agricultural growth and collective action, with consequences for historical and contemporary research. The book analysis the village level institutional arrangements in the context of irrigation and crop field were guarding. While comparing different villages in that area, the author found variations in social structure norms, basic tastes and technology. The book divided into eleven chapters. The first chapter talks about the village as a cooperative group. The second chapter highlights different circumstances of village organisation. The third chapter discusses the details of a village named Kottapalle. The fourth and fifth chapter is on the social response to open field farming and irrigation. The sixth chapter is on the range of council activities. The seventh chapter examines the mode of public choice. The eighth and ninth chapter is on the variation between different villages social structure and ecology and risk. Whereas the book provided two conclusion chapters, one is on the condition of collective action, and the second is on the theories of collective action. Overall the book is on the study of village-level development and collective action.

210. Wanmali, S., & Islam, Y. 1995. Rural services, rural infrastructure and regional development in India.

***Geographical Journal*, 149-166.** Based on data collected over three decades, this research examines the geographic distribution of rural services in chosen regions of three Indian states (Andhra Pradesh, Maharashtra and Tamil Nadu). The paper examines the functional, geographic and spatial features of these three regions. Since the late 1960s, rural service provision has vastly improved throughout the country, particularly in smaller settlements in these regions. During the early phases of the regions' development, the government played a significant role in this process, allowing the private sector to participate more fully later on. Changes in rural service provision are investigated further in the context of India's decentralised service centre planning. The analysis implies that the concepts and methodology used in this study could serve as the foundation for a more integrated regional approach to planning and policy creation for rural service provision in India's districts.

211.Yerankar, S. 2004. Village administration in ancient India. *The Indian Journal of Political Science*, *65*(1), 87-100. This paper analyses the village administration in the ancient period of India. The author argues that the village is the context where the administration process began in India. In ancient times, the town played less important in society than a village. The paper describes the Kingdom and the importance of the village. It's further enhanced the village in the Vedic age, where states were small. In modern times, governors frequently call a meeting of collectors to address major administrative policy issues; in ancient times, kings such as Alexander the Great held such meetings. Bimbisara used to call an assembly of local chiefs for this purpose in a similar goal. That village, without a doubt, was the real deal for significant units in the country's economy and centres of social life. They kept the national culture, prosperity, and administration afloat. The purpose of this study is to look for Village Administration or local self-government in ancient India.

Section-III
Regional Studies:
A Documentation from Odisha

1. Acharya, A., & A. K. Das. 2020. "District-level analysis of climate vulnerability and household nutrition status among rural communities in Odisha, India." ***International Journal of Population Studies*, 6(1), 41-55.**

The article attempts to grasp the impact of climate change vulnerability on household nutrition status through the agricultural production system in Odisha. The study used secondary data and an estimate composite index of climate change vulnerability at a district scale. The findings suggest that there is a wide variation in vulnerability indicators among districts. Climate vulnerability has a positive and significant relationship with forest area, grossed crop area, scheduled caste population, and per-capita income. The study suggests that climate vulnerability has a much more significant role in influencing household nutrition status, particularly among women and children.

2. Agasty, Mahendra P. 2016. "Migration of Labour and its Impact on Education of Left behind Children: A Case Study of Rural Odisha" ***International Journal of Research in Humanities and Social Studies*, Volume 3, Issue 4, April, pp. 57-63.**

On the basis of a sample survey of 200 households spread over six villages in three blocks of Kendrapara district in Odisha, India, this paper analyses the educational status of the children left behind. The results indicate that migration matters for the education of children. It is evident from the study that enrolment-wise children of migrant households are ahead of those of returned migrant and non-migrant households, in the case of school attendance, continuation in education and educational attainment they lag behind the children in the latter two categories of household.

3. Agasty, M. P. and R. N. Patra. 2014. "Migration of Labour and Left-behind Women: A Case Study of Rural

Odisha." *American International Journal of Research in Humanities, Arts and Social Sciences*, pp. 28-33.

Adult male migration from rural areas for harnessing better employment opportunities and other amenities to the urban centers not only brings economic gains for the households at the origin but also makes heavy demand on the women left behind. On the basis of a sample survey of 200 households spread over six villages in three blocks of Kendrapara district in Odisha, India, this paper analyses the status of women and their increasing responsibility due to migration of the male working members. The results indicate higher responsibilities and greater empowerment of women because of absence of male members. The authors also discover that male migration increases the household power and control over household management of the women. In the absence of the husbands, the wives' labour force participation increases to compensate for the loss of husband's labour on own farms and of their wages, more so when remittances are inadequate and irregular. Additionally, wives also take added familial responsibilities. The most startling observation that emerges from the study is that wives residing in nuclear families take on higher responsibilities and enjoy greater autonomy in comparison to those in migrant sending joint families.

4. Anjali, D. 2013. "Relates on tribal education and health: Evidence from rural Odisha, India." *International Research Journal of Social Sciences*, 2(11), 11-16.

The paper analyses the impact of education on health status of the primitive tribal people in tribal areas and rural areas. The paper uses both primary and secondary data to determine the correlation between health, education, and poverty status in the rural areas of Odisha.

5. Babu,A., S. Pattnaik, R.K. Sarangi, R. Panigrahi. T. Pradhan and S. Sarangi. 2005. "Development Policies and

Rural Poverty in Orissa: Macro analysis and Case Studies", Vasundhara

This study is undertaken in UpparaJaagar of Kumundi Gram Panchayat & UpparaKainsari of Suakathi Gram Panchayat of Keonjhar district and Jambahal Village of Patnagarh Block & Upparbahal Village of Louisingha Block of Bolangir District. The authors in this report focus on three sectors i.e., agriculture, forestry and industrial. The study begins with a description of the consistent efforts made by the state to make the centralised planning more people oriented and people centric. But it points out to the dilemma that the dichotomy between peoples' unmet felt needs and the fruits of development have got further widened ultimately reaching a point where serious questions are being raised about the planning process itself. This has assumed further significance in the light of the inception of the LPG regime in India in the 1990s.The study being a reflection of ground realities relates to the impacts of the development policies and programmes on the lives and livelihood of the poor in rural areas.

6. Bailey, F. G. 1957. ***Caste and the Economic Frontier: A Village in Highland Orissa.*** **Manchester University Press.**

The book highlights a study of a village economy and its interaction with its social system in Odisha. The study was conducted in the Kandhmal region of Odisha, which is dominated mainly by Konds tribes. The study reveals how the rural economic system changes with the gradual change in political adjustments within the village caste system. To answer the question, how does land come into the market, the author traces the role of commercial activities in the village and finds land is the primary source of their income. Gradually land becomes a marketable commodity as other capitals during the period of emergency. The emergency period, particularly in rituals and ceremonies (deaths or marriages) become the reason for the selling of land due to the lack of surplus wealth in the family. The author also examines the relationship between host and outside communities to understand the nexus. So, the author tries to reveal how social, economic, and political aspects of the village are linked to the commoditisation of land.

7. Bailey, F. G. 1970. *Politics and Social Change: Orissa in 1959*. United States, University of California Press.

The book examines the role of modern parliamentary institutions in social change in Odisha. In this context, the author has tried to rely upon the reports of local historians, verbal accounts of participants in movements, and interviews with politicians to draw out the nexus. The author compares two villages of Odisha, which are socially and economically unequal. The author notes that the introduction of representative institutions in such unequal conditions gave rise to different inter-communal and inter-personal interactions in the villages. The author highlights how new political conditions made changes in the social and economic condition of rural people. In analyzing the political situation in Odisha during the election, the author reveals that there has been a shift of loyalty irrespective of political parties and how unequal growth of Odia nationalism developed across the state.

8. Banjare, P., R. Dwivedi, & J. Pradhan, 2015. "Factors associated with the life satisfaction amongst the rural elderly in Odisha, India." *Health and quality of life outcomes, 13*(1), 201.

This article deals with factors associated with life satisfaction among the elderly population in rural areas of the Bargarh district of Odisha. The paper considers life satisfaction as subjective wellbeing. The study follows a cross-sectional survey and multi-stage random sampling method to collect data among the elderly. The study uses hierarchical regression analysis to assess socio-economic, demographic, health condition, social support, and multi-morbidity on life satisfaction. Findings of the paper suggest the cognitive health of men and women is the most influential factor in determining life satisfaction among the elderly, followed by individual social support. Those elderly living alone and with a disability have lower significance in life satisfaction. The study concludes that a better understanding of these associated factors can help remove the excessive anxiety of the old age population in the mindset of rural peoples.

9. Barnard, S., P. Routray, F. Majorin, R. Peletz, S. Boisson, A. Sinha & T. Clasen, 2013. "Impact of Indian Total Sanitation Campaign on latrine coverage and use: a cross-sectional study in Orissa three years following programme implementation." ***PloS one,*** **8(8), e71438.**

This paper analyzes the impact of the Government Total Sanitation Campaign on latrine coverage and use in villages of rural Odisha. The study uses cross-sectional investigation among 477 households of 20 villages in Odisha. The paper finds that mean latrine coverage among villagers is 72 percent, whereas 39 percent of members of families are not using the latrine. Over one-third of members in households with latrines report never defecating in their toilets. Further the study finds that 47 percent of the household members report using their latrine all the time for defecation, and 28 percent of households do not have toilets. Though large-scale campaigns have achieved substantial gain in open defecation-free villages, the paper finds open defecation is still a practice in rural areas.

10. Valerie, B., G. D. Sclar, A. Bisoyi , A. Owens, A. Ghugey and T. Clasen. 2021. "Experience of the COVID-19 Pandemic in Rural Odisha, India: Knowledge, Preventative Actions, and Impacts on Daily Life." ***International Journal of Environmental Research and Public Health.***

This group of researchers conducted 131 semi-structured phone interviews with householders in rural Ganjam and Gajapati district of Odisha. The purpose was to explore participants' COVID-19 related knowledge, perceptions, and preventative actions, as well as how the pandemic affected their daily life, economic and food security, and the village-level response to their needs. Interviews were conducted with 73 heads of household, 37 primary caregivers, and 21 members of village water and sanitation committees from 43 rural villages in the study areas. The study took place between May-July 2020 when many migrant workers were returning to their villages and cases were rising. The authors could note that though most respondents could name COVID-19 (they had very low knowledge about the causes of the disease and high-risk groups, and even the overall COVID-19 knowledge was lowest among caregivers. However, respondents reported high compliance with important preventative measures, including staying home as much as possible, social distancing, washing hands frequently, and wearing a facial mask. The common challenges reported by the respondents included jobless, financial challenges, changes in types and/or amount of food consumed, and adverse emotional effects as a result of the pandemic and lockdown. The results underscore the vulnerability of marginalised populations to the pandemic and the need for measures that increase resilience to large-scale shocks.

11. Beero, S. K., & A. Narayanamoorthy, 2014. "Irrigation Development, Agricultural Growth and Reduction of Rural Poverty Nexus in Odisha." *Growth of Unorganised Sector in India, 27.*

This paper tries to explore the irrigation impact on rural poverty in Odisha. The study takes the irrigation level, effectiveness, and trends in rural areas of Odisha to analyse its impact on rural poverty. The paper uses secondary data at four time points from 1970-71 to 1980-81, 1990-91, and 2001-01 in 10 districts of Odisha. The districts are selected on the basis of low rural poverty, agricultural development, and irrigation facilities, whereas rural poverty is considered the main variable. The authors use descriptive and simple, and multiple regressions analysis to study the interrelation between rural poverty and irrigation development. The study concludes that irrigation is predominantly impacting rural poverty. The paper recommends that authorities should work out irrigation development in rural areas for agriculture development and to reduce rural poverty in rural areas of Odisha. The paper also brings into focus the vital role of NGOs, Government poverty alleviation programmes, and other institutions in reducing poverty in rural areas.

12. Behera, D., & A. Kumar, 2015. "Predictors of exclusive breastfeeding intention among rural pregnant women in India: a study using theory of planned behaviour." ***Rural and remote health*, *15*(3), 62.**

This article documents the prenatal intention for breastfeeding among rural women. The authors here bring out the results of their cross-sectional study conducted among 218 pregnant women from rural Odisha. Structure data collection tool was used to measure the attitude, knowledge, subjective norms, perceived control, and intention for breastfeeding using continuous assessment scales. To analyse the data, the paper uses bivariate and multivariate regression models. The study finds that nearly 30 percent of pregnant women report a high intention for exclusive breastfeeding. Breastfeeding education is positively associated with knowledge, attitude, and subjective norms but inversely related to perceived control. Higher learning, positive attitude, supportive standards, and greater perceived control among pregnant women has a potential effect on their exclusive breastfeeding intention.

13. Behera, M. R., C. Prutipinyo, N. Sirichotiratana, & C. Viwatwongkasem, 2019. "Retention of medical doctors and nurses in rural areas of Odisha state, India-a policy analysis." ***International Journal of Workplace Health Management*.**

The paper aims to develop feasible retention strategies for medical doctors and nurses in rural areas of Odisha. The paper uses documentary reviews and key informant interviews to collect data. The article follows the World Health Organisation's framework to study policy relevant to human resources for health retention in rural areas. The paper finds that the district quota system for admission is not for practiced. Medical education has a provision of community placement a minimum period of three years in rural hospitals. Doctors also get location-based incentives to work in challenging and remote areas. The government also has career development deployment and promotion avenues for human resources. But the above provisions are not implemented effectively. The paper suggests putting the most effective policies and conditions for health human resources engagement in rural areas, and these activities need to be rigorously monitored and evaluated effectively.

14. Behera, M. R., C. Prutipinyo, N. Sirichotiratana, & C. Viwatwongkasem, 2018. "Living conditions, work environment, and intention to stay among doctors working in rural areas of Odisha state, India." ***Annals of Tropical Medicine and Public Health, 11*****(3), 70.**

This paper examines the work environment, living conditions, and other factors that influence doctors' intention to stay in rural areas of Odisha. The non-experimental cross-sectional study design is adopted to collect data from 233 rural posted working doctors. The logistic regression model is used to find out statistical significance between different variables. The study finds 57.6 percent of doctors want to stay and continue their work in rural areas. Age, travel, and work environment are significantly associated with the intent to remain in rural areas. The paper concludes by suggesting the need for effective strategies to bring improvement in the work environment of doctors in rural areas.

15. Biswal, S. N., S. K. Mishra & M. K. Sarangi, 2020. ***Rupkatha Journal on Interdisciplinary Studies in Humanities, Special Conference Issue*** **(Vol. 12, No. 5, 2020. 1-21) from 1st Rupkatha International Open Conference on Recent**

Advances in Interdisciplinary Humanities. Feminisation of Multidimensional Poverty in Rural Odisha

The present study is conducted with the basic objective of examining feminisation of poverty in rural areas of Jagatsinghapur district of Odisha. Seven socio-economic dimensions comprising sixteen indicators have been taken by the authors to construct the Multidimensional Poverty Index (MPI) using the Alkire-Foster (AF) Method at the individual level. The innovation of the study lies in analysing MPI at the individual level for rural Odisha. Higher female deprivation is identified across social groups and all occupation categories except services. Dummy variable regression analysis also supports the major findings of the study. Complementary Cumulative Distribution Function satisfies strict first-order stochastic dominance condition and substantiates the feminisation of poverty at each level of poverty cut-off across all social groups and occupational categories except for services. The findings of the study have significant implications for developing suitable policies for gender equalisation and poverty alleviation.

16. Bowen, Z. 2018. "Interacting circles of educational desire in rural Odisha: Students, schools, state." ***Modern Asian Studies*, *52*(5), 1639-1663.**

The paper examines students' engagement in school and argues that rural schools cannot be fully understood without examining the motivations and interaction between state, students, and local providers. The paper highlights the reasons, evaluations, and experiences of students that need to be brought to the fore light for their active roles in shaping the effects of schooling and village schools.

17. Caruso, B. A., T. F. Clasen, C. Hadley, K. M. Yount, R. Haardörfer, M. Rout & H.L. Cooper, 2017. "Understanding and defining sanitation insecurity: women's gendered experiences of urination, defecation and

menstruation in rural Odisha, India." ***BMJ global health*****,** ***2*****(4).**

This paper captures the frequency and range of women's sanitation-related concerns and negative experiences. The study is undertaken among Odisha's rural women across various life courses. The paper uses a mixed method of data collection followed by exploratory and confirmatory factor analysis to derive final measures. To measure the outcomes, the paper develops sanitation insecurity measures, including 50 items under seven factors across the physical environment, social environment, and individual constraints.

18. Caruso, B. A., H. L. Cooper, R. Haardörfer, K. M. Yount, P. Routray, B. Torondel, & T. Clasen, 2018. "The association between women's sanitation experiences and mental health: A cross-sectional study in Rural, Odisha India." ***SSM-population health*****, 5, 257-266.**

The paper aims to determine sanitation experiences and access among rural women of Odisha and how these aspects are associated with their mental health. The paper uses a cross-sectional design and collects data from 1347 randomly selected women across four life course stages among sixty rural communities. The paper uses hierarchical linear modelling to determine the association between the mental health outcomes, poverty, life stage, current health status, and social support. The paper finds that women in rural Odisha suffer assaults to their well-being and have higher symptoms of anxiety, depression and distress when urinating and defecating, even after toilets are available to them. The paper suggests that sanitation-related interventions should consider how to accommodate women's experiences beyond excreta management to impact health comprehensively.

19. Caruso, B. A., G. D. Sclar, P. Routray, F. Majorin, C. Nagel & T. Clasen. 2019. "A cluster-randomised multi-level intervention to increase latrine use and safe disposal of

child feces in rural Odisha, India" ***The Sundara Grama Research Protocol, BMC Public Health.***

This study evaluates the impact of a multi-level intervention that aims to increase latrine use by all, including safe disposal of child feces, in households that own latrines in rural Odisha. This study intends to study the effect of interventions designed to increase latrine use in rural Odisha. The intervention also includes a specific intervention component for safe child feces disposal. Odisha has the second lowest rate of latrine coverage in India despite SBM efforts representing a critical sanitation challenge. The authors derive the evidence that latrine use is still a distance dream in many parts of rural Odisha. This defeats the country's goal of becoming open defecation free by October 2, 2019. It suggests to inculcate sustained behavioural change to make cent percent latrine use among the rural dwellers.

20. Chand, D. 2015. "Rural Infrastructure: Emerging Trends and Perspectives." ***Orissa Economic Journal, 40.***

This paper makes a time series analysis of the trends of net sown area, net irrigated area, power consumption by irrigation sector, and power sold to other states over the years. Regression and analysis of variance technique have been used to find out the significance of each parameter. The paper emphasises on the creation of social forestry, dairy provisions, low-cost warehouse, cold storage, and market yard in rural areas.

21. Choudhury, P. K. 2019. "Pattern and Determinants of Household Expenditure on Higher Education: Evidence from Rural Odisha." ***In The Future of Higher Education in India*** **(pp. 165-180). Springer, Singapore.**

The paper analyzes the changeability of household expenditure on higher education in rural Odisha and examines how it has related to institutional, household, and individual factors. The data are collected from tribal, scheduled caste, and other backward class students across 19 colleges of two tribal-dominated districts in Odisha. The results suggest an average of

30 percent of the annual income of households is spent on higher education expenses. The paper further adds that students enrolled in government and aided colleges spend more. The pattern of spending on higher education by households varies significantly between hostellers and day scholars. The paper further finds that students who belong to poor households have invested less in higher education than better-income households. It also finds that there is a pro-male bias in pending on higher education by households.

22. Clasen, T., S. Boisson, P. Routray, O. Cumming, M. Jenkins, J. H. Ensink, & W. P. Schmidt, 2012. "The effect of improved rural sanitation on diarrhoea and helminth infection: design of a cluster-randomized trial in Orissa, India." ***Emerging themes in Epidemiology*, *9*(1), 7.**

The present paper evaluates the impact of the ongoing sanitation campaign in rural areas under India's Total Sanitation Campaign. The article selects a randomized 50 project intervention and 50 control villages without any intervention. The study finds delay in intervention rollout caused logistical problems for the planning of health outcomes. Latrine coverage at the end of the construction period remains far below the target. The paper assesses the health outcome measures diarrhoea, helminth infections, anthropometric measures, water quality, insect vectors, and exposure to faecal pathogens.

23. Clasen, T., S. Boisson, P. Routray, B. Torondel, M. Bell, O. Cumming, & W.P. Schmidt, 2014. "Effectiveness of a rural sanitation programme on diarrhoea, soil-transmitted helminth infection, and child malnutrition in Odisha, India: A Cluster-randomised Trial." ***The Lancet Global Health*, *2*(11), e645-e653.**

The present paper assesses the effectiveness of rural sanitation interventions to prevent diarrhoea, soil-transmitted helminth infection, and child malnutrition. The study has used the cluster-randomized controlled trial of 100 rural villages having 25984 households of Odisha. The finding suggests the mean village level latrine coverage increased after the intervention. The paper shows that increased latrine coverage cannot be assumed to reduce exposure to faecal pathogens and prevent disease.

24. Das, S. K. 2013. "Growth and Prospects of Odisha Tourism: An Empirical Study" Odisha Review, September.

The author describes that the state of Odisha with its rich and varied topography, vibrant culture and captivating festivities offers immense tourism delight and pleasure to the visitors. Tourism forms a significant aspect of the service sector which contributes largely to the Indian economic development. Odisha tourism industry is growing rapidly more than the preceding years. The scope of tourism as proposed by the author is expanding with greater diversities. The new varieties that have gained momentum are health tourism (medical tourism), religious tourism, sports tourism, educational tourism, agri tourism etc. The writer sees that Odisha have immense potential for such diversification. But it needs proper government incubation and support. If tourism can be strengthened in the state, it will give rise to employment potential, living standards of the locals and bring prosperity to the local communities and the state as well.

25. Das, S.S. 2019. "Diffusion of clean energy products in rural areas of India: A case study of Odisha". Centurian University.

The present study takes an ecosystem newline approach to study diffusion of clean energy products in the rural areas of Odisha. Globalisation and privatisation have swept the rural market in the state. Rural area is new line flooded with use and throws type cheap products without any services. Rural people also seek right value for what they buy. With saturation in urban areas, competition for new line reaching rural consumers is becoming stiff. Accordingly, marketing for rural consumers new line is becoming more challenging. A review of existing literature on rural marketing and new line characteristics of rural consumer is nicely undertaken in this thesis. Finally, the thesis provides input for rural centric model for clean energy diffusion.

26. Das, N., & N. Mishra, 2015. "Assessing the impact of coal mining on diversified sources of rural livelihoods: A case study in the Ib Valley coalfield area of western Odisha, India." ***International Research Journal of Social Sciences, 4*****(6), 83-88.**

The paper examines the impact of coal mining on livelihood sources in the Ib valley coalfield area of western Odisha. The study was conducted among six mining-affected villages around three opencast mines, in which the authors have surveyed 300 households from mining villages and 100 households from control villages. The recall method was adopted to collect the information on pre and post situation, followed by observation, case studies, group discussion, participatory rural appraisal. The paper concludes that though mining helps to increase in earnings, but halts diversified sources of rural livelihood in the region.

27. Das, S., S. K. Patnaik, & A. Patra, 2019. "Problems and Prospects of Rural Entrepreneurship in Mayurbhanj District of Odisha." ***SEDME (Small Enterprises Development, Management & Extension Journal), 46*****(3), 152-160.**

The paper attempts to study the present state of Micro, Small, and Medium Enterprises (MSME). It further analyses the amount invested and employment generated by MSME in the Mayurbhanj District of Odisha and highlights the problems and prospects of rural entrepreneurs of the districts.

28. De Shay, R., D. L. Comeau, G. D. Sclar, P. Routray, & B.A Caruso, 2020. "Community Perceptions of a Multilevel Sanitation Behavior Change Intervention in Rural Odisha, India." ***International Journal of Environmental Research and Public Health, 17*****(12), 4472.**

The paper examines the community perceptions on sanitation intervention, particularly latrine use behaviour in rural Odisha. The study was conducted in sixteen sex-segregated focus group discussion three intervention and non-interventions villages. The paper's findings show that it is challenging to understand community perceptions of past sanitation interventions and the level of collective efficacy to improve future programmes' effectiveness. Participants speak positively about intervention, but socially created divisions like caste, social conflict, and gender norms very often prevent villagers from getting such experiences. The paper concludes that in future interventions government needs to engage in a robust strategy to break the social barriers.

29. Gochhayat, A. 2013. "Political participation of women in Gram Panchayat elections in Odisha: A case study of Hindol block in Dhenkanal district." ***International Journal of Rural Studies, 20*****(2).**

The paper tries to analyze the political participation of women in the electoral and functioning process of panchayats. It further attempts to discuss the problems attached to women in the process. The study was conducted using 125 samples of five gram panchayats in the Dhenkanal district of Odisha. The findings expose that women's participation in election and panchayats activities is not satisfactory. Women are less aware of the name of political parties and have a great apathy towards politics. Low level of education, patriarchal society, and parochial culture are the responsible factors behind low participation.

30. Iwwage & Pci 2021. "Impact of Covid-19 on Rural SHG Women in Odisha" KREA university.

This study was conducted by the Initiative for What Works to Advance Women and Girls in the Economy (IWWAGE) and Project Concern International (PCI). The main objectives of this study were to (i) study the overall impacts on women's well-being during and post the lockdown period, and (ii) understand SHG participation in COVID-19 response activities. For the purpose, the study gave a coverage to a total of 423 SHG women in the districts of Deogargh and Jagatsinghpur in the month of July 2020 for the study. The study finds that SHG members are well aware of COVID-19 related health information, with a large majority of respondents reporting that they receive health advisories/information. The findings demonstrate the immense source of support that the SHG movement has given to the rural women of the state. The study notices that women could reach out to their SHG in times of need. The SHG also emerged as the preferred avenue for women to access emergency loans, savings and gain information, proved to be an important space where women formed social bonds. Respondents reported they missed the socialisation spaces and the financial opportunities the SHG provided during the lockdown period when all SHG activities had come to a halt.

31. Jena, S., K. C. Sahoo, M. Samal, P. Kripalini, C. Shrivastava, H. Anand, P. Mahapatra & S. Pati, 2020. Rural community attitude towards mental healthcare: a mixed-method study in Khurda district of Odisha, India." ***Middle East Curr Psychiatry*** **27, 48.**

This study examines the attitude of rural people towards mental healthcare in rural Odisha. An explanatory mixed-method study was conducted by the group of researchers among 395 participants age between 18 to 65 years in two rural blocks of Khurdha district, Odisha. A total of 16 in-depth interviews were also conducted among the caretakers of the patients. The educational level, religion, age, and gender are found to be significantly associated with attitudes towards mental healthcare facilities. Female having lower-education had more negative attitudes towards mental healthcare facilities. The major barriers for the mental healthcare are the rejection of mental illness by patients due to fear of societal stigma, faith on religious healers, and lack of availability of mental health services.

32. Johnson, L. 2019. "Rural sanitation: A charter of demands", IDR, https://idronline.org/rural-sanitation-a-charter-of-demands/

In this article, the author, the executive director of Gram Vikas, Odisha throws light on some micro–level issues, based on more than two decades of experience in rural Odisha. To him, Gram Vikas under the integrated water, sanitation, and hygiene (WSH) intervention has tried to create toilet facilities with hundred percent people's participation in 1,400 villages, covering close to 90,000 households. Over the years, the author marks bringing attitudinal and behaviour changes towards safe sanitation is very difficult in rural Odisha. Financial incentives to rural households for constructing individual household latrines, mostly likely in recognition of the fact those rural households need the financial incentive as motivation to change sanitation behaviour under different schemes has enabled households to construct toilets and the Government records the number to be perceptibly high. But the ground reality as the author portrays is that the actual coverage of usable toilets is likely to be much less than what the numbers show, households are in need support for repairs and upgradations of the already built latrines. In addition, he suggests that two categories of rural population i.e. who have not constructed latrines so far; and new households that have come up in villages that have already been declared open defecation free (ODF) need financial assistance to build toilets.

33. Johnson, L. & B. Peter. 2020. "Safe and Dignified Migration for the poor in rural Odisha" ***Blog Gram Vikas, June.***

The authors in this article try to project the multiple yields of migration in the poverty stricken areas of rural Odisha. There are some positive yields. These yields include: improved quality of life of the migrant families, increased private investments in human development through better education and healthcare, better use of productive resources. The negative costs are: the social and emotional stress migration causes are too high. Through a multi-stakeholder assessment conducted by Gram Vikas and the Centre for Migration and Inclusive Development (CMID), the authors have identified these impacts which they elaborate in this paper. Migrants have limited information about jobs at the destination, remain deferred paid, underpaid and unpaid at the destination, face unexpected termination, suffer from poor health conditions, face issues in remitting money to their families. They explain the Odisha-Kerala corridor of the Safe and Dignified Migration Programme being taken jointly by Gram Vikas, Centre for Migration and Inclusive Development (CMID) Kerala, ESAF Small Finance Bank and Prachodhan Development Society. They hope this agency can erode some of the formidable issues faced by the rural migrants and convert the present threats into opportunities.

34. Kalyani, M. 2011. "Structure, Policy and Prospects of Rural Industrialisation in Orissa, India: A Strategic Approach for Sustainable Development." ***Journal of Management and Public Policy*, 2(2), 70-98.**

The paper looks at the poor living condition of poor people in rural areas of Odisha and the steps that are taken to improve their living conditions through rural industrialisation. The paper highlights and discusses different rural industrial ideas and activities and how they can bring sustainable development to an agrarian society. The article suggests for interconnecting and integrating rural industrialisation with rural entrepreneurship for sustainable development in rural industries.

35. Kumar, S. S., P. Rabindranath, P.M. Ranjan & B.L. Mohan, 2012. "Traditional knowledge of Medicinal plants against birth control by the tribals and other rural people of Bargarh district in Western Odisha, India." ***Global Journal of Research on Medicinal Plants & Indigenous Medicine*, 1(12), 670.**

This article relates to the use of medical plants for birth control by tribal and rural people of Bargarh district of Odisha. The article surveys medical plants at different forest pockets and rural areas of the district and captures medical plant-related information collected from local peoples. The paper reveals that 20 plant species belonging to 20 genera and 16 families are used for birth control. The article elaborates on the plant species, parts used, drug preparation, and their doses for respective treatment.

36. Madiath, A. et.al. 2004. "People, Communities & Development in Rural Orissa: A compendium of case studies from Gram Vikas, Orissa".

This compendium of case studies carries the experiences of the development practitioners of Gram Vikas. It states the way in which these practitioners deal with people attempting to bring about changes in their quality of life by providing some tangible and intangible benefits. They aim at generating 'self-reliance' and 'self-esteem' among the people with whom they engage which they consider as intangible transformations. The processes of such change are slow and often imperceptible. At the same time, they provide some tangible benefits like safe water, disaster-proof housing, forests and plantations, schools and medical facilities, etc. The compendium also describes the need of 'inclusion' of all and creation of a level playing field for development processes to take off. The authors describe the activities of social mobilisation, resource mobilisation, environment management, appropriate technology, habitat development, education, etc. which they take up for rural development. The entire compendium is arranged into six sections and each section reflects the practitioners' experience with the community on various facets of development. In the first section the case study of the Kerandimals movement is reflected, the second section relates to interventions in renewable energy and alternative technologies, the third section focuses on women's role in creating space for them in households and communities and taking the lead in carrying forward the process of development in the rural areas, the fourth section traces Gram Vikas' work in education, the fifth section relates to the current spearhead intervention of Gram Vikas in the Rural Health and Environment Programme (RHEP) and the sixth section focus on livelihoods, linked to natural resource management and the Gram Vikas experimentations.

37. Majumder, J., & L. K. Sharma, 2014. "Composition with Aging Among Adult Rural Population of Odisha, India." ***Indian Journal of Biological Sciences, 20.***

The paper investigates the body composition from adult to old age rural population. The study has taken 263 males and 286 females from different age groups from the Ganjam district of Odisha. Anthropometric measurements – height, weight, skinfold, were recorded to calculate the body fat, mass, and surface area. Results indicate that increases in age in men shows weight reduction, abdominal skin folds, and percent of body fat. In contrast, in the case of women significant difference in reduction of these parameters is observed. Further, there is a reduction in anthropometric characteristics of body composition among rural men and women. The results also show that rural men show rotundity-oriented susceptible anthropometric characteristics of body composition with increasing age.

38. Mallick, R. K., S. K. Dash, & G. Pattnaik, 2016. "Socio-Economic Determinants of Women Leadership in Panchayati Raj in Odisha." ***Journal of Rural Development, 35*****(1), 115-130.**

The paper tries to report the socio-economic determinants of women leadership and participation in local government – Panchayati Raj, in Odisha. The paper has adopted a random sampling method, followed by qualitative and quantitative approaches to analyze the variables like caste, age, education, marital status, family and political background, and the training exposure of women in defining their leadership in the local government. The paper describes how these variables determine the role women play and change their skills, knowledge, and attitudes confirming their ability to become local leaders.

39. Mallik, S. 2016. "Industry and Rural Development with Reference to Odisha." ***Productivity*, 57(2).**

Despite being one of the most mineral-rich states in India, the present paper reveals that Odisha remains the most impoverished state in the country. Industrialisation in rural areas has accentuated social inequalities in society. The process further damages the backbone of the rural economy i.e. agriculture, and alienates poor farmers from their habitats leading to uneven development. The paper concludes that industrialisation is not the solution for rural development and argues that a participatory, inclusive balance between industry and agriculture can bring people-centered growth.

40. Mishra, A. K., & B. P. Mohapatra, 2015. "Decentralised Governance and Devolution of Funds to the Panchayats in Odisha: A Critical Review." ***Madhya Pradesh Journal of Social Sciences*, 70.**

The paper examines the issues attached with decentralised governance and devolution of funds to Panchayats, particularly to the Odisha context. The article focuses on four aspects i.e. the evolution of the Panchayats in Odisha, institutional arrangements and legal provisions associated with fiscal devolution, the institutionalisation of the State Finance Commission, and finally, gaps associated with fiscal devolution in the state of Odisha. The findings highlight that rural local bodies' fiscal position in the state has been disturbed due to missing cases of horizontal equities and efficiencies. The paper concludes fiscal autonomy can be promoted to the local level if State Finance Commission can recommend building financial capability of local bodies.

41. Mishra, A., S. K. Mishra, I. Baitharu, & T. K. Das, 2020. "Food Security and Nutritional Status among Rural Poor: Evaluating the Impact of Rural Livelihood Mission in Odisha, India." Journal of Reviews on Global Economics, 9, 141-148.

The paper examines the impact of the National Rural Livelihood Mission on respondents' food security and nutritional profile in rural areas of Odisha. The data are collected from beneficiaries and non-beneficiaries through structured questionnaires to evaluate the program's impact on rural people. The paper finds better food consumption patterns among beneficiaries, and NRLM positively impacts rural people's food security.

42. Mishra, C. 2021. "Decentralised Renewable Energy and Rural Development: Lessons from Odisha's First Solar Village." Journal of Land and Rural Studies, 9(1), 178-192.

The paper studies the effectiveness of renewable energy projects by examining villagers' experiences of the first solar village of Odisha. The author uses the participatory rural appraisal method to determine the energy use pattern, issues, and challenges the communities face. The paper concludes that though the solar project initially was a success, due to the lack of maintenance and technical matters there was a decline in the use of solar energy. Looking into the issues, the paper suggests incorporating Nai Talim approach of Gandhi to resolve the hurdles in the success of the solar projects.

43. Mishra, D. K. 2011, April. "Behind dispossession: State, land grabbing and agrarian change in rural Orissa." In International conference on global land grabbing (Vol. 6, No. 8).

Looking into the history of marginalisation and dispossession due to land grabbing for development purposes in Odisha, the paper analyzes the diverse forms and implications of land grabbing in Odisha. The paper finds that there is a linkage between catastrophic land grabbing and the classical process of land alienation. The paper further highlights the importance of global and local political economic forces in land grabbing in Odisha.

44. Mishra, J. &A. Singh, 2017. "Rural Market in Odisha: A Case Analysis w.r.t K.B.K., Odisha." ***International Journal of Research and Scientific Innovation (IJRSI)*** **| Volume IV, Issue XII, December.**

This paper examines the impact of marketing strategies on rural Odisha with special reference to KBK areas. The study is undertaken after the MNCs started penetrating into the rural markets. The authors define rural marketing as a function that manages all activities involved in assessing, stimulating and converting power of rural consumers into an effective demand for specific products and services and moving these products and services to the people in rural areas to create satisfaction for a better standard of living and there by achieving organisational goals. To them very often, rural marketing is accepted as agricultural marketing. It is just a narrow interpretation of the term. But recently they note a transit in the nature of rural markets in KBK region. Rural markets are stimulated through the organisation of Trade Fair and Cultural Fests. But they are not sufficient to vitalise the rural markets. Rural markets in these areas still cripple with many problems which need a solution by the involvement of multiple stakeholders.

45. Mishra, N. 2015. "Coal Mining, Displacement and Rural Livelihoods: A Study in Mahanadi Coalfield Odisha" ***National Institute of Technology (NIT),*** **Rourkela.**

In this NitiAyog sponsored project, the researcher focuses on the various implications that coal mining has on social structure and culture of the mining affected areas. He clearly establishes that coal mining has its adverse impact on the health of women and children, on local biodiversity, agricultural productivity, employment and livelihood. The study also explores the strategies adopted by the Corporate Social Responsibility of Mahanadi Coalfields Limited (MCL) in helping rehabilitation of displaced people and restoration of ecological resilience and the roles played by Gram Sabha/ Gram Panchayat/Non- Government Organisations/Forest and Tribal Affairs Department on mitigation of and adaption of livelihood. The project report also looks into the role of both mining companies and forest department in use of Compensatory Afforestation Management and Planning Authority (CAMPA) fund for ecological restoration. The researcher concludes that mining has both positive and negative impact on the people's way of living. The positive gains include economic gain for the local people, better work opportunities. The negative costs include a highly polluted environment, mining induced diseases, the pain of displacement, ruined life and livelihood. The impact on biodiversity, agriculture and health sector is equally negative. At this juncture, he suggests that improvement in the overall condition of the environment and the quality of life should be the prime responsibility of the mining company.

46. Mishra, N. 2014. "New Agro-Technology and Traditional Rural Family and Rural Power Structure: A Case Study from Odisha." Indian Sociological Society XL (40th) All-India Sociological Conference on Development, Diversity & Democracy,Varanashi, 29- 30 Nov & 01 Dec, 2014.

The paper aims to analyze the impact of new agro-technology on the rural social institutions in Odisha, particularly to traditional family and power structure. The paper findings suggest agro-technology and education, westernisation, and modernisation helps in increasing productivity and brings change in the structure and function of rural family structures. The paper also finds the rise of class feeling and weakening of traditional caste feeling in the studied villages.

47. Mishra, R. 2015. "Assessment and Comparison of Service Quality of Regional Rural Banks and Co-operative Banks in catering to the need of Rural Mass in Western Odisha." ***International Journal on Global Business Management & Research*, *4*(1), 13.**

The paper assesses the service quality of regional rural banks and cooperative banks in satisfying the needs of rural masses of Western Odisha. The paper uses a multi-itemized rating scale to evaluate the quality of services of both banks. The study finds that service quality is not meeting the expectations of rural customers irrespective of their dimensions.

48. Mohanty, B. 2015. "Empowerment of Excluded Groups Local Democracy and Social Change in Rural Odisha, Eastern India." ***Governance, Conflict and Development in South Asia: Perspectives from India, Nepal and Sri Lanka*, 6.**

The paper investigates the unequal distribution of power across the caste, class, gender and political party affiliations in the local bodies of Odisha. It throws light on the process by which women, scheduled caste, and tribal people are excluded from the decision-making processes in rural areas of Odisha. Though there is a moderate inclusion of women in local bodies after the introduction of the 73rd Constitutional Amendment, higher caste people still find an over representation. The paper notes that though formally institutional inclusion has been implemented, but still excluded groups are discriminated. The author in the findings expresses his doubt that whether the institutional steps have been effective in the reduction of persistence inequalities in rural areas.

49. Mohanty, R., S. K. Sadual, and A. Samal, 2019. "The scope of rural tourism in Odisha: A case study", ***Pramana Research Journal*, Volume 9, Issue 2, 2019 ISSN No: 2249-297, Volume 9, Issue 2.**

The authors in this article talk about the huge scope of rural tourism in Odisha. To them, "Rural tourism" is a new trend gaining rapid momentum all over the globe. Rural tourism becomes an attraction for the tourists as it showcases the rural life, art, culture and heritage of village area. It also brings economic prosperity for the local community. It creates an enabling interaction between the tourists and the locals for a more enriching tourism experience. The authors conclude that Odisha having 74% of its population residing in rural areas in its almost seven lakh villages and a dense population of tribals living in the remote villages showcasing their living styles has enough potential for rural tourism. The distinct cultural identity of the rural areas of the state, with archaeological treasures craft traditions, with their age-old institutions like Bhagabata Tungis, folk arts like chawdance Daskathia, Naga Dance, Samprada Dance, Medha Nacha, Pala, Kela Keluni, Kandhei Nacha, Jhoomar Dance, Ghoomar Dance, ChaitiGhoda Nacha, Ghanta Patua, Danda Nata, Dalkhai Dance, Paraja Dance, Kharpa Dance etc. and the rural cuisines can provide a solid base for rural tourism.

50. Mohapatra, A. 2015. Study Report on "Evaluation of Rural Housing Programme (IAY) under Economic Stimulus Package (ESP) in Selected Naxal Affected Districts in Jharkhand, Bihar and Odisha".

The author of this report tries to trace out the systems and processes adopted in operationalising ESP under IAY at the grassroots; the process of planning, execution and time bound realisation of objectives pertaining to ESP under IAY; to assess the socioeconomic impact of IAY on beneficiary households and (to draw action interventions based on the study findings so as to strengthen ESP component in general and over-all IAY implementation in particular in areas affected by LWE.ESP stands for **Economic Stimulus Package** and LWE for **Left wing extremists.** The GoI for the first time in the year 2009 allocated a total package of Rs 3050 crore for rural housing under

Economic Stimulus Package (ESP) to LWE affected states, of which, Rs 2429 crore was as part of normal Indira Awaas Yojana (IAY) and Rs.413 crore was allotted for building houses for poor in 33 LWE affected districts in 8 states. The study is based on a participatory and consultative approach. The author records poor utilisation of ESP allocation by states and terms it as one of the major shortfalls noted under the study. Poor utilisation of ESP allocation also results owing to the inabilities of the state governments to adhere the timeline for release the state share to the district. The author suggests that transparency needs to be maintained for beneficiary selection, quick disbursal of the money to the districts to be made and system of supervision, compliance and complaints redressal need to be set up preferably at the local level to bring in efficacy.

51. Mohapatra, I., S. C. Das, and S. Samantaray 2018. "Health impact on women using solid cooking fuels in rural area of Cuttack district, Odisha" ***J Family Med Prim Care.*** **2018 Jan-Feb; 7(1): 11–15.**

This current study is an attempt to evaluate the impact of solid cooking fuels on health of rural women in age group of 20–40 years. It tries to establish the relationship between the duration of exposure to cooking fuels and various health problems. The study records that dry cough, followed by eye and nose irritation, headache, and hypertension (HT) are the associated health outcomes of cooking with solid cooking fuels. The morbidities are increased with increase in duration of cooking. Knowledge related to health effects of cooking fuels seems to be poor among the participants.

52. Mukherjee, A., A. Dwivedi, and N. Agarwal.2021. "Rural Sanitation Practices: A Rapid Assessment Study for Odisha" ***Centre for Policy Research.***

The authors in this report point out that Odisha is a lead state in terms of creating a changed sanitation practice in its rural areas under the aegis of 'Swachha Odisha, Sustha Odisha', and the national imperatives set by the National Rural Sanitation Strategy, 2019-2029. The state has created a systematic framework towards the achievement of total sanitation in the form of the Odisha Rural Sanitation Policy, 2020. It has made an unprecedented stride in increasing access of individuals to toilets from 14% in 2011 to a purported 100% in 2019 under the Swachh Bharat Mission. The present report discusses different aspects of rural sanitation. It ranges from trends in toilet use and on-site sanitation systems to the availability and state of Solid and Liquid Waste Management (SLWM) infrastructure.

53. Nayak, C. 2011. "Rural Infrastructure and Cropping Intensity in Odisha." ***IOSR Journal of Economics and Finance*, *2*(6), 6.**

The present article tries to explore how rural infrastructure helps in raising cropping intensity. The paper takes secondary data of rural physical, financial and social infrastructures into consideration and develops a Rural Infrastructure Index to analyze the impact on cropping intensity. The study finds that regional disparity exists in the existence of rural infrastructure. The study further reveals that regional disparity is lesser in cropping intensity and only rural infrastructure impacts cropping intensity in agriculture.

54. Nayak, C. 2014. "Rural Infrastructure in Odisha: An Inter-District Analysis." ***PRAGATI: Journal of Indian Economy*, *1*(1), 17-38.**

The present paper examines the inter-regional disparity of rural infrastructure in Odisha through the Rural Infrastructure Index. The study finds the existence of vertical inequality in a different category of rural infrastructure in the state. The study further finds that the underdevelopment of rural infrastructure persists mostly in KBK districts and some western-central regions of Odisha. The disparity primarily exists in financial infrastructure followed by physical and social infrastructure.

The coastal region of the state is better off than other regions in rural infrastructure. The paper suggests a time-bound delivery system and measures for better off the rural infrastructure.

55. Nayak, C. 2015. "Crop diversification and land productivity in Odisha: role of rural infrastructure." ***PRAGATI: Journal of Indian Economy*, *2*(2), 1-18.**

The present paper analyses the role of seed, rural credit, fertilizer, surplus and rural infrastructure in crop diversification and land productivity in Odisha. Using the crop diversity index and rural infrastructural index, the author attempts to examine the regional divide in land productivity and crop diversification vis-à-vis rural infrastructure. The study reveals that rural infrastructure has a significant positive impact on land productivity. The study further observes the existence of regional inequality in rural infrastructure.

56. Nayak, C., C. R. Kumar, & M. Nayak, 2017. "Gender Perspective of Rural Livelihood in a Backward Village of Coastal Odisha." ***Orissa Economic Journal, 162.***

The paper analyses the role of gender in determining occupational structure and migration as a livelihood strategy. The paper investigates employment, income distribution, and family income and how gender plays a role in determining these factors. The study finds that gender plays a significant role in occupation, work participation, income, and migration, but lack of access to ownership of land deprive the rural dwellers from availing the facilities of formal credit. The work participation rate is also found lower among the women in the study area.

57. Nayak, S. 2013. "Determinants and Pattern of Saving Behaviour in Rural Households of Western Odisha", Department of Humanities and Social Sciences National Institute of Technology Rourkela.

The present thesis submitted to NIT, Rourkela analyses the determinants and patterns of saving behaviour in rural household of western Odisha. The author visualises that the determinants and patterns of saving differ from rural to urban region. In rural areas, the consumption is always prioritised over saving. The study is conducted through primary survey with 300 households drawing a sample from rural villages of Sundergarh district of Odisha. These 300 households from Sundergarh district are selected and a cross-sectional primary data is collected through personal interview method. The determinants of saving are analysed empirically by a linear regression method. The income, level of expenditure, consumption pattern and saving behaviour are taken as the criteria for drawing the samples. The present study reveals that the rural households vary in terms of the distribution of income and occupation i.e. in other words, the lowest income groups (the agricultural labours and the non-agricultural labours) have the highest marginal propensity to consume which leads to lowest marginal propensity to save as compared to the other occupational groups. The study finds that most of the rural households have low educational status which results in less awareness of the people towards the benefits of saving. They are even careless towards their health standards. Consumption of local liquor is very prominent in these households which detoriates their health as well as their financial conditions.

58. Nayak, S. 2020. "Dispossessed Women's Work: The Case of Talcher Coalfields of Odisha." ***Economic and Political Weekly*****, Vol. 55, Issue No. 20, 16 May.**

This paper examines the experiences of dispossessed women in terms of accessing work opportunities in a setting of opencast coal mining in Talcher coalfields of Odisha. Drawing its understanding from the framework of social exclusion and adverse inclusion, it argues that the variations in the changing lives of rural women as an outcome of the dispossession process, needs to be viewed in terms of the pre-existing agrarian inequalities shaped by caste, class and gender positions that is used by capital for constructing its division of labour. Coal mines are male-dominated capitalist settings that have created three categories of work for rural women as evident in Talcher. First, the work of "miners' wife," a process of housewifisation, which is basically their unpaid labour contributing to the social reproduction of the miners, and restricting the women to household work. Second, work in the coal mines, the process of becoming women miners, which are not the jobs of "coal miners" in a true sense, but rather the jobs that facilitate coal production. Third, moving between low-grade works such as sanitation work and other casual labour in and around coal mines and primarily, coal collection. Women belonging to landowning households (majorly upper-caste Hindus and OBCs, and a small minority of Dalits and Adivasis) are working in the first two categories. Landless Dalit women are, however, carrying out menial jobs. In all these cases, the entry of women (across the caste and class positions) into different forms of work is under unfavourable circumstances. Women have been subjected to exclusion by the state's compensation policy, the gendered coal mining industry, and existing social norms. Where included, the manner of inclusion and the conditions they face are adverse. Marginalisation in the process of dispossession affects landless Dalit women, as the most vulnerable, the hardest.

59. Odisha Review (2017) Vol. LXXIII No. 9, Government of Odisha.

This special volume brought out as the Odisha day special volume contains almost twenty-two articles contributed by authors. These articles are vital resources to unfold the history, culture, lives, resources and governance of the state. It describes nicely the contributions of the legendary leaders who are considered as the makers of Modern Odisha. It also contains articles which look into the culture, cuisine and the craft traditions of the state. It has placed within its pages some great social movements of the state, the historicity of this state and the status of women and the system of governance and articles revealing the typical cultural traditions of the state. The volume is a must read for the researchers and students to get a foundational knowledge base on the state with its manifold facets.

60. Panda, H., S. M. Panda, & R. Lund, 2013. "Environmental insecurity and social friction: Links in rural Odisha." ***International Journal of Rural Management*, *9*(1), 17-43.**

In the wake of neoliberal policy, this article explores the relationship between environmental insecurity and social friction in rural Odisha. The connections are intertwined with the destabilisation of natural resource-based livelihood systems, degradation of water, forest, and land. The paper notes that loss of natural resources base for livelihood leads to underemployment and unemployment among people. This ultimately leads to increased morbidity, social disharmony, and distress migration at the family and community level. From rural Odisha, it is observed that scarcities, deficits, and disparities create environmental security and resulting social friction around the state. The social frictions resulted in conflict in mining areas, which ultimately leads to new stakeholders. These stakeholders can establish co-operation among them for desired development goal.

61. Panda, P. K. "Inclusion and Economic Empowerment of Rural Tribal Women in Cashew Value Chain and Market: A Case Study of Nabarangpur District in Odisha." ***Orissa Economic Journal, 104.***

The paper tries to analyse the impact of the Cashew Livelihood Model on the income of tribal women in the Navrangpur district of Odisha. The study finds that employing strategic, participative, and scientific technology among the tribal women for the Cashew livelihood model increases their income. The study provides evidence that these women are capable enough to acquire new skills and leadership if provided with appropriate training and skill-building.

62. Panda, R. K. 2013. "Rural Poverty and Access to Land-A Study of Odisha." ***IASSI-Quarterly*, *32*(4), 31-44.**

The paper analyses the impact of land reform measures on rural poverty in the state of Odisha. It reveals that land distributions across the state are unequal, and poverty reduction remains slow in the state. The paper suggests the overall development of the population, and the training of the rural youths need to take up various off-farm activities to overcome different odds of rural poverty.

63. Parida, J. 2016. "MGNREGS, distress migration and livelihood conditions: a study in Odisha." ***Journal of Social and Economic Development*, *18*(1-2), 17-3**

Based on a primary survey of 400 households from the Mayurbhanj and Jajpur districts of Odisha, this article finds that Mahatma Gandhi National Rural Employment Guarantee Act is playing an important role in the agricultural slack seasons by providing job opportunities to needy poor and socially marginalised groups. The primary survey conducted in two districts, viz. Mayurbhanj and Jajpur, shows that the workforce participation rate in NREGS is very high among the households belonging to poor, landless and socially disadvantaged communities. Availability of guaranteed employment during the slack agricultural seasons with relatively better wages in NREGS in the study region (as compared to both agriculture and other non-farm wages) has restricted the potential seasonal migrants who would have migrated elsewhere otherwise. NREGS increases the purchasing power of the people and as such the consumption rate takes an upward turn. The author is optimistic that this flagship programme will cause a substantial decline in rural poverty on the one hand and increasing aggregate demand for consumer goods, help to boost economic growth in the rural sector in the long run. This will also ensure higher participation among women and by that gear social change in the study region through improvement of the socio-economic conditions within households, which has implications for women's empowerment.

64. Patel, S. K., B. Mathew, A. Nanda, B. Mohanty, &N. Saggurti, 2020. "Voices of rural people: Community-level assessment of effects and resilience to natural disasters in Odisha, India." ***International Journal of Population Studies, 6*****(1), 3-15.**

The paper explores the effects of floods, droughts, cyclones, and heat waves on Odisha and the resilience strategies adopted to mitigate these disasters at rural community levels. The article relies on both primary and secondary data to analyse the natural catastrophe's effects and resilience. The finding reveals that these disasters severely affect people's livelihood, health, water, food security, and sanitation. The government strategies like Early Warning System, Public Distribution System, Multipurpose Cyclone Rehabilitation Centers, Seasonal Residential Care Centers, and Indira Awas Yojana play crucial roles in mitigating the effect on rural communities in Odisha. The study highlights that these disasters impact the rural communities physically, socio-economically and psychologically. Looking into the findings the paper suggests to focus on reducing vulnerabilities of communities through taking proactive measures to sustain their livelihood.

65. Patnaik, U., P. K. Das, & C. S. Bahinipati, 2016. "Coping with climatic shocks: empirical evidence from rural coastal Odisha, India." ***Global Business Review, 17*****(1), 161-175.**

The paper examines the traditional coping mechanisms and consumer behaviour of the vulnerable households in the flood and cyclone-prone rural areas from the coastal districts of Odisha. The findings of the paper suggest that disaster sink the consumption capacity of the rural households, increases the health expenditure which becomes difficult to meet with. The paper reveals no exact coping mechanism to mitigate the shock generated from the disaster, but suggests the government needs to create a business environment with multi-stakeholders' participation to better deliver safety nets to reduce the risks created by the disaster.

66. Patra, C., & S. K. Mahapatra, 2020. "Statistical Study on Role of Migration in Agricultural & Rural Development of Odisha." ***Biotica Research Today,*** ***2*****(6), 510-512.**

The paper studies the role of migration in the development of rural and agricultural sectors of Odisha. The article concentrates on the major migration-prone districts of Odisha, which includes Bargarh, Bolangir, Kalahandi, Nuapada, Sonepur, Ganjam, Gajapati, Nowrangpur, Koraput, and Khorda. It establishes that migration of an area significantly depends on the areas and their crop production pattern. Those areas have produced higher cereals, pulses, and oil seed crops and have attracted more migrants from 1991 to 2011. The paper concludes that migration linked with the nature of workforce and natural resources have a definite role in rural development.

67. Patra, S. K., & D.M. Mahapatra, 2017. "Perceptions and Image Attributes of Tourists towards Rural Tourism: A Study on Pipili Village of Odisha." ***Training & Development Journal,*** ***8*****(1), 67-74.**

The paper analyses the perception of tourists towards destination travel and tourist satisfaction. The study conducted in the Pipili village to examine the components, factors influencing, and attributes towards the tourist destination image. It also examines tourist satisfaction and determinants of destination loyalty. The findings suggest that the travel attributes have satisfactory predictive relevance. The paper explains the changes in the variance of the endogenous variable tourist satisfaction.

68. Patra, S. K., D.S. Murthy, & S. Rath, 2013. "An Evaluation of the National Rural Health Mission (NRHM) in Odisha." ***Journal of Health Management,*** ***15*****(3), 471-480.**

The paper makes an impact assessment of the National Rural Health Mission on the health indicator in Odisha. The study was conducted at Kharagaon village of Puri district of Odisha. The paper tries to examine how the schemes under the NHRM are working and how the programme helps in the transition of the state of health status in the state. The paper makes use of both primary and secondary data to analyse impact. The author also uses multiple regression analysis to know how state government capital expenditure and revenue expenditure on health and family welfare influence the health indicators like birth rate, mortality rate, death rate, etc. The study finds that the health status of the study area is very poor and is slowly increasing its status after the execution of NRHM. The research suggests more funds are needed to implement the programme successfully, and scarcity is the major cause of poor implementation. The paper also highlights the primary reasons for poor health status and concludes illiteracy, low income, unwillingness of doctors to go to remote areas, shortage of doctors, lack of proper health care facilities, and laboratory technicians contribute significantly for the poor health conditions in rural Odisha.

69. Pattanaik, D. K., & P. Mohapatra, 2010. "Ethno-medicinal studies in the weekly fair of Koraput, Odisha." *Biohelica: Sci. J. Biol. Sci., 1*, 52-55.

The paper explores the list of plants used by tribals in districts of Koraput Odisha for the cure of the different types of diseases they encounter. Most of these plant-based medicines are sold by tribals in the weekly fairs held from time to time in their local areas. The tribals use these medicinal plants for various medical purposes. It reveals that tribals mostly use medicinal plants for dysentery, bone fracture, diarrhea, lactation in mother, gonorrhea, worm infestation, muscular pain, piles, and injuries and for easy child birth.

70. Pattanaik, S. 2017. "Development or Disaster? Land Acquisition and Dispossession in the Mining Belts and

Coastal Zones of Rural Odisha, India." ***In Land Policies in India*** **(pp. 105-125). Springer, Singapore.**

The paper examines the question of whether development-induced land acquisition and dispossession leads to development or disaster in rural spaces of Odisha. In analysing the Land Acquisition and Resettlement and Rehabilitation Bill of Odisha, the author argues that the two bills allow the state government to capture the land for private players and extend its power beyond the ideals of a welfaristic state. In investigating the rural mining and coastal zones of Odisha, the paper reveals that state in the name of development grabs the land of poorer and results in the marginalisation and put the people out of their sustainable culture. The study highlights the resistance, dispossession, and role of the neo-liberal state in settling POSCO project in Odisha. The anti-POSCO movement sends a message that the Bills or Policies of Land Acquisition needs to focus on solving problems of local people than capitalist or industries.

71. Phalkey, R., S. Dash, A. Mukhopadhyay, S. Runge-Ranzinger, & M. Marx, 2012. "Prepared to react? Assessing the functional capacity of the primary healthcare system in rural Orissa, India to respond to the devastating flood of September 2008." ***Global health action*****, 5(1), 10964.**

The paper aims to study the functional capacity of the primary healthcare system in response to a devastating flood in rural areas of Odisha. The study was conducted in five rural blocks of Jagatsinghpur district in Odisha. The study reveals that healthcare facilities are poor in rural Jagatsinghpur. Poor supplies of essential medical stuff and facilities, lack of human resources, missing standard operating system, lack of effective leadership, weak financial capacity, and lack of electricity backup, make the district ill-prepared and lowers the capacity to handle the flood situation. The flood situation challenges the primary preventive and curative healthcare facilities in rural areas. The paper suggests building of vital primary healthcare services and facilities to tackle the situation in rural areas in the post-disaster period.

72. Pradhan, A. K., & R. Patra, 2012. "Common property forest resources and rural livelihoods: an empirical investigation in the state of Odisha." ***Journal of Resources, Energy and Development*, 9(1), 23-34.**

The paper tries to study the degree, extent and determinants of common property forest resource dependency at a household level in the villages of Odisha. The study finds that CPR forest dependency is directly related to household size but inversely related to economic condition and agricultural land holding.

73. Pradhan, J. and D. P. Misra, 2014. "Rural Brand Awareness and Preferences for FMCGs: An Empirical Study on Keonjhar District of Odisha, India" ***IOSR Journal of Business and Management (IOSR-JBM)*** **e-ISSN: 2278-487X, p-ISSN: 2319-7668. Volume 16, Issue 9.Ver. IV (Sep. 2014), pp. 17-29.**

The authors in this article explore the rural consumer buying behaviour through brand awareness and the influence of demographic factors on brand preference. This paper is based on primary as well as secondary data. The sampling regions include one of the rural districts of Odisha viz, Keonjhar. The results indicate that brand preference is conditioned by age, gender, family type and education. But the researchers find no significant linkage between occupation and annual income with the brand preference.

74. Pradhan, L., A. Das, & H. S. Rout, "Local Self-governance: A Case Study in Odisha." ***Orissa Economic Journal, 69.***

The paper aims at examining the extent of devolution of power by government of Odisha to PRIs and ULBs and also evaluates the participation of elected representatives in the decision making of PRIs. The study finds that low-income generation capacity of local bodies is a major problem. Low level of local participation is influenced by low level of education, lack of employment opportunities and awareness of constitutions.

75. Pujari, S. 2018. "Local governance and management of health care services: A community-based case study in rural Odisha." ***Indian Journal of Public Health Research & Development*, *9*(10), 91-95.**

This paper looks at the different ways the gram panchayat functions, particularly its role in the areas of providing health, hygiene and sanitation. To the author, availability, accessibility and affordability, of facilities to maintain the maternal and reproductive health is the chief matter of concern in rural areas. The author also takes care to elaborate vividly the role of local self-government in the management and delivery of public health services.

76. *Pujari, N. K.* **"No smartphones, internet access: Odisha's rural kids caught in digital divide."** ***Down to Earth.***

The author quotes the Economic Survey Report (2018-2019) which says 20 percent (11,000) villages in Odisha do not have mobile connectivity and the state has just 28.22 percent internet subscribers. Under such situations, COVID-19 has taken the state far behind in fulfilling the children's right to education envisaged in RTE. It makes it difficult to achieve the minimum level of learning.The author records that at least 80 percent parents of such children in Malkangiri, Kandhamal, Nabarangpur, Rayagada and Deogarh districts do not have a smartphone. At least 40 percent parents in Kandhamal and Malkangiri districts do not have a regular mobile phone. Of 67,128 government elementary schools in the state, only 27.68 percent have initiated online education so far. The number of children who attend online classes through a smartphone was 31.95 per cent, the report revealed. This digital divide as per the author's version is going to aggravate the disparity and inequality in imparting online classes. It is also in violation of the fundamental Right to Education Act of these children.

77. Rath, A. K. 2013. "Role of Self-Help Group/Micro Finance in Rural Odisha-An Opportunity and Challenge." *Siddhant-A Journal of Decision Making, 13*(3), 196-202.

In this article, the interplay of socio-economic development and saving mechanism has been explained in the context of microfinance evolution in Odisha.

78. Rath, N.1996. *Women in Rural Society: A Quest for Development,* M.D. Publications, Pvt. Ltd. New Delhi.

The author in this book tries to connect the macro policy intervention with the micro implementation and assesses the efficacy of these policies on the rural women. In this context, the book tries to locate the rural women in the present development process. The author begins by describing how since the beginning of the sixth plan period, massive efforts have been undertaken by the government to bring the rural women into the orbit of the development network. Different policies and programmes have been initiated by the government to change the status of the rural women. The book comprises of three parts; the first two parts are based on a macro-study and the last part is based on micro-study. The first part makes a situational analysis of the women in India in past and present, the rural setting of the country and the plight of women therein. Part two of the book makes a policy analysis by discussing the planned proposals launched by the government for rural development and the women specific rural development programmes. The third part consists of a micro-analysis; to be more specific a role-analysis of the rural women in the development programmes. This role-analysis embraces an assessment of their awareness, and their perception of the rural development programmes, their participation in the planning and implementation of the programmes and finally the benefits they have received from the programmes.

79. Ray, G. K. 2017. "Analysis of food security in rural Odisha." ***IJAR*, *3*(8), 550-553.**

The study tries to analysis the determinants of food security in rural Odisha. The data is based on 400 marginal farmers and landless labourers. The study reveals massive welfare programmes are responsible for ensuring basic food security in rural areas. The author concludes that food security needs to be prioritised in the rural development agenda.

80. Reddy, M. G., B. P. Mahapatra, & J. Naik 2019. "Current Implementation and Impacts of MGNREGS in Rural Odisha: Does this Solve the Problems of Unemployment and Migration?" ***IASSI-Quarterly*, *38*(3), 506-526.**

The paper reveals that the implementation issues of MGNREGS and the way it affects the livelihoods of people. It shows that proper implementation of MGNREGS would certainly help the rural people for a better livelihood. At present, the insufficiency in quantum of job, lower wage rate and delay in wage payment are the major reasons for rural to urban migration.

81. Routray, P., W. P. Schmidt, S. Boisson, T. Clasen, & M.W. Jenkins, 2015. "Socio-cultural and behavioural factors constraining latrine adoption in rural coastal Odisha: an exploratory qualitative study." ***BMC Public Health*, 15(1), 880.**

This paper examines defecation patterns of different groups of people in rural areas of Odisha to identify causes and determinants of latrine non-use, with a special focus on government subsidized latrine owners and shortcomings in household infrastructures. Habits, socialisation, sanitation, sanitation rituals and daily routines vary with caste, gender, marital status, age and lifestyle. These factors hinder the adaptation of latrines. Providing infrastructure does not ensure use when there are significant cultural barriers. Behavioural changes should be address before the implementation of any scheme.

82. Routray, P., B. Torondel, T. Clasen, & W. P. Schmidt, 2017. "Women's role in sanitation decision making in rural coastal Odisha, India." ***PloS one, 12*****(5), e0178042.**

This paper examines the association between women's decision-making autonomy and latrine construction in the rural areas of Odisha. Mixed method is used to conduct the research in Puri district of Odisha. Cross-sectional survey among 475 randomly selected households indicates that though government emphasises women's involvement in decision-making in sanitation programmes but cultural and household dynamics prevent them. Gender power relation and familial relation influence latrine adoption and use immensely.

83. Routray, P., B. Torondel, M.W. Jenkins, T. Clasen, & W.P. Schmidt, 2017. "Processes and challenges of community mobilisation for latrine promotion under Nirmal Bharat Abhiyan in rural Odisha, India." ***BMC Public Health, 17*****(1), 453.**

This paper documents the strategies and processes of NBA (Nirmal Bharat Abhiyan) in rural Odisha. It looks at the pattern of mobilisation for latrine promotion in these villages and assesses the strength and limitations of the mobilisation activities. Lack of consistent implementation strategy, lack of capacities and facilitation skills of NGOs staff to implement sanitation programmes, political interference and challenges in accessing to government financial incentives leads to the failure of schemes. Community discussions are found to be dominated by upper caste males which exclude lower caste males and women.

84. Roy, D. 2012. "Rapid appraisal of the rural water and sanitation sector in Orissa."

This paper describes the concept of "problem villages" i.e. villages which do not have drinking water source within 100 mts or the source of water has problems with the quality. According to the Seventh Five-Year Plan, the norm of 40 litres of water per capita per day is introduced in the ARWSP. The reform initiative is launched on a pilot basis in 67 districts of 26 states by government of India. Balasore, Sundargarh and Ganjam are covered under the scheme from Odisha. The author concludes that the programme has not yet achieved its full success and needs to take a momentum and needs seriousness.

85. Saha, G. S., H. K. De, L. Safui, A.E Eknath, S. Adhikari, N.K. Barik, & S. Chandra, 2013. "Status and economy of community fish farming in rural Odisha." ***Indian Journal of Fisheries, 60*(4).**

This study reveals a low level of technological adaptation of aquaculture with traditional method of crab culture. 81 ponds from Khurda and Puri were under investigation. The author concludes that techno-input intensification and socio-political problems needs need to be resolved which can enhance fish production, family income, improvement of the livelihood and nutritional security of rural poor.

86. Sahoo, P., D. Sahoo & S. Chandra. 2020. "Changes in Rural Poverty Among Occupational Groups in Odisha: An Analysis of Post-Reform Period." ***Journal of Land and Rural Studies, 8*(2), 150-165.**

This article studies the changes in rural poverty and its link with growth of farm sector output for Odisha in the post-reform period. The Odisha economy has recorded high growth in net state domestic product (NSDP) in the post reform period. During 2000s, the farm sector reported high growth, higher rural poverty reduction and occupational mobility within the farm sector. So, the growth of the farm sector is the major driver of rural poverty reduction in Odisha as per the conclusion of the authors.

87. Sahoo, R. R. 2021. "Weaver and the Woven".

The article delves into the philosophy of Odisha's handloom and hidden meaning of motifs. She recaptures the work through the artist's intention and perception as the spiritual journey. It explores the meaning attached to the work and the reality of weavers' socio-cultural milieu. It unrevealed the multilayer meanings of social reality attached to the handloom sector and the people engaged in it.

88. Samal, M., N. Khara, S.Pati and K.C. Sahoo. 2019. "Treatment by untrained providers among sick infants in rural Odisha, India." ***Primary Health Care Research & Development,*** **26 June.**

This study assesses the diagnosis, treatment and referral service provided by untrained providers for sick infants in three rural blocks of Odisha. The study is a cross-sectional study. Lack of trained providers causes inopportune treatment of sick infants and results in increase in child morbidity and mortality. The untrained providers deliver a significant proportion of healthcare for rural infants; however, there is a paucity of information on their treatment practice. This study recommends there is a need for training on common disease algorithm and treatment using a standard guideline for untrained providers to reduce inopportuneness in the treatment of sick infants, promoting early diagnosis and referral services to public health systems.

89. Samal, P., B. Mondal, & A. Pandit, 2016. "Rural Livelihood Diversification in Flood Prone Ecosystems of Odisha." ***Indian Journal of Economics and Development, 12*****(3), 413-420.**

This paper analyses secondary data for the last 64 years which reveals that the percentage contribution of primary sector has reduced considerably where as other sectors have increased. Factors like frequent occurrence of natural calamities, no proper irrigation facilities and no storage have reduced the profit from agriculture.

90. Satapathy, S. S. 2014. "Information and Communication Technologies: An Agent of Social Change for Rural Women in Odisha." ***Sociology and Anthropology*, *2*(4), 152-158.**

This paper tries to establish the relationship between women's' access to ICTs and empowerment. A large portion of rural women in the state are reeling under poverty and lack of awareness regarding technologies and its benefits. The author notes that socio-cultural barriers discourage their public participation and decision-making ventures.

91. Satpathy, I., B. C. M. Patnaik & P. K. Pradhan. 2011. "Empowerment of Rural Odisha through Connectivity (A case study of Khurda District of Odisha)".

The present paper makes an attempt to study the implementation of Prime Minister's Gram Sadak Yojana (PMGSY) in rural area and its impact on the lives of the rural people. Roads constitute the life line of rural people. The authors have taken recourse to questionnaire to collect their data. They detect that the PMGSY has made significant contribution to the lives of the rural people. It has transformed the life style of the people. Due to this connectivity, the rural people are able to find new markets for their products. They are also enabled to access basic medical and education facilities now within their reach.

92. Sedlander, Erica, et.al. 2021. "How gender norms affect anemia in select villages in rural Odisha, India: A qualitative study" ***Nutrition Volume 86*, June.**

This study aims at examining the role of gender norms in promoting anemia prevalence among women in rural India. For the purpose the researchers conducted 16 focus group discussions. Their total sample size was 124 covering women of reproductive age, husbands, and mothers-in-law and 25 key informant interviews in four villages in Odisha. The research discovers that due to a double burden of work outside the home and completing the majority of unpaid work in the home, women lack time to visit health centers to get tested for anemia and to obtain iron supplements. Women are expected to prioritize the health of their family over their own, thus affecting their access to healthcare. Women's autonomy to leave the house to seek health care is limited. In many households the expenditure made by the males on alcohol consumption limits the supply of iron-rich food for the household. Intra-household food allocation favours men, in-laws, and children; thus, women serve their family first, often being left with little food. So, the study concludes that anemia reduction interventions need to include examination of the whole social context to successfully increase iron supplement use and iron-rich food intake. Understanding how gender norms contribute to anemia could change the narrative from a biomedical to a social justice issue.

93. Xaxa, J., 2013. "Empowerment of Women in Panchayatiraj System : A Study in Odisha" ***Odisha Review*****, February-March.**

The author in this article tries to assess the role of the Panchayati Raj system in the process of women's empowerment. To her with the initiation of the 72nd Constitutional Amendment Bill and the commencement of the 73rd Constitutional Amendment Act with effect from 24th April 1993 reservation of seats have been ensured for women in the panchayati raj system across states. But Odisha has been a frontline state in making this provision for women's reservation and participation in the PRIs before it was introduced at the national level. The author notes that the women who came reluctantly to adorn the positions have become proactive in the decision-making process today, women from marginalised communities find themselves in a different footing due to their participation in the decision-making process, their role in the democratic and decentralised process has increased phenomenally. All these signalise the greater empowerment experienced by women in the rural areas. Some important recommendations she suggests through the article are the government needs to provide greater security to women, campaign vigorously with local organisations to bring attitudinal changes among men and women representatives needed to be encouraged for greater participation in the Panchayat meetings.

The Epilogue

At the end of a serious six months endeavour, we are now ready to write the epilogue. The hunt to discover articles, books, blogs, journals, reports was serious. We have been selective in our identification of the articles from the available sources. In every section, we could note that studies on rural societies are done from multiple facets. In each section some strong points relating to rural studies and some weaknesses in their process and outcomes have been detected by the authors.

In the first section 197 international studies have been reviewed and placed. These international studies could generate a clear-cut impression that rural studies have a strong base in the United States of America followed by United Kingdom. Over the years they have become the thrust of research in other countries of Africa, Australia and Asia. We have tried to select some studies which are classic and can influence the insight of the present generation academia, researchers and policy planners. There are good studies on the theoretical perspectives to study rural societies. But their numbers were found to be limited confined to the western world, particularly, U.S.A. With the process of urbanisation and developmental interventions, particularly in the Asia, Africa and Latin American countries, there has been a proliferation of literature on the rural space. Similarly, with the syndrome of over urbanisation and urban addiction coming to an end, studies have grown on rural spaces in Europe and Australia. The articles, books reviewed and incorporated in section -I contain literature on rural economy, technology and agriculture, climate change and its subsequent impacts on rural lives and livelihood, rural social systems, institutions, their continuity and changes, rural development policies in different countries, their comparisons, the scenario of poverty in rural space across nations, rural education, healthcare, development policies and programmes impacting rural lives. Added to all these broad categories articles on rural tourism, rural reversal, rural-urban migrations and vice versa have adorned the pages. A good number of articles are their on-community participation, community development, emerging livelihood opportunities, women, their roles in rural economy, changing patterns of leadership in the rural political set ups and rural demographic dividends. On the whole, the section provides an international perspective on the dimensions and dynamics of rural studies.

The second section is a repository of the studies on rural society in India. There are almost 211 books, articles and reports annotated in this section. These articles cover a wide range of issues from economy to polity and from rural issues to rural services. To be more specific they focus mostly on rural economy, employment, poverty, agriculture, migration, village structure, culture and life, social security, social class and division, gender, environment, forest resources and energy, cooperatives, rural finance and bank, local governance, rural livelihood and development, rural public policy, rural industrialisation, rural education and health infrastructure and services. Added to these, some articles on rural violence, movements in rural spaces are also placed in this section. Reviews also deal with the impact of media and ICT, CSR, transport and communication services and their galvanizing role in bringing changes in the rural society of India and the challenges faced by them. As India is predominantly rural, rural issues have been the area of concern and rural development being on the frontline of the planning process of the country, a good number of studies do exist in the archives on India's rural society. But studies are still awaited in the fields of conflict over resources, digital lagging, impact of globalisation on rural space etc.

The third section is dedicated to compile the rural studies in Odisha. This section is quite crucial for the researchers working on the state. Till date studies on rural society of Odisha were scattered. So, in this section we have made an endeavour to bring them together. But, during our search for literature, we selected only 97 literature and dropped some overlapping literature. In this section, we have tried to place some reports of the development agencies who have been working in the rural sector for a pretty long time. The major works relate to such areas like agriculture, social system, education, health, sanitation, common property, banking system and rural political institutions.

The distribution of the literature annotated can be presented in the Graph below.

Hope this academic endeavour of ours will cater to the needs of the readers, researchers, academia, policy planners and development activists. It will provide a repository as well as can serve as a road map for furthering rural studies. With this expectation we await the valuable comments and feedbacks of our readers which we will try to accommodate in our next edition.

Navaneeta Rath — Rath Yatra

Rashmita Sahoo — 12-07-2021

Archita Bala Patra

Bishnu Prasad Mohapatra

Chinmayee Mishra

Subhrajit Rath

Index

D

E

F

G

J

K

L

M

N

Q

R

S

T